MEMORY PIECES

MEMORY PIECES

MAURICE GEE

VICTORIA UNIVERSITY PRESS

VICTORIA UNIVERSITY PRESS
Victoria University of Wellington
PO Box 600 Wellington
vup.victoria.ac.nz

A catalogue record is available from the
National Library of New Zealand

ISBN 9781776562077

Several passages in these memoirs were published in an earlier
form in *Creeks and Kitchens* (Bridget Williams Books, 2013)

Printed in China by 1010 Printing International

To the memory of my parents, Lyndahl and Len Gee,
and my brother, Aynsley,
and for Margareta, Gary, Nigel, Emily and Abigail.

I want to thank Geoff Walker for helping me get this book into shape, and for friendship and support in his many years as my publisher. Jane Parkin too has been a sympathetic and friendly help over that time, using her editorial skills to my and my readers' benefit. Thank you, Jane.

CONTENTS

'Double Unit', the first of these three pieces, includes a description of her childhood written in middle age by my mother, Lyndahl Gee. She was the eleventh of the fifteen children of James Chapple, a Presbyterian and later Unitarian minister, and his wife Florence. Lyndahl published stories and poems as a young and youngish woman but, for reasons 'Double Unit' makes clear, never went on with a writing career.

My father Len Gee's story is here too. He was boxer, builder, man's man, and no less remarkable in his way than Lyndahl.

As one of three sons I've confined myself to a third-person role in their story.

'Blind Road' is my story up to the age of eighteen, when my apprenticeship as a writer began.

'Running on the Stairs' describes the early life of Margaretha Garden who, in 1940, the year of her birth, travelled with her mother Greta from Nazi-sympathising Sweden to New Zealand – an overland, sea and air journey of six weeks through Russia, the Middle East, India and South East Asia to Sydney, from where their last leg to Auckland was flown by her father, Oscar Garden, a TEAL captain. After that, through childhood, girlhood and young womanhood, Margaretha never stopped running – until in 1967 she met me and managed at last to stand still.

In writing these pieces I've relied on memory, mine and other people's, rather than research. Where the two conflict I've usually gone with memory.

DOUBLE UNIT

Including an account of her childhood, and other writings,
by Lyndahl Chapple Gee

ONE

I'm Captain Armadilla Joe
      a fierce old pirate don't you know
And I live on the sea
      as happy as could be
What! with the treasures I
      find, great small every kind
'O' a pirates life is worth
      all its toil,
Take the sea boys the sea
      not the land and soil.

When me and my crew are in a
      bad mood any prisoner
      we have goes for fishes
      food
But when there is wanting
      a little more fun he is
      used as a target for
      each man's gun.
                 Lyndahl Chapple

It's a surprising poem. Lyndahl was a gentle child whose father, a Unitarian minister, was in prison for preaching pacifism in a time of war. Perhaps, as a reader in 'the wider bible of literature', James Chapple forgave his daughter because she could rhyme. While the poem shows no promise, except in its rollicking first two lines, on the page facing it Lyndahl drew a girl wearing a college uniform: neat embroidered collar, knotted tie, pleated skirt. She's in profile, calm-faced, with dark hair hanging in ringlets to her shoulders. Her small delicately drawn hand holds a rose by the stem. Lyndahl did only moderately well in English but was always top of the class in drawing. She was also good at plasticine modelling. Her knight mounted on a charger, with a darning needle for a lance, was displayed for several months in a Christchurch shop window. Later, her father sent her to an art school, where the naked models embarrassed her. She chose the sculpting course instead of the drawing.

She was Harriet Lyndahl, the eleventh of the fifteen children of James Henry George Chapple and Florence Eugenie Chapple, née Gough. (Nina, the fifth child, died shortly after birth, from 'an infection caught from an unhygienic midwife'.) The name Lyndahl is a misspelling of Lyndall, the heroine of the 1873 novel *The Story of an African Farm* by Ralph Iron (Olive Schreiner). It displaced Harriet right from the start, fitting the quiet child better than the sharp-edged first name.

She was born in Timaru in 1907. James Chapple was minister of St Andrew's Presbyterian Church, several miles south of the town. At the date of his seventh daughter's birth he was forty-one and his wife Florence thirty-seven. James's father, William Sandy Chapple, had emigrated from Ashcroft in Somerset to Australia, where he met Elizabeth Bancroft, originally from Manchester. They married in 1864 and lived in Rockhampton. James was one of two children. He was born in 1865. A younger brother died at eleven weeks and Sandy, the father, drowned soon after, while fording a river on his horse. Elizabeth Chapple sent James to Sandy's sisters in Ashcroft to be brought up. They looked after him well and he grew fond of them. He was to name his seventh daughter Harriet after the older of the two. There's a story, impossible to verify, that he had his early education in a school for girls. True or not, his lessons were orthodox. He became proficient in Latin and acquired a good knowledge of the scriptures. His first job though was as a plumber, and he worked at this trade on his return to Rockhampton as a young man. It's not known what took him to Ballarat, where he chanced to meet Florence Gough, a young woman from that town. Perhaps he worked there for her father, a plumber too.

Henry Gough came from Gloucestershire and his wife, born Mary Froome, from Middlesex. In a letter written to a niece in 1973 Lyndahl tells how her maternal grandmother, an innkeeper's daughter in Somerset (actually Middlesex), fell in love with a young plumber 'in a brown corduroy jacket'. The couple emigrated to Australia, where they had seven children. Lyndahl's mother, Florence, was the youngest. In her old age she told Lyndahl 'her very first memory': 'I was sitting on my father's knee in my nightgown. There was a fire and it was cosy and I was ready for bed. I must have been very little because my father was holding my two bare feet in one hand and was smoking his pipe with the other. There was no one else in the room – no sound except the fire spitting sparks and my father puffing his pipe.'

The loving father does not seem to have been matched by a loving mother. The innkeeper's daughter worked hard for respectability. Florence was never allowed to climb trees or sit on the ground or sit with her legs the least bit apart. When hard times arrived Mrs Gough gave lessons in French and music. But along came another young plumber, James Chapple, a short, lively, red-headed man who, like Florence, was a Salvation Army officer. Lyndahl writes: 'One day at a church picnic he saw my mother, a demure young girl, cutting sandwiches and making tea for the elders. How to meet her was James's problem. He couldn't just stroll up and say, "Hi." So he found out her name, Florence Gough, and where she lived (Ballarat) and saw in the window a notice reading: French and music lessons given . . . In he went to learn the piano in the front parlour. He sat through a lot of lessons before meeting Florence, who was no doubt peeking at him through the lace curtains or a crack in the door . . . Suddenly the great day! Mrs Gough had to go out. She pulled on her gloves and said to my dad, "My daughter will give you your lessons today, she is quite proficient."'

James Henry George Chapple of Rockhampton married Florence Eugenie Gough of Ballarat at Newcastle, NSW, on 27 August 1890. Fifty years later, writing their Golden Wedding notice, James included the number of their children, fifteen, and added 'Sursum corda' [Lift up your hearts].

Shortly after their second child was born they emigrated to New Zealand, where, for four years, they served in various South Island towns. Three more babies were born before, in 1898, they moved to the mining town of Kumara on the West Coast, where James became a Presbyterian home missionary. It was not an easy posting. The Kumara station was a large one, taking in the settlements of Dillman's, Greenstone, Stafford, Humphrey's Gully and a number of isolated gold workings and sawmills. James Chapple worked long hours, cycling on bush tracks to outlying preaching stations, then studying into the night – and his wife worked equally hard, running the house, visiting parishioners deep in the bush, giving birth to babies and caring for them. She seems not to have complained about overwork and having babies one after the other. Obstinately, she called her husband 'the minister' although he was not yet ordained.

They stayed in Kumara for six years. In a short autobiographical piece written in her old age, Florence describes how, leaving the children with her home-help, she went with James to visit an old couple deep in the bush. James doubled her on his bicycle. He carried her over streams, which made her laugh with delight, and when night trapped them in the parishioners' 'tumble-down house almost overgrown with weeds', and 'the minister' had read from the Bible, and they had eaten bread that looked dark with dirt in some places and drunk condensed milk mixed with hot water, they climbed a ladder to a bed made of straw and sacks and slept the night with a string of onions hanging over their faces and a chamber pot on the floor. James laughed as he pulled her up the ladder. She wore a pink flannelette nightdress loaned to her by the old woman.

They may have been 'the minister' and his wife but alone together they were Flo and Jim.

The family shifted to Eltham in Taranaki, where James, although not yet ordained, began to show signs of what his future would be. He was a strong-minded man, and obstinate. He knew right (his right) from wrong and not surprisingly he was in trouble at once. First he opposed the renting of pews. There was no place for precedence in a church, he said. Then he spoke from his pulpit against the use of young children as early-morning helpers in milking sheds. He had had reports of them falling asleep at their desks at school. His arguments did not go down well in a farming community.

Trouble was to be the story of his professional life. It followed him to St Andrews, a town just south of Timaru, where he was ordained a Presbyterian minister in 1903. There he preached in support of the miners in the 1908 Blackball strike. It was plainly wrong, he said, that mine owners above ground should deny their workers down below half an hour for lunch instead of a quarter. His radicalism came from reading and thinking and observation, and soon it widened from politics into matters of religion. He began to question the doctrines of his church. 'Wouldst make a jail to coop the living god?' The widening of his mind went on until, in 1910, after being called to explain his behaviour in taking the chair at a lecture given by the evolutionist Joseph McCabe, he resigned from the Presbyterian Church ('that great lying Church'). A Unitarian church was being built in Timaru, and James became its first minister.

Meanwhile, the family increased. Lyndahl was the twelfth child born, and the third in Timaru. Writing of her parents in 1937, she says: 'Their love deepened with the years, although it was sometimes tough going. Only porridge and bread and dripping to feed the children on.' She never met her grandparents across the Tasman Sea. Her mother hinted to her once that her own mother was 'ashamed of her daughter, Florence – fifteen children was a bit much. As for her son-in-law, he should have known better – a parson and all.'

What was it like growing up in a family of eight girls and six boys, with a father always in trouble, money scarce and food hard to come by? Lyndahl answers the question herself, in an account of her childhood written in 1954. It's called 'The Change' and it takes her from the age of five years to sixteen, where it stops in mid-sentence on page 37. There must have been more, or more intended. The title suggests she meant to bring the story up to her present day, or at least to the end, a few years earlier, of her hard menopause.

The script is typed on foolscap paper, with alterations inked in here and there. She does not name the family and she changes the names of her siblings and calls herself Lynda, but they're the Chapples, no mistake.

'The Change' follows, making up the whole of Chapter Two. Except for one or two spelling and punctuation changes I've left it exactly as she wrote it.

TWO

'The Change', by Lyndahl Chapple

Timaru, about 1912

There are deep ditches on the way to school and there is a man who drives a horse and cart along the road. He talks out loud to himself. His horse always only walks. It is best to hide in a ditch or behind a hedge when he goes by. His cart is full of lumpy looking sacks and someone said he likes little girls best.

The stone cracker man never stops cracking stones with a heavy mallet. He makes big stones into little stones; big piles of big stones into big piles of little stones. He's always there somewhere or other along the road to school. The blacksmith is always hitting something with a hammer too. In the blacksmith's shop it looks black and warm and dirty. Girls aren't allowed. Only boys go in there. Boys can go anywhere.

Nearest the school is the house where Rose lives. It is behind the highest hedge ever. Rose is always staying away from school. She has something wrong with her bones; she has broken her arms and legs lots of times and doesn't mind anymore. You can see through the hedge if you lie down almost under it. Rose sits on the veranda in a big chair.

It's hot in our classroom and teacher is cross. She threw a piece of pink chalk at a boy.

What a horrid feeling to know that you are going to wet yourself before teacher notices your hand is up. The form gets wetter and wetter and warmer and warmer the harder you sit on it. Now you can't leave the room. Everyone will see you have wet yourself if you walk out.

When will the bell ring? When the bell rings who will be first to get the seat in the tree for the lunch hour?

Spit on slates has a sicky smell. I'm going to ask Diamond to make me a slate duster like Mary Smith has only I'm going to have mine made of red velvet better than hers. Mother has red velvet cushions in our best room. I wish we had them to sit on in school instead of wooden forms. Wood makes my bottom sore; bottom is a rude word but I don't care. I wish the bell would ring and I hope I've got a better lunch than Mary Smith. I wish she wouldn't sit with me at lunch time.

Teacher's going to let us go.

If I get to the tree first Mary Smith can't sit with me. There's only room for one. Me.

Behind our playground is a big yellow quarry. The blasting blows rocks into our playground and sometimes it is very dangerous. One little boy got hit with a rock and our headmaster swore; some big boys heard him. He said damn I'll blast them.

It's a long way home from school and I'm hungry. My brothers and my sister have run away from me. I'm going to tell on them when I get home. They cracked my slate too. I'm not going to school tomorrow now. Nobody can make me. I'll hide. I hate school like anything and I'm hungry as anything too.

It's the sack man! I can hear his cart coming and his horse walking. Where can I run? Where can I hide? It's dirty in the ditch and I've got my new school frock on. I can hear the man talking to nobody coming nearer. Quick. Quick. Get in the ditch. Get right down so he can't see you. Never mind the spiders and frogs. Oh Mummy. Mum. The sack man's coming. He's stopped. I can see the wheels of his cart. He's looking and looking. He's laughing at something. I mustn't cry. He'll hear me. I mustn't cry yet.

Still as still I am way down in the wet ditch.

The man's talking to himself some more. 'I'll skin 'm alive when I catch 'm.' He's laughing again and slapping the reins and the horse is slowly walking away, slowly, slowly down the road.

The sack man's gone. He's round the corner and out of sight and I am crying. I am crying and running home. It's hard to cry when you're running and it's hard to run when you're crying. I've left my slate in the ditch and my dress is wet and dirty and I'm crying loud as anything and running fast as anything too.

The cherries are ripe. Our orchard is big and has high wire netting all round it and a wire netting roof. The blackbirds love our cherries and get into them no matter how often the netting is mended. Blackbird hunts are exciting. Round and round the birds fly, forgetting the way they got in. They shriek as loud as we do chasing them with long sticks. Lower and lower they fly as they get more and more tired. When they are too tired to fly anymore they cling to the netting with their claws. Their orange beaks and black wings are wide open. We catch them easily and feel their hearts bumping in our hands. We wring their necks, jerking downwards and upwards hard. Sometimes we pluck them and make them into blackbird pies in our outside play oven. They are greedy birds and they eat our cherries. They look sick without their feathers on.

We have been good and can have our candles alight for a little while longer before going to sleep. I am in the black double bed with the gold knobs on it with my two sisters. It's my turn to sleep in the middle.

Diamond is going to tell us a story when she has put the boys to bed. Mother is too busy. Baby is sick and our father is worried about something.

Why doesn't Diamond come?

The boys are fighting in their bedroom. It sounds like a pillow fight.

It's real night now. The moths are flying round and round the candle nearer and nearer. That one flew straight into the flame. It's shivering in the grease.

It's warm under the blankets. Why doesn't Diamond come and tell us our story? I wish baby would stop crying. I wish my sister would stop curling her legs round mine and let me go to sleep. I don't want a story now.

I went to the end of the pines today. My brothers are making a hut in the top of a pine. It's a secret hut but I followed them. They pulled up the rope ladder to their hut so I went on to the end of the pines a long long way. Funny things live under the pines. Monster spiders and monster toadstools. It got darker and darker and quieter and quieter as I went and the world changed and I got a little bit frightened but not much. I got to the end of the pines where our father's paddocks end and stood in a little corner full of pine needles and looked over a stile into someone else's paddocks. It was a long long way from home. It was a funny feeling. I ran and ran home over the slippery needles. I didn't stop until I could see our house. I didn't look behind me until I was in our backyard. I hopped and skipped and jumped to the open back door. I'm glad I went to the end of the pines by myself now that I am home again.

The traction engine comes when the wheat is cut. It chugs across the paddocks pulling the cook house and the bunk house behind it. Its belt flies round and the chaff flies up and wheat runs into the sacks and looks like water pouring out. It's best of all sitting in the cook house with the cook. Outside it is hot and the sunshine is full of flying chaff and the traction engine is shaking the ground and making a lot of noise. It hurt our feet coming over the stubble to the cook house. I wish I could sleep in the bunkhouse instead of going back home over the stubble. It hurts our bare feet more going home when the men are finished work and stop the engine and the sun goes down. Our feet sting till we go to sleep but tomorrow the engine will start chugging again and the gold chaff will be flying up into the air and falling like another kind of rain and the cook said he would cook us something nobody has ever tasted before – tomorrow.

Our Father is worried about something. We can tell by his nose. It looks white as if it has been pinched. Our Father eats his meals in his study where we are sent if we have to get the strap. Our Father is deaf. If we knock too softly on the study door he doesn't hear us and we don't always get the strap. We tell Mother our Father didn't hear us and she knows we are telling the truth. Our Mother always tells the truth no matter what. When she can't tell the truth she won't talk. She just looks at us or goes on working or sends us outside with a scone or biscuit. Sometimes I tell a lie and it makes me feel sick and funny inside. But I don't care.

'Sticks and stones will break your bones but names will never hurt you.' Mother always says this when we call each other names that make us cry. There is one name we are frightened to call each other. Somebody made it up and after a while it was the worst word. My brothers kick and punch each other if they are called this name. Sometimes they start a little fight and then hurt each other too much and then yell this word and the fight gets a big one and Mother calls our Father and my brothers get the strap in the study. We don't know who made the word up. It is Bellbail.

The Sunday school picnic is held at our place this time because we all have the mumps and our Father is the minister. We are in the front bedroom where the veranda is so we can watch the games and races on the lawns outside. The boys and girls are allowed to come and see our mumps through the window. We are the most important people at the picnic.

Our Father is talking to all the ladies in their hats on the lawn, and Mother and Diamond are making lots of pots of tea in the kitchen. Diamond is our grown up sister and we love her next best to our Mother. I don't know why we call her Diamond. Her real name is Dora. She is a teacher but not at our school.

Our Father has a fishing hut on the Opihi River. We went there in our trap one day with Mother and baby too. Our Father made the horse gallop and Mother made him stop and let the horse just trot. All its muscles went the other way when it trotted. It is a very shiny horse and shies a lot and Mother was glad to get out of the trap and go into the hut. She put baby on the bottom bunk to go to sleep and after a while we went on the river in our boat. Our second littlest brother fell out filling a rusty kettle with water. He went right under and we couldn't see him for a long time. When he came up Mother caught him by his jersey and pulled him back into the boat and we all went back to the hut. Our Father was making fishing flies with coloured feathers and wasn't very worried. Mother wanted to go home and our Father got cross with her and she cried and we cried too.

Saturday is a different sort of day. Diamond bakes and sews and Mother irons our Father's stiff shirts and collars. The shirts stand up almost by themselves after Mother has ironed and ironed them until they are shiny. The kitchen is hot with the black irons on the stove and things in the oven. Our Father is writing his sermon in the study and we can go where we like. We like it best in the kitchen but we have to go outside. Our big brothers have to weed two rows of vegetables before they can go where they like.

We are making a house in the macrocarpa hedge and Diamond has let us have an old mat to put in it. The hedge has got a nice smell because it has just been cut. If we are good and don't quarrel Diamond is going to give us some hot scones to play afternoon tea with. We have an enamel tea set in our hedge house.

Yesterday one of our brothers said 'bum' and nearly got the strap in the study but he didn't knock loud enough so he has to weed three rows in the garden instead of two. Mother said so. He's not weeding very fast because he's reading a book behind the bean sticks. It is Saturday night in our wash house and the copper is steaming hot. Annie and I have our baths first always in the two wash tubs. Diamond fills the tubs with hot water from the copper and when we are in we are allowed to splash each other a bit. Our brothers have their baths after we all do. Our brothers are not allowed to see us undressed and we are not allowed to see them undressed. Boys have something girls haven't got and it's rude to try to see what. But Mary Smith told me one day. It's a sort of teapot.

Sunday we are dressed up most of the day. We don't like Sundays much except Sunday dinner. It gets a bit exciting when we know that soon we will be called for dinner and there are red jellies and junket with nutmeg on to have after our vegetables. Everyone goes away after dinner to do things alone. Our Father goes to sleep in his chair in the study and our Mother sometimes has a rest on her bed with baby beside her. Diamond goes away to write poetry and won't answer if we call her. It's dull till everyone wakes up again.

Sometimes we go to Sunday school and sometimes we don't. Our Father is a funny sort of minister. Mary Smith said her mother said so. He should make his own children go to Sunday school always her mother said. Her mother said our Father shouldn't give our Mother so many babies. Her mother said she wouldn't be our Mother for anything. Mary Smith is a Bellbail. She's a bino too. She's got pink eyes like a white rabbit.

A boy at school said our Father was a pacifist and he said the policeman would put him in jail if there was a war. Some people at our church don't like our Father because our Father doesn't believe in kings and queens and wars. Most people like our Father a lot and are always shaking his hand. Mr Wells likes him a lot. Mr Wells has a lot of money. He was our baker until his uncles in Australia left him all their money. He doesn't sit up on the baker's cart now. He is going to build our Father a new church if some people don't stop talking about our Father.

We aren't exactly poor but we aren't exactly rich either. The Robinsons are rich. They always have ribbons in their hair and shoes on and icing on their cake. They don't play with us but we have lots more fun than they do. They said parsons are always poor people. But we aren't a poor family. We just aren't very rich that's all and sometimes we have to wear one another's dresses and coats if it rains too long and sometimes we have porridge for tea as well as for breakfast but not often.

I'm up a gum tree nearly near the top. There's a big hard wind blowing and a lot of noise. All the trees are bending backwards and forwards and the hedges too and the fowl house roof is clapping. The wind won't let the smoke from our chimney go straight up. It blows it round and round and down. If I close my eyes the noise is like the sea smashing and my stomach feels funny. If I look up the top of my tree is going round and round like seaweed does round a rock. But it makes me dizzy if I look up and I mustn't fall. The wind is blowing the hens the wrong way. They look silly when they run with their feathers blowing the wrong way. The rooster won't run; the wind can't make him. He looks annoyed but he won't run. Annoyed is a new word. I like saying it. Annoyed. Annoyed. Words are funny. They are only sounds coming out of your mouth. Annoyed annoyed annoyed. It doesn't mean anything now. Nobody knows where I am. Nobody in the world knows where I am. The wind is annoying a seagull trying to fly home. He's nearly got nearer and nearer twice but he's slipping sideways again down to the treetops and away out of sight nearly. But he won't give up. He's trying again. Why doesn't he walk back to the sea? He'd look funny walking down our road into town and down to the beach. That was a bigger noise somewhere like a barrel rolling. Maybe a tree has fallen down. Maybe it was thunder. Maybe I had better get down. It looks like a long way down and I'm not sure which way I got up. If I turn round backwards it might be better. If I can reach the first branch down I'll be all right but my foot can't reach the branch I want, nearly but not quite. Another thunder bang. I don't like thunder. I must get down even if I fall a bit of the way. If I let go to the next branch I'll be down quick. But I mustn't fall too far. Why doesn't someone call me and find out where I am and help me get down? It's no use shouting. There is too much noise and nobody would hear me. It's no use crying either. When I count three I'll let go a little bit. One. Two. When I count three this time I'll let go. One. Two. More thunder close as anything and big raindrops. One. Two. I want to cry but I won't. I want to let go but I can't and it's raining. The seagull tried again and he's probably home. Quick before more thunder comes. One. Two. Three. I'm on to the branch! Now I can get the rest of the way. I'm on to the ground safe. I am running for home. I didn't cry either. The wind is blowing my hair and dress in front of me. I hope I get to the back door before more thunder comes. The wind blows the door open out of my hand and I'm inside the kitchen with my brothers and sisters and Mother.

'Where have you been?' Mother says and I say up a gum tree.

My brothers and sisters laugh and I hate them all suddenly but I like being inside with them.

'By gum she's been up a gum tree,' my brother says.

'Did you get stuck up a gum tree?' my other brother says and they laugh a lot more.

Mother says don't mind dear but I do mind and I'm nearly crying. I didn't cry properly before when I was stuck up the tree. Why did nobody miss me when I was stuck up the gum tree and nearly in a storm, not even my Mother? I hate everybody for laughing but still I'm glad to be inside even though I am crying now.

Diamond says our Father is worried because the war has started and he doesn't believe in fighting. She says our Father believes in peace and truth and beauty. She says God is love and nobody must hate anybody if they believe in God. She says we must be good as gold if we want to help our Father.

Our Father and Mother and Diamond talk a lot in the study. It's secret talk and we are not allowed in. Yesterday my brothers saw some soldiers on Caroline Beach and one was the Robinsons' big brother. They are going to fight the Germans soon. They were singing songs.

I have got more brothers and sisters than anyone in Timaru. I have got six brothers and seven sisters. I was born on the 7th of May in 1907 and I am the seventh daughter so I make seven my lucky number. My name is Lynda.

*

It's not a secret anymore. We are all going to America except our two big brothers. Woodrow Wilson lives in America and he is a pacifist too. Diamond says we will all be happier in America and our Father can preach peace there and not be put in jail. We are going on a train and a big boat but not if we aren't good. Diamond says just be good and try and forget we are going away and we will soon be there. She says just to play until the day.

I don't like playing anymore. I want to be inside with Mother and Diamond. They are sewing our clothes and Annie and Jeannie and Hannah and me are going to have navy serge dresses all made the same except for the embroidery on them. Mine is going to have blue forget-me-nots on it and Annie's is going to have purple violets. We are going to wear ribbons in our hair too like the Robinsons, and shoes. Why doesn't the day come? And why is everyone so cross even Diamond? Our sister Ruth doesn't want to come to America. She's got a sweetheart she kisses down our drive but our Father says she's got to come and no nonsense. She cries and cries.

Our second eldest brother is a sailor. He ran away to sea. He isn't coming to America. Our other big brother is a teacher and will be a soldier soon. Our Father is disappointed with him for not being a pacifist. It's nearly the day and we are allowed to play in the passage if we want to. The house makes a lot of noise when we run in it. It hasn't got any carpets or curtains and all our things are in boxes and suitcases. Our Father's books went yesterday and tonight some of us are going to sleep at other people's places and some of us are going to sleep on the floor. We have only got breakfast at our house now and then we are going to the station and then to the boat and then to America.

It is night now and our room looks funny from the floor. The ceiling is too high. The floor is hurting my back. It's hard whichever way I turn but Annie is asleep sucking her thumb with her head off the pillow on the floor. She always goes to sleep first. I wish all my other brothers and sisters were home. What will school be like in America? Will they talk a different language there? I wish I wasn't going now. I wish the furniture was all back in the house and I was going to school at our school tomorrow and our Father wasn't a pacifist and there wasn't any war.

I can't go to sleep. I want to be in the kitchen where Mother and Diamond are drinking tea and Baby and Dickie are asleep in the cosy corner. Everyone is up except Annie and me and Jeannie and Hannah. Ruth is outside somewhere talking to her sweetheart. I saw her go along the drive under the trees. Caroline and Vera are up somewhere too. I wish the moon would stop staring in the window. There aren't any blinds to pull down. The floor is getting harder and harder and I don't want to go to America tomorrow. I wish Diamond would come in and tell me a story. I can't go to sleep and I left my blue tea set in the hedge and I don't want Mary Smith to find it when we've gone away to America. I hate America. I can hear everybody talking in the kitchen. Talking and talking and talking.

It's tomorrow! We are really leaving Timaru now and we are at the station and the train is waiting. There are people everywhere. People we know and people we don't know and there is Mr Wells and where are my brothers? What if they miss the train? We are all going in one carriage our Father says. We must keep together or get left behind he says. Mother is keeping hold of Dickie and Adrian is asleep on her shoulder: he doesn't look like a baby anymore in his first pants and jersey even with his curls on. Annie and Jeannie and Hannah and I have to keep close to Diamond. John and Leigh have to help our Father with all the luggage but where are they? Our Father is looking cross a bit and our Mother too and the train has whistled. Now we are getting on and everybody is moving quicker and a lot of people are by our carriage to say goodbye to our Father and Mother, and John and Leigh are the last to get on the train. Our window is open and Mr Wells is giving Diamond a big tin of mixed biscuits to eat on the journey: he's got a kind face and he looks as if he's going to cry; he shakes hands for a long time with our Father. The train is whistling again and we are moving. We are really leaving Timaru. It's true at last! Everybody is waving goodbye to us. Lots of our Father's church people are running beside our carriage calling out good luck and God bless and one man is shaking his fist and a red white and blue flag at us but we can't hear what he is shouting there is so much noise. And now there is only the noise of the train and our Mother is crying a bit and our Father is patting her shoulder and Timaru is a long way behind already.

*

Christchurch about 19–

Mother has some funny sayings. One of them is that it's 'another shake of the kaleidoscope'. I got a kaleidoscope for a present last Christmas; it never shows the same picture no matter how often you shake it. Mother says that every shift to a new house in another town is a shake of the kaleidoscope. Mr Jutsum gave me my kaleidoscope. He has a toyshop in Christchurch and he is a pacifist like my Father and goes to my Father's lectures in the Trades Hall. He is a bachelor and loves children. At Christmas time he gives toys away. He just leaves boxes of toys on poor people's front verandas on Christmas Eve and nobody knows who leaves them. He loves my Mother because she has so many children and he loves my Father just like Mr Wells did because he is a pacifist. Not many other people like us; that's why we left America and came back to New Zealand. When America went into the war my Father had to stop preaching peace or else be put in prison. He says he would rather be put in prison in New Zealand.

The last shake of the kaleidoscope left some bits out. Our sister Ruth got married in America and didn't come home to New Zealand. She married an American mechanic. And Caroline stayed in America too to keep Ruth company in case she was lonely. And Diamond fell in love with a Dutchman there and is going back to be married soon. She only came back to New Zealand to help our Mother with us children on the trip.

I am not a child anymore and I am not a pacifist. I am nearly ten years old and I had a fight with my fists last week with Pamela Hammel next door. She called my Father a coward because he didn't believe in fighting so I hit her and pulled her hair and pushed her in the gutter on the way home from school. I enjoyed not being a pacifist and not turning the other cheek. I called her a witch. She has white hair like string and a sharp nose.

We go to Shirley School now. When we were in America we went to a two storey school called Oxford School. Our New Zealand teachers ask us to tell the class what Oxford School was like. It makes us feel important telling the class about the school in America. It makes us forget we are pacifists. A Japanese boy and two German girls and two French boys were at Oxford School when we were there but everybody was more interested in us because we came from New Zealand and nobody knew where New Zealand was. We used to tell our playmates over there that New Zealanders talked a different language and we would say a lot of Maori names jumbled up to prove it. We had fire drill twice a week and stood on drying grates if we got wet coming to school. Coming to school we used to see snakes in the gutters and once we saw a huge tarantula spider come out of a rock wall. Near our house in Oakland lived a millionaire family and they had a swimming pool and let us swim in it; there were yellow water snakes in it but they didn't bite. All the children at Oxford school were rich; they brought grapes and water melons and things in jars in their lunch baskets and nobody was a bit hungry there. We only came back because America went into the War and our Father wouldn't stop being a pacifist and my brother Dickie and I didn't grow. Dickie and I got thinner and thinner and our Father and Mother said we were two trees which didn't transplant so we all came home to live in Christchurch.

We have a nicer house than we had in Timaru because it is new with a tile roof. We have an orchard and a rose garden and a creek. We have play houses under the willows down by the creek and my brothers have a willow swing. It's very dangerous because you have to hold on to long willow branches tied together and swing way out over the creek and land back on the bank again. The other day Leigh wouldn't let John land and he just hung over the water in the middle of the creek until he had to let go; he was in his school clothes and our Father was very angry and Leigh had to weed the rose garden and had a clod fight and got the strap in the study so it wasn't a very nice day.

I only have one playmate. Her name is Madge and she lives over the road from us. Her father is at the war and her mother is supposed to be half German so doesn't come out of her house much. I like going to Madge's place to play because she has lots of toys and dresses and learns music. But I'm not allowed to play with her for a week because one night in her bedroom we cut all the pearls off her mother's wedding dress to make a long string of pearls right down to the floor and now Madge has to sew them all back on again, so many every night until they are all in place again. It was the longest string of pearls in the world.

I'm clever at school except at arithmetic. I am bottom of my class at arithmetic. When we are doing sums something happens to my head but the teacher won't believe me and makes me stand up and do the sum out loud and everybody laughs. But I am best at drawing and always come top in it. Our teacher is a returned soldier and was gassed at the war. He has a sick stomach and keeps lots of pills in his pocket. His eyes look just like our gooseberries when they are half ripe.

We have a big bad boy in our class and he is in love with my sister Annie. He writes her notes and waits in the grass on the way home from school to talk to her. He doesn't like anyone else in the world not even his mother and father. He steals things and dresses like a robber with a black cowboy hat and a black belt. Nobody can stop him doing anything he wants to. Only Annie isn't frightened of him. Once he jumped down out of a tree right in front of Annie and Madge and me and pointed a pistol at us. He was going to kidnap us but Annie made him let us go. Annie is very pretty with black hair and black eyebrows but she's got a pug nose; my brothers sometimes call her pug. Madge is very pretty too: she's got real yellow curls and dimples and some freckles she doesn't like. I haven't got much; my hair is brown in a not very long plait and my teeth aren't straight but I don't mind much.

Our Father has been in the papers and everybody is talking about him again even children at school. Our sister Jeannie cries about it and won't go to school anymore. She is going to work instead; she is fifteen and prettier than Annie even, only she has long fair hair almost down to her waist. She says our Father should stop talking peace and be like other fathers.

I like best being away from all my brothers and sisters and playing actresses and princesses with Madge down the creek in our secret place. We have grown up dresses to wear hidden in a butter box. Madge's mother gave them to us. Next best I like to hide in the orchard when I come home from school with a book from the school library to read, only Mother gets cross when she finds out because she says I'm spoiling my eyes reading until it gets almost dark. Sometimes I do wish and wish I was pretty like the princesses I read about.

We have to salute the flag at school now before we go in to class.

One day I'm not going to. I've made up my mind. Maybe tomorrow I won't. I can read the paper easily now but Mother doesn't like us to read the Killed and Wounded and Missing part. I had a dream about the Germans the other night. I dreamt that Dickie and I were in the vegetable garden and we heard the Germans coming. We hid way under the trellis with the scarlet runner beans on it and we could see the German boots marching past us and then one German stopped and lifted up the runner beans and saw us and I woke up! Sometimes at night when I'm in bed I wonder and wonder where the Missing are. It must be funny not to be anywhere at all like them. I don't like thinking what I think in bed sometimes.

The Insurance man has just been and he made our Mother cry. He said he doesn't want our insurance because somebody might set fire to our house because we are pacifists. I wish he had fallen off his bike and broken his neck. I wish and wish and wish there was no war.

I did it today. I don't quite know why I did it. I didn't salute the flag when we marched into school. When I said I wouldn't no matter what my teacher sent me to the Headmaster's office and I had to wait for him. I was very frightened when I heard him coming and nearly ran home but didn't. When the Headmaster asked me why I wouldn't salute the flag I didn't know exactly why I wouldn't. He said was it because my Father was a pacifist and I said yes my Father didn't believe in war and I was on his side. He asked me would I salute the flag tomorrow and I said I still didn't want to so he said I have to go into class five minutes early every morning to miss saluting the flag. He didn't growl at me once and when he opened the door for me to go he smiled at me as if we had a secret. I am not frightened of him anymore.

I wish and wish the war was over and Madge's father was home and my Mother and Father would talk about other things beside peace and war. It's nearly Christmas and nobody seems to care but me. I am making my Mother a dust cap over at Madge's place for her Christmas present. Madge's mother gave me the patches for it from her patch bag. It is going to be very pretty and it doesn't take much sewing. It has a covered button on it in front to fasten it with. The button part is going to be the hardest to sew but Madge's mother is going to show me how to do it. My Mother doesn't know a thing about her present so it will be a big surprise for her on Christmas morning.

Sometimes I hate everybody and everything. Mother says I have 'a little black dog on my back' when I feel like this. It's another one of her sayings. But I only feel like this when everybody looks sad and serious and there is no fun. Sunday is a serious sort of day. On Monday after it there is always something in the paper about our Father preaching peace, and lots more names of soldiers killed and missing in the war. In our house the people who come to see our Father say that something will happen soon. Our eldest brother who went to the war is a captain now and our Father isn't pleased. Everybody else is pleased when somebody is made a captain. The world is a silly place.

Our Father is in prison and has to stay there for a year and Diamond is away too back in America. She has a different name now and it's too hard to say. It's Dutch. Our Mother often cries and goes out to the kitchen so we won't see her. Our sister Vera stays home from work to help her. Leigh and John don't quarrel much anymore to help our Mother too. Only Jeannie isn't nice sometimes; she says she is ashamed of our Father and the girls at work won't sit with her. Hannah might have to go to work soon too but she doesn't mind doing anything to help our Mother, she said so.

On Saturdays our Mother goes to see our Father and takes him things and a lot of Church people and pacifists go too. So many that they have to have a special bus but most people are glad our Father is in Gaol. I think my teacher is.

This Christmas was the best I remember. Mr Jutsum brought us all a big box of toys and stayed to Christmas dinner and after tea we all went out onto the lawn and let off fireworks. Mr Jutsum brought a big box of crackers and rockets from his shop, more than anyone else in our street had, and a lot of children came to watch us let them off but they didn't come right in to our place because their mothers and fathers wouldn't let them. My Mother liked her dust cap but the button came off it and I have to sew it on before she can wear it again. She wants to wear it very soon again she says. It is a bit too big but she doesn't mind. I got a doll just like a baby and Annie got its twin so we are going to call them Paul and Pauline. I don't like dolls much but I wouldn't tell Mr Jutsum. I like books best and my Mother gave me Grimm's fairy tales with pictures for every story in it. It's the biggest book I've ever got but I'm not allowed to read it in the orchard after school Mother says. I've got to do my work and home lessons first. I've promised. It was a lovely Christmas.

*

It's peace time again and my Father is home and I have passed my proficiency exam. I am going to High School next year. Hannah is going to work. She isn't very clever at school and likes being home best but she doesn't mind working in Mr Jutsum's shop. The epidemic is on and a lot of people are dying of Influenza. Our Father says it is the war's fault. Nobody in our house has had it yet but two people in our street have died. We see funerals every day. There is a tram near our place where everyone goes to have nose sprays and breathe in and out. You go in one end of the tram and get sprayed and come out the other. It's to kill the Flu' germs. Everyone has S.O.S. stickers to put in the window in case they get the Flu' bad and need help. There is one in the corner house where some rich people live. I don't know their name. They don't like ordinary people so nobody near knows them very well. Most rich people have gone away from their homes to stay in the country or at the beach while the Flu' is on. There are a lot of burglaries. I suppose the burglars aren't nervous of germs.

There are hundreds of girls at High School and we learn French and Latin. I catch the tram every day and cross the Square and walk up a busy street to the school. The boys' High School is near our school. Our Head Mistress won't let us walk up the same street as the boys do. We aren't allowed to talk to boys. But some girls do when they get round the corner out of sight. Madge doesn't come to our High School. She is going to live in Wellington soon. My best friend at High School is called Louise and she is as pretty as Madge only she has dark curls. Her father is manager of the picture theatre in the Square. He buys Louise the best clothes of any girl in our form. She doesn't talk about her mother much. She isn't happy at home, only when she is with her father or with me. We are writing a book in our lunch hour. Louise is doing the writing part and I am doing the pictures for it and lots of girls come into the shelter shed at lunch time and ask us to read it out loud. It's about a man called Eric and a girl called Magic. Last chapter a bad man called Alec has Magic tied to a tree and is going to torture her. Next chapter Eric is going to save her and in the last chapter he is going to marry her. Louise and I have got it all worked out. I do a drawing for every chapter and paint it when I get home at night. I'm still top of my class at drawing.

I got into trouble at school today. We have a horrid little man for physical drill. All the girls hate him. He says girls shouldn't wear stays or elastic in their bloomers and to find out if they are he feels them. He is a military man and a captain and comes all polished up in uniform to teach us drill. He is so small he looks silly. We nickname him Rooster. Today a girl called Evelyn who hates him most wouldn't stop talking when we were marching in a big circle. Rooster stopped the march and made Evelyn come and stand in the middle of the circle and said, 'Now to prove how uninteresting your chatter is I am going to ask any girl who likes talking to you to come out here.' Nobody was going to until I did then everybody came out of line to talk to Evelyn and nobody was left to march. Rooster went red and made me stand by myself in the circle and sent me to the Head Mistress when drill was over. I was frightened but I was wild too and told our Head Mistress that all the girls hated the drill master but I wouldn't tell her why because it didn't seem nice to. She just said, I think I see and You may go now.

It was very exciting last night. We were all in bed when the widow lady next door ran in and said her boy had jumped out the window and was away down by the creek. He has got the Flu and was too hot in bed and wanted to get cool. John and Leigh got up and went to find him. They pulled him all the way back and he bit Leigh's finger. He didn't mean to. He only did it because he has fever and was too sick to know what he was doing. I hope he doesn't die.

We are going to the beach too at New Brighton like rich people. Mr Jutsum has found us a house. He is worried about us all in case we catch the Flu and won't let our mother say no we can't go. He won't let our Father pay for the house either. So next Saturday Adrian and Dickie and Annie and Hannah and John and Leigh with Mother and me are catching the tram to New Brighton. Vera is staying home to look after our Father and Jeannie is going to stay at a friend's place. Mr Jutsum wants our Father to come to the beach too but he is still writing the book he started to write in prison and he doesn't want to leave his study and he lectures a lot still too. He's allowed to now and not so many people think what he says is wrong like they used to.

It's just lovely at New Brighton. There is hardly any work in the house to do and we can stay away at the beach or in the sandhills nearly all day if we want to. I like the sandhills best. It's easy to get lost in them. Each one you go over is just like the next one until you're right in the middle of them like in a desert. There isn't a sound either unless you remember to listen for the sea. I found a grave in them one day. At least I think it was a grave. I didn't dare dig it up to make sure in case it was. It was the shape of a grave and had a jam jar with red geraniums at each end of it. It wasn't long enough to be a grown up's grave. I sat down by it and felt very sad and queer in case somebody was really in it. I wondered if someone's child had died of the Flu and there weren't enough proper people to bury her. I was sure she was a girl like me and wondered what it was like to be dead. And then I got frightened and went home. I told my brothers about the grave but when I tried to find it next day to prove it I couldn't. They said I was dreaming it because I am so romantic and it's not fair because I really did see it.

I know I'm romantic. Annie isn't a bit. She does things I wouldn't. She sneaks out after tea and meets Nicky. He is still in love with her. He is still a bad boy. He has got two black moles on his face and wears cowboy clothes still and hides down by the creek. He hates me because I try to stop Annie from meeting him. Annie doesn't like me much either. She quarrels with me and calls me a sap. John and Leigh are going to catch Nicky one day and give him a hiding for meeting Annie and giving her violets he steals from other people's gardens. Our Father and Mother don't know about Nicky and Annie.

I don't like boys very much. I like Madge still. But Madge likes boys now too. She has got lots of them. They are always writing her notes about being in love with her. She shows them to me. She doesn't like playing actresses anymore and doesn't like reading books as much as she did. I like one boy a bit. He is John's best friend at High School and his name is Simon but John doesn't like me to like him. He's got a mole on his face too but he doesn't look like Nicky. He blushes a lot and Nicky never blushes. I know Simon likes me but he won't let John know and they go out to football together every Saturday and sometimes on Sunday they go out together in Simon's father's Ford to the Waimakariri River to fish. One day Simon is going to take me out in his father's Ford even though he hasn't actually said so. He almost asked me last weekend but John called out to him to come and he didn't ask. He blushed a lot and went off to play football with John. John says I'm a romantic idiot and it's time I woke up and stopped reading books and pretending. Only my Father likes me to read and I'm allowed in his study any time I like, to read anything I like. I have read a lot of his Greek Myth books and enjoy knowing about the Gods. Sometimes I feel very lonely but I don't mind the feeling. I enjoy the feeling because there is no end to it and I can be lonely for as long as I like even when everybody is around me. Perhaps I am too romantic. Dreaming is nice. It's next best to reading.

I got my essay on gardens in the school magazine and came top of my form in drawing. Louise came top in French so her father is giving us the very best seats upstairs in his theatre next Saturday to see Mary Miles Minter act. She is my favourite actress. And my Father says I am to go to School of Art evening classes once a week, for coming top in drawing. There is another girl at school I like but Louise doesn't like me to like her. Her name is Ruby and she is not a bit pretty but all the boys like her and take her to surprise parties. She wants me to go to a surprise party soon but she won't ask Louise to go to it. Louise doesn't like boys at all. She says they bore her ever so. Ruby says there is a boy who wants me to go to the surprise party but she won't tell me his name. He goes to High School and has seen me and asked Ruby about me. If I go I have to meet him in the Square and he will take me from there to the party. I don't know if I want to go to it or not.

I went to see the School of Art teachers about taking lessons and took some of my drawings to show them. I like drawing people best. The head teacher said I am very good and he asked me how old I was. He wants me to do drawing from life. He took me into a classroom to show me what life pupils were drawing and I felt very uncomfortable because the pictures were all of naked men and women. He said all the pupils in life class had to be over sixteen but if I wanted to very much I could start before I was sixteen to draw from models. I didn't want to very much because all the pictures of bodies made me blush all the time he was talking. So I have decided to take Sculpturing for a while.

I am going to the surprise party and Hannah is lending me her violet voile dress with the frill round the bottom and arms of it to wear. Mother said I can go as long as I am home by twelve o'clock. I'm pinning my hair up in a plait round my head and wearing a pair of Jeannie's silk stockings only she doesn't know that I am. She mightn't lend them to me if I asked so I'll just take them out of her drawer and put them on last thing of all. I am catching the seven o'clock tram. I wonder what the boy is like who is meeting me. I know his name is Lester.

It is the night of the party! My dress looks very pretty and Hannah has helped do my hair. I feel a little bit sick but perhaps it's because I couldn't eat any tea. I've got ten minutes to catch my tram. If Jeannie would go out of the bedroom I could get her silk stockings. I just can't wear my black school ones. They would look too awful. I almost don't want to go to the party; then I could eat the cakes I am taking for supper and read my library book and be perfectly happy. Lester is a silly name for a boy and I mightn't like him a bit. If my stomach grumbles like this at the party I'll die. I'm perfectly hungry and I know I won't be able to eat a bite at the party, it's too awful eating in front of strangers especially if they are boys and you are trying to eat nicely. There's the phone and maybe there isn't going to be a party or perhaps Lester can't meet me. I do wish he couldn't. It's for Jeannie and she's going out of the bedroom. Now for her stockings. They feel nice on my legs but I wish the silk part came up far enough; my dress doesn't quite meet the silk. But I must go or else I'll miss the tram and I mustn't forget my basket of cakes and I must kiss Mother goodbye and promise not to be home late. Hannah is lovely. She has just given me her best lace hanky to take. I've never been so excited!

There is another girl on the tram who is going to the party. She goes to our school but I don't know her very well. She is wearing a blue lace dress and has pinned a blue artificial flower in her hair. She looks very pretty but I don't think she wants to speak to me. She keeps looking away out the window. I wonder if Jeannie has found out about her silk stockings yet? If she doesn't miss them tonight she needn't ever know I wore them. I'm dreadfully hungry.

I can see two boys standing waiting for someone. If one of them is Lester what shall I say to him first? Oh what shall I say first? Just hello and something about the weather; about what a lovely night it is. One of the boys is coming over to the girl in blue. He looks nicer than the one coming over to me. I wish he was Lester. I wish I hadn't come.

Lester is nearly fat. He says hello Lynda and I say hello Lester and then we both say nothing and walk to another tram. It's worse sitting in the tram with nothing to do but try not to look at one another. The girl in blue is laughing a lot and she is smoking a cigarette her boy has given her. People are looking at her but I think she likes it.

I must say something soon. But what? What shall I say first? I say it's lovely this time of year isn't it? And Lester says invariably so and we don't talk anymore for a while. It's getting sillier and sillier just sitting and saying nothing and not knowing where I am going so I say this is a pretty suburb and don't the trees make everything nice and Lester says invariably so again. I ask Lester what he is taking at High School. He says Science is his main course and I say how exciting I love reading about Science and isn't it a wonderful world when you read about it? Lester says invariably so and we are nearly at the party.

The blue girl's boy's name is Jacob and he looks rich. He is the best dressed boy at the party and the only one who has got a cigarette case. He has got fair curly hair and looks like a picture of one of the Vikings in a book of my Father's. He has looked at me three times now but his girl hasn't spoken to me yet though I know her a bit; she keeps pulling him away into a corner and smoking his cigarettes. Lester won't leave me alone for a minute. He keeps saying invariably so to everything I say and keeps sitting beside me and bringing me cake I can't eat because I don't feel a bit hungry now.

There is a boy playing the piano all the time. Ruby is sitting next to him although the piano stool is only made for one. Ruby looks beautiful. She is all in red and has got some red on her lips and powder on her face. She looks quite different from what she looks like in school uniform. She is not a pretty girl really. Jacob has brought a lemonade bottle into the room and is spinning it on the floor. Everyone is sitting in a circle and when the piano stops and the bottle stops spinning too whoever it is pointing at has to go out of the room and be kissed by someone in the passage. It's an awful feeling waiting and hoping it doesn't point at you, and not knowing who is waiting for you in the passage. I knew it was Jacob before he kissed me in the dark. I could smell cigarette smoke on him. Our first kiss missed and when we tried again it was a long kiss and I wriggled and pushed him away. I couldn't breathe properly with his mouth on mine for so long. He said what's the matter and I said nothing only I don't like cigarette smoke much. He said that's because you don't smoke I'll give you one afterwards. Supper is over and it will soon be time to go home. Jacob's girl won't let him give me a cigarette. She said out loud for everyone to hear, you shouldn't start babies on bad habits, and she pulled him away from me. Lester keeps on saying it's time to go home so I had better go. I'm very hungry again now. It's after eleven o'clock and I haven't eaten a bite since lunch time. I hope Lester doesn't want to kiss me goodnight. There is something dirty about kissing. I've wanted to wash my face ever since Jacob kissed me in the passage. It's a lovelier night than ever and it's nearly twelve o'clock and funny to be outside at the gate with everyone inside and probably asleep. I wonder is Mother awake waiting for me to come inside? Lester says he wants to meet me again and take me to the pictures on Saturday afternoon. I think I'd like to go. I've promised to ask Mother if I can. I wish Lester would go now, I'm tired and I want to go inside and one silk stocking keeps slipping down. Lester is saying I want to kiss you goodnight Lynda, may I? I say that I think kissing is silly don't you? He almost said invariably so then said sometimes, it depends. We shook hands instead of kissing. Oh bed you're nice when I'm so tired and I don't like silk stockings much they are hard to keep up and isn't night lovely to be out in when everyone else is asleep? Asleep is best of all.

Jean is the prettiest of all my sisters but not the nicest. She found out about her silk stockings because I got a run in them the night of the party. Hannah didn't complain when I found I'd lost her lace hanky at the party. Jean hates work and only goes to get some money for herself she says and she doesn't always give Mother all her board money. She says she was meant to be a lady that's why she was born with such small hands. One of our ancestors was a real Lord. Mother has told us about him and I think Jean thinks she is too good to have to work in a shop sewing silk shades for rich people's homes. She calls Hannah 'little angel' because Hannah always gives Mother all her board money and never growls if tea isn't very nice. Ours is a funny house. We don't always have interesting things to eat but we have interesting pictures on the walls and a big bronze statue in the hall and our Father's study is full of valuable books. Our Father says that food for thought is more important than ordinary food and he says that to clothe the mind well is more important than to buy dresses and things. Jean doesn't believe him but I do, nearly always.

We have funny visitors sometimes. An Indian fruit shop man comes to see our Father. He is quite black and very shy of our Father, and a German lady we call Tanta comes too. She brings Mother pickled cabbage called sauerkraut which we don't like much. Mr Jutsum is our best visitor and he comes a lot. He used to be a rich Englishman but now he is a poor shopkeeper. He has given nearly all his money away. He always sells things at half price to poor people who come into his shop. I've been to his shop to have tea on Friday nights a lot so I can go to School of Art easier afterwards instead of going home for tea. He likes me and John best of all our family except for our Mother and Father of course. His shop is on a corner and is very narrow and dark and full of toys and things which are very dusty. Mr Jutsum lives upstairs over it in his storeroom. His bedroom is the funniest I've ever seen. It's like a box in the very middle of the upstairs part and nobody is allowed to go in and dust it not even Hannah who hates dust on anything. One day she went into it and tried to tidy it up but Mr Jutsum was so annoyed with her that she cried and told Mother all about it. She says she won't ever go into his horrible little bedroom again not even if Mr Jutsum drops cigarette butts round his bed as deep as a carpet. I love being invited to have tea upstairs with Mr Jutsum on Friday nights. He pushes all the broken toys and things off a long table and puts a newspaper down and sets all sorts of nice things to eat out in tins and pots. There is always a big tin of fancy biscuits on the table and a tin of any kind of jam with a tin opener beside it and hot pies from the shop next door and new bread and he never does the dishes straight after eating.

There is a man who comes into the shop every Friday night to see Hannah but I don't think she likes him very much. He is a lot older than her, nearly ten years older. He is a travelling salesman and a returned soldier. He's nice looking but Hannah doesn't like going out much; she is very shy and likes staying home best when she isn't working so she doesn't take much notice of him and won't go out with him. John often has tea with Mr Jutsum too. John likes lots of fun and teases everybody a lot and is no good at school. He doesn't work at his lessons enough. Leigh is going to be a teacher and is very serious and passes all his exams, but nobody likes him as much as they like John. John's last school report was a very bad one so he stood on a bridge over the Avon river and let the wind blow it out of his hand into the water and went home and told our Father that the wind blew his school report out of his hand into the river and of course it was the truth and our Father couldn't be cross.

Nothing is very fair. It's weeks since I went to the party and I never went to the pictures with Lester and still Louise hasn't spoken to me. Diamond has got a baby boy and Ruth is going to China to live

49

for a while, she has got a little girl. And our eldest brother is getting married soon to a society girl and Annie has got a new sweetheart and Nicky is jealous. Something is happening to everybody but me. Next week my Mother is taking me to a doctor. The school doctor said I might be getting a goitre and I must see a specialist soon. I heard Mother talking about me to Vera the other night. They said I was late or something. I wish Jacob would ring me up. He could easily find our telephone number from the book and I know he liked me. Simon hasn't asked me to go out in the Ford yet. I think he is frightened John will make fun of him if he does. I think Annie likes Simon too. She always lies out on the lawn when he is around on Saturday. Her new boy only comes to see her on Sundays. I think she is mean and silly the way she looks at boys, fluttering her eyelashes and showing all her teeth at them. She only does it to make me feel uncomfortable because my eyelashes aren't as long as hers and my teeth aren't as straight as hers. Nobody is very nice to me only my Mother and Father and Hannah. And I don't feel very well sometimes.

I got a surprising letter last week. It was from Louise's father and it had two tickets for the pictures in it and asked me to be friends with Louise again because Louise has been very unhappy. So I have written to Louise to ask her to be friends and come to the pictures with me again. I hope she does but I wish she wouldn't like only me at school.

I cry more easily now. Once nothing could make me cry if I didn't want to. I sometimes cry for nothing now. The other night I cried more than I ever have over anything. I was reading Seven Little Australians and came to the part where Judy dies after the tree falls on her and someone in the room was playing The Glow-worm on the gramophone and suddenly I began to cry and couldn't stop. Next day when no one was in the room I put the record on again and read over again the part where Judy dies and cried some more. It was all so sad again I nearly sicked up.

The Doctor has told my Mother that I must have iodine in water to drink so there is always a big jug of water with a few drops of horrible tasting iodine in it on the sink bench. I hate it but I have to drink it. The day I went to the doctor's I heard him talking to my Mother when I wasn't supposed to be listening. He said a word I've never heard before. I thought it was a disease so looked it up in Father's big dictionary when I got home. I wish I hadn't.

Nobody knows I'm meeting Simon round by the bridge next Sunday afternoon. He is taking me for a ride in his Ford. Only he has told John he is going to see his Auntie Sunday afternoon so I have to pretend I'm just going for a walk when I go to meet him. I'm going to wear an American dress Ruth sent me for my birthday. It's gingham and has a velvet bow at the neck. I tie a ribbon in my hair when I do it up now. I like Simon very much. I'm getting very excited about meeting him and hope I can get away without Annie guessing anything. She still likes Simon too.

I had the same dream last night. I've had it a lot of times. It came just as I was waking up. I think it's the dream that wakes me. Every time I'm in a desert somewhere all alone and standing still and without ever seeing it I know there is a caravan coming nearer. I don't know how I know it's a caravan just out of sight. As it comes nearer I can hear a bell tinkling. The tinkling bell is always the very last part of the dream and I hear it still even as my eyes are opening. It's a strange dream but I rather like it when it comes. I feel certain I'll see the caravan some time and understand something important.

John did a mean thing. I went out with Simon on Sunday. I got away all right. Annie was lying on the lawn with her hair she had just washed all over her face and I don't know where John was. I walked off in the opposite direction to the bridge and right round the block as if I was only going for a walk. When I got to the bridge Simon was waiting. He looked smart in his school blazer. I felt smart in my new dress too and it would have been lovely if John hadn't been so mean. He was hiding under the bridge and climbed up and sat on the rail of it and watched Simon and me until we drove away. Simon blushed and blushed and couldn't start the car properly. When it did start John called out give my love to your little Auntie and we nearly went into the gutter. I haven't spoken to John since and Annie calls me Auntie every time she can without Mother hearing. Just the same I'm going to meet Simon again in spite of John and Annie.

I didn't get my Senior Free Place. I don't know what happened to me in the examination room. I couldn't seem to get started and I got worse and worse each question I tried. Everybody else was writing fast and I got frightened in the end and never properly finished one question. It was so horrible I don't want to think about it. Louise passed so will be going to College next year. I'm going to work but Louise says she will still see me at the pictures on Saturday afternoons if I will go. Louise still doesn't like boys.

My Father is a Socialist as well as a pacifist and gives lectures on politics. He is still a minister too and believes in God but doesn't believe that the poor should always be with us like it says in the Bible. He believes in Darwin too and says man will evolve into something much better than he is at present. He says that when everybody is well fed and clothed and educated then Mankind will have time to discover Truth and Beauty and Love. I believe my Father. I sometimes go to his lectures. Mother plays the organ at them, a hymn to start with and a hymn to finish with. I walk home from them round the Avon river. I like walking alone. There is a lady I meet sometimes walking round the river alone too. She has told me her story and I don't like meeting her much. She told me her husband and only son were killed in the war. They used to walk round the river with her too before the war and feed the seagulls which fly up from the sea and sit on the banks. She still feeds the seagulls for her husband and son. When she got word from the war office that her family was killed she got such a shock that a blood clot went into her eye and she is half blind now. I don't like meeting her because she tells me the story all over again each time and her blind eye looks ugly. I don't like looking at it but pretend I don't mind.

This year our Father is going to England to visit two old Aunties and to get his book published. His two old aunties are paying for his trip because they want to see him before they die. I am named after one of them, great Aunt Harriet. Also our Father has got a touch of asthma and a sea trip is supposed to be good for asthma. Jean says his book won't make any money because it's all about Pacifism and Socialism and everybody is sick of everything except making money. It's just as well our Father is deaf or he would hear what she says. Jean is engaged to be married to a man who looks like Raymond Novarro the actor. She isn't very kind to him sometimes and I don't think she is very much in love. I could fall in love with him any day but he doesn't take any notice of me. He's mad about Jean and loves her long fair hair. I saw her take it down for him one night and he kissed it. Jean is so pretty a photographer asked her to pose for a picture he could put in his shop window in town. He gave her an enlargement of it free.

I'm still not very pretty but I don't mind much. Hannah is growing prettier but she is very shy. She is most like Mother with brown green eyes and dark hair. The commercial traveler still likes her and she goes out with him sometimes. Jean's sweetheart liked Hannah first until Hannah brought him home and he met Jean. Jean is like Annie. Men can't help falling in love with her. John says that when fellows meet Jean and Annie they can't see for looking poor saps.

I don't like my job very much. I work in a shop which sells frocks and fancy work and crockery. I have two men bosses and a head woman over me and a girl below me. I detest one of my bosses although he is good looking. He came into the shop the other day and said how's the enemy? I didn't know what he meant. He got wild and said what's the time, what's the time? And then one day he said there's fourpence on the floor Miss and I looked and couldn't see it. He said pick it up, pick it up, and pointed to a skein of fancy work silk which had fallen out of a drawer. The head lady worships him and runs when his bell rings from the office. I detest her too. She sold a frock we have had in the shop for ages to a nice woman who wanted a frock to wear to the races. The head lady said it was a frock from the last shipment and the woman believed her and bought it. It looked awful on her and the head lady laughed behind her back. When a hard to sell frock is sold in the shop whoever sells it gets a commission.

There is a boy who works in the next building who likes me. I make him a morning cup of tea sometimes if the head lady is out. He is trying to become a doctor and is saving to study in Otago University. He has a sad face and is very shy. He wants me to be engaged to him and marry him later on when he is a doctor. I would like him if he laughed sometimes but he never does. I never feel very happy with him. I still like Simon and wish he wasn't so frightened of John finding out about us liking each other. John likes plenty of girls. Simon is silly to keep everything so secret. He meets me after work sometimes in his father's Ford but he doesn't like John to know. Louise meets me too sometimes. She still dresses better than I do but always in tweed things and flat shoes. She doesn't like boys yet and says she never will. We go to the pictures at her father's Theatre sometimes on Saturday afternoons. She calls her father Dearest. There is a mystery in her life. She doesn't know what it is yet but her father is going to tell her one day and she is going to tell me.

Our Mother is very very upset. The commercial traveller wants to marry Hannah and Mother wants him to wait until our Father comes back from his visit to England so our Father can see if he likes him enough to let him marry Hannah. Hannah wants to get married but doesn't mind waiting until our Father comes home. The trouble is the commercial traveller doesn't want to wait that long and talks and talks to Mother to try and make her change her mind and I think he will win.

Jean is married to Jack, the handsomest man I've ever seen. Jean got married just before our Father went to England. She had a little wedding because she couldn't have a very big one; our Father couldn't afford to give her a big wedding. Jean said he could have if he hadn't spent money to go to England but she needn't grumble because she has a two storey house to live in and her husband's father is rich. There must be something in Jean that won't let her be glad about anything. If I was as pretty as she is and had a husband as handsome as hers and a two storey house to live in I'd be as happy as anyone in the world. I'm very sad sometimes. Things I read make me sad and music makes me sad too. There is something wrong with the world and I don't know what it is. I have written two or three poems about what is wrong with the world but they don't say quite what I mean. Diamond writes a lot of poetry now and gets it published; her poetry is very hard to understand but a lot of people understand it. We get letters and parcels from America nearly every mail. Ruth is in China and says she will come to New Zealand on her way home to America. It would be lovely to see her again and Mother is excited at the thought. I wish Diamond was coming for a visit too but she has two children now and not very much money though she is very very happy she says. Caroline got married in America too but doesn't write letters home much. Vera has gone to Wellington to work with a woman who has a dressmaking shop there. Only Hannah, Leigh, John, Annie, Dick, Adrian and I are home with Mother. We are a small family now. Whoever shakes the kaleidoscope has forgotten us for a while I think.

I couldn't sleep last night. The moon was shining in my bedroom window. It was perfectly round and I sat up and looked at it for too long. Annie was out somewhere in the rose garden with Nicky. The longer I looked at the moon the worse I felt until I felt so queer I hid under the blankets and cried. I felt sure something terrible was going to happen to me and to everyone I loved. It was no better under the blankets so I got out of bed and prayed on my knees to God to look after us all and not let any of us die too soon. I got back into bed and tried to imagine God but couldn't. I could only think about dying some day and what it would be like if everyone in our family died first and left me behind. I was glad when Annie crept in. She got into bed without putting on the light so Mother wouldn't know how late she had been out. I said I couldn't go to sleep and tried to make her talk but she wouldn't and went to sleep straight away. She looked black and white and beautiful asleep in the moonlight. She is exactly like Renee Adore the actress. I felt terribly lonely and sad. When I did get to sleep I dreamed and had a nightmare. I thought I was standing on the banks of the Avon River and as I looked at the water my Mother floated past drowning and then one by one the rest of my family. I tried hard to catch them but couldn't and was crying so hard I woke myself up.

It was wonderful waking up and knowing it was all a bad dream but then I couldn't get to sleep again for thinking about the dream.

Simon and I are going together seriously. John doesn't seem to mind us liking one another anymore. He likes a girl seriously himself so doesn't tease me like he used to. Annie makes fun of me still but Mother stops her from being too mean. Yesterday Mother patted my face and said I had a good kind face and Annie came in and said Yes just like a cow, Moo. I think she is jealous because Simon likes me. Next Sunday Simon is taking me to a picnic at Corsair Bay and I am

THREE

It's not possible to discover who Simon was or if he and Lynda carried on with their romance, but it's plain to see the sort of boy Lyndahl wanted for herself. And plain to see too the sort of child she was: dreamy yet adventurous, loyal, loving, intelligent, sentimental and brave.

She returns to her childhood again and again in stories and poems written throughout her life, and in recollective and meditative scraps put down in intervals in her busy days as a housewife and mother, and in the long sad times of her middle and old age.

In several pieces she alters the story set down in 'The Change', gives a sharper account, sees a different reality standing beside the one portrayed there. The conflicting narratives have an equal truth.

The idyllic side of a childhood in hard times goes on:

Saturday night baths in the washhouse
In the twin wooden tubs . . .
Dippers of rain-water soft-warmed poured on our dusty heads,
And home-made soap to scrub with down to our heels . . .
Then off to bed, two to a bed
In a tall room with one candle
Burning softly yellow on a white table cover,
Pale curtains gathered together
Against the blue night
And Sunday school tomorrow.

Our Father which art in his study
Writing a sermon is a good man . . .

She suggests, not very convincingly, that her father is 'like God'. But in an unpublished story, 'The Meek', written at about the same time as 'The Change', we find Mrs Calthorpe, a Florence Chapple figure, opening her eyes 'to the first thin light of another day' and holding her sleeping husband's hand between her own. "'Please God," she murmured, "love my children and keep them from harm . . . Help me to be a good mother and a good wife to John. Blessed are the meek. Amen.'" She then shuts her mind to thoughts of God and opens it to 'the crowding problems of meals and clothes and bills and cash in hand', and to a daughter's waywardness and a son's growing antagonism towards school. She looks at her husband again, 'such a good man and so clever with all his books and reading; always speaking up for social reform and the betterment of the human race . . .'

Later, after giving her children their breakfast – there are four in this family, not the Chapple fourteen – Mrs Calthorpe places the morning paper on her husband's tray. She goes down the hall, opening and closing doors so he will not hear his daughters quarrelling: 'it would upset his day's work'. She settles him with the tray on his knees and two pillows at his back. Then she shuts herself in her daughters' room to sort out their argument. These two are, unmistakably, Lyndahl and Joyce, called here Margot and Rae. Rae has 'startling good looks', a 'brilliant smile', 'white even teeth'. Margot has a 'pale soft-featured face', crooked teeth and straight light-brown hair. She works in an office. Rae is doing dental training.

This morning Rae has Margot's new stockings on. "'Yes I have, Mother. She's got another pair and all mine have runs.'" She does not turn round from the mirror, but peers into it 'with open conceit'.

Sorting out the quarrel is beyond Mrs Calthorpe. She sighs deeply and turns to Margot 'a face lined with uncertainty, the eyebrows raised above distressed eyes'. She is asking Margot to give in.

'Oh! let her have them then,' Margot says.

Her mother rewards her by saying, 'You're a dear good girl . . . You've got a good kind face.'

'Like a cow,' Rae says.

The day goes on. Another crisis. Conrad, or Brer (in the Chapple family he's Maurice or 'Dick', Lyndahl's favourite brother), announces that he's leaving school to become a fisherman and, when he has saved enough money, a farmer.

John Calthorpe is outraged: 'This boy says he wishes to literally sweat for his living?'

Would James Chapple have said that? A working man's sweat was 'honest' in his belief. But John then carries on as James probably would have. He begins to feel the need for his books, for the privacy of his study, and after telling the boy to come and see him tomorrow, that's where he goes. His wife soon arrives with 'a nice cup of tea, dear'.

The story covers several years. Conrad becomes a fisherman, then a farm hand, drain digger, fruit picker, road maker. Margot steals Rae's boyfriend and marries him. The younger son, Emerson, is shown by hints and nudges to be homosexual (as the youngest Chapple, Aynsley, was). And all the while John Calthorpe sits in his study, waiting for his wife's appearance with his slippers and a cup of tea. He tinkles his spoon on the saucer for a second cup. Or he nods his way out of 'the bedlam in the kitchen' and goes to bed.

This is as close as Lyndahl comes to criticising her father. In an earlier non-fiction piece called 'Potato Peelings' she writes of the 'stark and dark days that followed our return from the States when my Father . . . was put in prison for a year's hard labour. That year was as bitterly hard for my Mother as it was for my Father. I can recall, and always do so with an impulse to weep, my Mother bending over an iron boiler full of stew while we children sat at table waiting to be served; the wait was so prolonged that a questioning silence took hold of us all. But even then Mother couldn't turn round to face us; she was crying over the stew.'

There are several childhood memories in 'Potato Peelings'. On board the ship to America, 'sitting perilously on its high prow and looking down to where it split the water cleanly on both sides . . . listening to the coconuts somewhere aft rolling about during the uncanny nights at sea. Lying in a bunk and first seeing nothing but grey sky and then nothing but green water through the porthole as the ship rolled on her way.' She recalls again that her parents described her as 'a tree that would not transplant', and for this and other reasons they came back to New Zealand – where James Chapple went to prison and Florence Chapple cried into the stew.

When James came home from prison and resumed his work as a Unitarian minister good times of a sort returned. He was though 'a tired old man'. The family had shrunk. Several of the sons had left home, and Mercy and Jean had stayed in California to marry. The oldest girl, Dora, went back and married too and spent the rest of her long life in Carmel, where she was widowed twice, brought up two sons, married a third time, and wrote to Lyndahl all her life. Dora is Diamond in 'The Change'. 'Diamond is our grown up sister and we love her next best to Mother.' She 'bakes and sews', she 'fills the tubs with hot water from the copper' for the children's baths. In 'The Meek' she appears, less convincingly, as Deborah, a dark-haired girl with 'a face too long for beauty'. She has an 'arched nose and a wide tender mouth'. Deborah is Mrs Calthorpe's live-in help.

She is loving and patient and takes the mother's place in many of the young Calthorpes' activities. The real Dora was a teacher and wrote poetry. She remained, all her life, Lyndahl's touchstone for wisdom and spiritual peace.

FOUR

The school Lyndahl mentions in 'The Change' was Shirley School. From there she went to Christchurch Girls' High School. She writes little about those years or about her work when she left. By that time only the four youngest children were at home: Lyndahl, Joyce, Maurice (Dick) and Aynsley, the four who appear, in disguise, in 'The Meek'. The relationships were probably happier than those in the Calthorpe family but Lyndahl's memory can be trusted in the descriptions of daily life.

In 1925 James Chapple retired from his ministry. He and his wife and their shrunken family shifted to Tauranga where they bought a house and named it Dove Cottage after Wordsworth's house in Grasmere in the English Lake District. Lyndahl was eighteen, the oldest of the children left. She seems to have been happy in Tauranga but writes nothing about it in her later years. Further great changes were coming for her. The dreamy, sentimental girl was about to be picked up and shaken and never let go.

For a while she worked as a teacher's aide at Te Matai Native School near Te Puke, where her brother Kingsley (Leigh in 'The Change') was head teacher. Although unqualified, she became second assistant in October 1928. The memorandum of appointment notes the Department's understanding that she would not be able to continue much beyond the end of the year. Her salary was 'at the rate of 65 pounds per annum plus 35 pounds per annum lodging allowance'.

She boarded with Kingsley, called King in the family, and his wife Winnie. It's doubtful that she was happy with them. King was seven years older and had never been close in affection or interests. Lyndahl always held that he and Winnie were snobs, at least at this time. Perhaps they simply wanted what they saw as best for her. Both were highly regarded as teachers later in their lives.

Lyndahl got on well with the pupils. Māori children appear, sentimentalised in varying degrees, in stories and poems she wrote over the next twenty years. When she left Te Puke, a girl pupil made her the gift of a greenstone tiki. Lyndahl kept it as a treasure for many years before giving it to the Māori partner of one of her sons – who gave it, to Lyndahl's distress, to an American friend.

A teaching colleague of Kingsley fell in love with Lyndahl and proposed. She turned him down, to Kingsley's annoyance. There was also a young parson, who survives in a half-page scrap written many years later 'in vino veritas'. Lyndahl remembers taking her class to the Kaituna River in Te Puke. The parson was also there. 'We sat on the bank, watching the Maori kids swimming. I had to make up my mind; he offered me his mother's pearls as an inducement. But I was bewitched, a mere girl in love with a carpenter in Tauranga.'

A carpenter, when she could have had a teacher or a parson. No wonder King and Winnie were not pleased.

The carpenter in Tauranga was Leonard William Gee, the son of a builder, Henry William Gee, always called Harry, and his wife Helen, also called Ellen and sometimes Marmee after the idealised mother in Louisa M. Alcott's *Little Women*. Len's background is harder to fill in than Lyndahl's. A year older than her, he was born and grew up in Sydenham, Christchurch. He had an older brother, Alf, and two younger sisters, Rona and Kathleen. Carpentry was the Gee trade. His father and grandfather were both born into it, and Len followed. His mother, Helen Davidson, was the daughter of a mine manager and her family considered that in marrying

Harry Gee she had married beneath her. Helen, though, was unaffected by snobbery and Len always remembered her as a loving mother.

At Christchurch Technical High School he was good at arithmetic and geometry and technical drawing, but he left early to become apprenticed to his father. It wasn't a happy relationship. Harry Gee was a hard man and Len was tough and stubborn and quick tempered. He was, though, good at his job and was soon a skilled carpenter and joiner. In the 1920s Harry was subcontractor to Armstrong Whitworth and Co. who were building a railway in the Bay of Plenty. Len's reference, written by the Armstrong Whitworth manager, states that he was employed from July 1924 to June 1928 and 'worked on Station Buildings, Platelayers' Cottages, Huts, Bridges, Culverts, and other work necessary to the building of a railway . . . He is a skilled tradesman thoroughly competent, intelligent and industrious.'

Len played rugby and was good at that too, but his real sporting skill was in boxing. He won many fights, often with his father in his corner, and when the family shifted to Tauranga became a main-bout performer in amateur tournaments in North Island towns. In 1928 he fought his way to the final in the welterweight division in the New Zealand championships, where he lost on a points decision. He was still boxing when he met Lyndahl, but gave it up, to Harry's disgust. Did he stop to please her? The pacific and gentle-natured young woman cannot have liked such a violent sport.

Lyndahl though was no home body. She was active and athletic. She loved the beach and swimming and learned how to ride on a board towed behind a speedboat driven by one of Len's friends.

Many years later they enjoyed telling their children about the early years of their marriage, but they never said how they met. They might have gone to the same dance in a Tauranga hall – Lyndahl enjoyed dancing – or been introduced at the movies – she liked those too. It's unlikely they met at her home or his – the daughter of a retired parson, the son of a rough-mannered builder only half broken-in socially. Somehow they came together and Lyndahl was 'bewitched', and Len, although it's not a word to use of him, must have felt something similar.

There are not many photographs of them from this time, either singly or together. Those that survive show two attractive people – a pretty girl, a handsome young man. Lyndahl had learned to pose. She seems to have decided that a thoughtful look suited her better than smiles. In her bathing suit she displays a well-shaped figure but is serious still. A tiny smile breaks through as she stands on a flat rock, showing off a dress with a frilled hem and leather boots shaped and decorated at the top. One hand rests on a sash at her waist, the other on her hair, which is done in a style she adopted in her teens and gave up only in middle age: plaited and rolled into buns over her ears. She had abundant hair, often worn in a fringe. But the smile is gone as she poses at Ocean Beach, sitting on a rock. Her hands are beautifully placed, one on her knee, the other resting at her side. Then she stands, arms raised and hands behind her head. It's a Hollywood pose. Later in her life she sometimes spoke of her supposed resemblance to the silent-screen actress Mary Miles Minter, mentioned in 'The Change'.

Perhaps she had learned not to smile because of her crooked teeth.

Len is more natural. He seems at ease with himself, at the beach too with a group of friends. He wears a hooped football jersey, possibly red and black, and he's turning to look at the camera, ready for whatever comes next. He's a man who likes the sun and sea, likes doing things that test his strength. Later he often spoke of fishing trips on a friend's launch out to Mayor Island and beyond. Sometimes they spent the night on the island.

There's only one photograph showing Len and Lyndahl together. They're dressed formally, Len in a suit and tie. One hand fits in his pocket and his other arm is bent so that Lyndahl can hold it comfortably, which she does although her fingers do not show. She has a large purse slung over her shoulder and holds what seems to be a wrapped gift in her hand. Her dress is black and fashionable and the brim of her puffed hat shades her eyes. She wears a string of pearls, almost certainly artificial. Lyndahl doesn't look bewitched or even happy. Len, handsome as a film star, is stern. It might be a wedding photo or a photo taken as they set off on their honeymoon.

The parson she had turned down married them in the Tauranga Baptist Church. His name was J. Simpson. In the fragment that describes his proposal Lyndahl writes: 'He kissed me at the altar after the ceremony! A fallen woman! "My privilege," he said, blushing.'

Did Mr Simpson know she was 'fallen'? Perhaps she confessed it to him on the river bank. A Chapple genealogical chart prepared in the 1980s gives the date of her wedding as 16 February 1928, but someone was guilty of misdirection. The marriage certificate shows that she and Len married on 16 February 1929. Their first child, Aynsley, was born five months later. In 1973 Lyndahl, alone in the house while Len was at 'the second day of the up-north races', turned to the pencil and paper that now formed much of her company. 'To think we married for love,' she wrote, 'or was it because we had to?'

'Had to' and 'for love' are both true.

There's no record of what James and Florence Chapple thought about their daughter's union with the carpenter from Tauranga.

Len is called 'Building Contractor' on the marriage certificate. Lyndahl is 'Teacher'. He was twenty-two. She was twenty-one.

FIVE

The early years of their marriage were the years of the Great Depression; but Depression, great or not, was a name Len and Lyndahl seldom used when describing that time. To them it was the Slump, an ugly word that captures the reality of the event. It affected the newlyweds almost at once. Where they lived in the first few months, before the economy finally slumped, can't be determined exactly. How they lived isn't certain. Harry Gee's business collapsed. As well as having the railway contract he had built houses and bridges – all the wooden bridges between Tauranga and Te Puke, he once claimed. There's a family story that several years into the slump the only job he could find was painting median lines on the roads, although it's unlikely that many Bay of Plenty roads were sealed at that time. The end of his father's business put Len out of work. He travelled to wherever there were jobs. He and Lyndahl were in Te Puke, Auckland, New Plymouth, Auckland again, Whakatāne, Auckland a third time between the years 1929 and 1933. Their first son, Aynsley, was born in Auckland in 1929; their second, Maurice, in Whakatāne in 1931; their third, Gareth, in Auckland in 1933. From the stories they told about those years, they survived through Len's strength and determination, Lyndahl's fortitude, and the resilience and, frequently, the high spirits that filled them both. They were young, they were in love, and the slump was not going to take those things away.

Before it began to bite, Lyndahl kept on with her teaching job in Te Puke. Len worked there, possibly still for his father. They boarded with Kingsley and Winnie. Sitting down for his meal after a hard day's work, Len saw Kingsley served with a large flounder while he got a bit of warmed-over stew. 'You don't mind do you, Len?' Winnie said. 'King needs fish because he's doing brain work.' Len did mind. He 'minded' that pair all his life. It wasn't long before he and Lyndahl were off to Auckland, where they stayed until their first son was born. Then it was New Plymouth, to one in a line of smoky tin shacks on Ngāmotu beach.

In a story written in the 1930s, 'when I was a mother, a wife, and my husband was on relief', Lyndahl renamed the settlement. 'To the transient poor who rent its summer cottages through the winter it is known as Tiger Town; holiday makers no doubt refer to it only by its correct and beautiful Maori name. It is a strip of black sand beach, its front door the open Tasman Sea, its back step a low cliff upon which stands a town of some importance.'

The story is about Madge, who comes up from Wellington to spend the 'wind-driven winter' with her brother Budd and his pretty, melancholy wife Tessa, who is expecting a baby. Budd is on relief, which 'doesn't seem to mean what it says'. There's 'unrelief' in Budd's eyes. He's 'humbled'. On his 'off work' days he has 'a habit of sitting and staring at his fists'.

Budd is Len in many ways, although 'humbled' doesn't suit Len. Staring at his fists? Lyndahl must have seen Len do that. She is not Tessa, the melancholy, helpless wife. She must have wanted to be like – probably was like – proud, outspoken, intelligent Madge, who takes a job at the Tiger Town tearoom and grocery shop.

'From where she served, Madge could see the busy wharf life, the black iron sand beach and the tall spume-topped breakers of the Tasman. The beach was a highway for the "wharfies" who tramped it to and from work, night and day, in storm and out.'

Standing by her rattling window one stormy night, she sees a match flare on the beach. It was 'ringed in protectively by men's

faces as pipes and cigarettes were lit from it. The wharfies who had
been working overtime were only just getting home and it was after
midnight. These work-toughened men were not afraid of the storm;
listen! They were laughing! The wind was tearing the words from
their mouths and tossing their laughter high and far . . . From that
hour onwards her regard for the manual worker grew; she came to
call them "the inner circle" . . . closer to the heart and throb of life
than the "nine to threes" and "collar and ties".' Budd accuses her of
being a snob and says she'll end up marrying a business magnate
or a bank manager.

'"Never!" Madge denied stoutly, "nothing less than an engine
driver will suit me. I like my men sweaty."'

Tessa tells her she's being disgusting. Some of Lyndahl's sisters
would have said the same.

The rest of the story supports Madge's judgement. One
afternoon, a 'mood of boredom' drives a young man, Colin Jefferies,
down from the golf club to the shanty town. He 'noses his shining
car on to the beach' and comes into the tearoom for cigarettes;
sees Madge; stays for a cup of tea. 'He liked the way her coarse
healthy hair curled about her wide forehead . . . He was pleased to
see her teeth were natural and not false, as were those of so many
working girls.' He chats with her and makes a crude pass: 'Are you
as friendly by night as you are by day?'

Madge studies him, 'his well-brushed hair and faultless clothes
and especially his hands'. Colin tries to repair his mistake, but she
tells him, '"You're out of your depth down here . . . better swim
back to the shallows."'

We meet other Tiger Town residents, an old sailor, Captain
Elms and his 'missus'. The captain has a growth like a berry on a
stem on one of his eyelids. Madge longs to take scissors and snip
it off. There's also Piri Paeora, who has two wives, a Māori one
who 'did the work and bore the babies' and a white one who 'was

for ornament and like an incense burner smoked for hours on end'. Perhaps these people were actual residents of Ngāmotu beach. Colin Jefferies, on the other hand, is there to make Lyndahl's point. Budd is 'relief worker'. Colin is 'son of society'. Madge is intrigued by him, goes out with him, and he falls in love with her. She comes to like him 'more than she wished to'. After two months he asks her to meet his parents at a ball they are giving. The reception room is 'full of gay-gowned girls and black-clad men'. Madge thinks they look like butterflies and beetles.

Later in the evening Colin's father takes her into his study to look at the portraits of ancestors lining the walls. His real motive is to tell her that he 'would rather see Colin dead than married to you'.

Madge looks at the ancestors and shivers. She thanks Mr Jefferies for her lucky escape. She leaves the ball and sets off home. Colin overtakes her in his car. He leads her 'somewhat roughly to the Cadillac', where he makes it clear that no matter what his father says he will marry her. Before she can 'kill his love for her' with the lie that she loves someone else, 'a beam of light reached out of the darkness . . .' A train smashes into the car. Colin is killed.

'"I think the girl's all right," said the engine driver and Madge felt a strong arm under her shoulders.'

The story winds down quickly: 'Three years later the "slump" for New Zealand was over and Madge married her engine driver, the man who having once held her in his arms could not forget her.' Their baby is born in a railway settlement. A smiling nurse tucks Madge into bed. It is midnight.

'As the nurse switched out the light the silence of the sleeping countryside was broken into by the whistle of a train; nearer it came, a long steady whistling for her in the night. Madge breathed softly, listening, until the sound died on a low crooning note far out in the country.

'"What on earth?" said the nurse from the dark doorway.'

It's a story full of interest, full of close observation and well-turned phrases and sentences, although it's marred by sentimentality and moralising. Written in Auckland several years after that winter at Ngāmotu beach, it can be read as Lyndahl's statement of allegiance. She never varied from her belief in 'the inner circle' of working men. 'Honest sweat' was a term she used all her life.

There are bits of autobiography in the story. Len brought home a sack of swedes, given to him by one of his mates. There were too many to use, so he and Lyndahl threw half a dozen over the fence for a neighbour, then some for the neighbour on the other side, a snooty woman (called Mrs de Winter in the story). As the last one flew over it passed the first one coming back.

Madge, 'almost in pain with silent laughter', calls her thanks through 'the furze fence' to Mrs de Winter and tells her swedes are delicious mashed with butter and they'll have them for tea that night. It's Lyndahl's voice – or perhaps, more accurately, a voice she was learning.

She and Len never forgot their winter in 'Tiger Town'. They crept away early one morning when there was no money for the rent. Len carried their belongings in two cardboard suitcases, and Lyndahl the baby, Aynsley, wrapped in a blanket. A friend of Len's drove the Auckland service car. He let them on free, sat them at the back. If an inspector was waiting at one of the stops they had to get out without raising his suspicions or the driver would lose his job. So they came to Auckland and for a short while Len went back on relief. It must have been the chance for better work that took them to Whakatāne early in 1931. Their second son, Maurice, was born there in August.

Whakatāne doesn't figure in any of the stories they told, and Lyndahl never wrote about it. They probably knew the town from their Tauranga days. It sits on the south side of a river mouth, with white-sand beaches north over the river and south beyond a hill – beaches unlike the black-sand one on the other coast. Whale Island squats close to shore and White Island, a volcano, smokes on the horizon. But there would have been little time for beaches and the sea. Survival was their concern. It's possible that Harry and Helen Gee were in Whakatāne at that time. A whisper of memory says they were, and that Lyndahl and Len lived with them, but it's impossible to be sure. Their second son's birth certificate is one of only two pieces of hard evidence that they ever lived in Whakatāne. The second is a telephone call Maurice received in 2005 from a woman whose grandparents lived there in the early 1930s. She told him that her grandfather hired Len to build a dining table out of kauri planks he had stored. Len finished the table. It's beautifully made and is still in use in that family.

SIX

Again they packed up and left for Auckland, where Lyndahl's parents now lived. Four of her siblings were also there, in Henderson, a small town ten miles west of the city. James Chapple had bought a bungalow on Millbrook Road, a mile from the town centre. It had two bedrooms, a sitting room and a study, that essential feature of a Chapple house. Here James read and wrote, while Florence ran the house and garden. Her two youngest children, Dick and Aynsley, both in their early twenties, were still at home. Aynsley lived in the house and Dick had a detached room out the back. He worked in the garden and made the remnant of the family almost self-sufficient. There were apple and pear and plum and citrus trees, a row of guava bushes and a large vegetable garden. Dick milked a house cow. Aynsley was a teachers' college student. He was, by Lyndahl's account, a beautiful young man and his mother's favourite child.

A small creek ran down from the cow paddock, went under a brick bridge and round the side of a rose garden beside a wide lawn, then through a culvert under Millbrook Road, where it dived down a rockslide into Henderson Creek. Dick built a tea-tree summerhouse on the lawn. Over the tributary creek was a small cottage, also part of the property. James rented it out.

Dick painted the name 'Peacehaven' on a board and screwed it to a barred gate at the bottom of the drive.

It seemed to Lyndahl an idyllic place, but the first house she and Len found was worse than the shack on Ngāmotu beach – two rooms, with a washtub out the back fed from a rainwater tank.

There was no stove. Lyndahl cooked on a sheet of iron over a fire that burned in a hole cut in a bank outside the back door. The one advantage was that Peacehaven was only half a mile away. Lyndahl went there as often as she could – down the View Road hill to the wooden bridge over Henderson Creek and along Millbrook Road, which ran beside the creek all the way. Halfway along was a small orchard behind a macrocarpa hedge. The second Chapple son, Hollis, lived there for a short while with his wife Connie and their four children (there were two more to come). Peacehaven was several hundred yards further on, past the rented cottage where the Henderson School dental nurse lived. On either side of the Chapple five acres was a large house in wide grounds, each owned by an elderly couple. They were snooty, Lyndahl believed, and they never made friends with James and Florence Chapple and their sons. It did not bother Lyndahl. It strengthened her belief that Chapples were set apart and special.

But now she was a Gee, with her husband on relief. A third baby was soon on the way. They left the shack in View Road for a house at the very end of Henry Street, a blind road running from the heart of the little town to the creek. It was, at last, a proper house, although tiny: a kitchen/living room, two bedrooms, a bathroom and a washhouse. Standing at the end of the narrow gravel road, it had unused farm land at one side and the back, the creek, deep and dark, on the other side, and empty paddocks over the road. The only neighbour was Pat Phillips, a retired soldier who had been in the Indian Army. He lived over the creek in a small house with a persimmon tree in the yard. Access was by a swing bridge that bounced and swayed when walked on. Pat Phillips and Lyndahl became good friends, although they disagreed about most things – Empire, militarism, socialism – and had many vigorous arguments. But they both disliked what they called 'church religion'.

Lyndahl walked the quarter mile to Station Road to do her

shopping. Norcross's grocery, Walker's butcher shop, Scott's chemist shop were opposite Henderson railway station, where the trains ran in from Auckland and left for Swanson and Helensville. Further along towards the Great North Road was the Town Hall, a large concrete building where movies were shown on Saturday nights. The Town Clerk's office was at the back. A secondary part of the town (soon to be more important) stood at the junction of Station Road and the Great North Road. The post office was there, with two more grocer shops, Reanney's and Dollar's, Holborows' butchery, a blacksmith's workshop, and a boarding house that had been a pub before West Auckland went dry. The school was back along the Great North Road, over the creek and up a hill. All three Gee boys had their primary schooling there.

That was Henderson in the early 1930s. Lyndahl was happy. Her parents lived close by and she soon made friends. Len liked the town too and he made friends easily wherever he was. He was to leave his mark on Henderson. But for the time being he stayed on relief or took odd jobs where he could find them. He got hold of an old bicycle, repaired it, and rode out to the work sites. At other times he waited at the sawmill for loaded timber trucks to come out. He pedalled after them with his toolkit on the handlebars, and if he could keep up might get a day's work unloading the truck and stacking the timber. There might even be a bit of carpentry. Now and then a driver would slow down so he could keep the truck in sight.

They were hard days for Lyndahl but perhaps even harder for Len, who all his life prided himself on his strength and skill and his ability to provide for his family. At home the couple seem to have been equals, but Lyndahl ruled in the naming of their sons, where her pride in being a Chapple came to the fore. Len wanted to call their first son Nelson. Lyndahl would have none of it – an English aristocrat, a naval hero, was not getting into her family.

The boy became Aynsley after her youngest brother. The second son was Maurice, after her second youngest brother. And the third, Gareth, born in 1933, following an anxious taxi ride to the hospital in Auckland, was named after Sir Gareth, a knight of King Arthur's Round Table (she mistook Gareth for Galahad, who had seen the Holy Grail). For good measure, Aynsley was given the middle name Emerson, one of James Chapple's favourite writers. Gareth became Gareth Carlyle (another). It's doubtful that Lyndahl had done more than dip into either writer's work. Maurice scored Gough, his grandmother's maiden name. But Lyndahl's naming went awry. To avoid confusing him with his uncle, the boy Aynsley soon became known as Junior in the family and among his friends. Even Lyndahl called him that. Maurice became Moss or Mossie and answered to those names all through his schooldays and beyond. Gareth's was the change Lyndahl fought hardest against. He became Gus. There's a story that a neighbour, Mrs Flynn, said, 'He doesn't look like a Gareth to me, he looks like a Gus.' The name stuck, and when the boy was old enough not to want it anymore he did not revert to Gareth but chose Gary.

Len was always Len, except with several sisters-in-law who preferred Leon. Lyndahl was Lyn or Lindy. But when she began to submit poems and stories for publication she became Lyndahl Chapple Gee. It's not certain when Len began to think, Bloody Chapples, but he said it aloud now and then most of his married life, with amusement sometimes, and sometimes not.

As the slump went on he fought against it as though he were in the ring. Lying awake, Lyndahl heard the night cart arrive and the night man carry out the can from the dunny at the back of the house. Then she heard something soft thud on the front porch. In the morning she found a sugar sack of children's clothes, used but still wearable. She was pleased. Her children had not much more than the set of clothes they wore each day. But Len was furious. It was a blow through his defences into the solar plexus. He grabbed the sack from Lyndahl and rode his bicycle round to the night man's house, where he threw the used clothes on the porch and yelled that he could look after his family, he didn't need help from a bloody night man. Lyndahl never forgot. It was a mark both for Len and against him.

They stayed in Henry Street for two or three years, then shifted to a rented house in Newington Road, a blind street running off View Road almost opposite the shack they had lived in when they arrived in Henderson. It ended in farmland after a quarter of a mile. There were seven houses, four of them railway houses, on the north side and seven on the south side, two of them also railway. The house Len and Lyndahl rented was on the high south side, with a view across Henderson Valley to the Waitākere Ranges. It had two bedrooms, a living room, a kitchen/dining room, a scullery, a bathroom, a washhouse, and a front porch that Len saw at once could be made into a third bedroom. He and Lyndahl must have felt they had bettered themselves, even though their water still came from rainwater tanks and the night man (perhaps the one who had tried to give them clothes) made his weekly call for the dunny can.

The section covered a quarter acre. Len started a garden at once. Soon he managed to come off relief and find carpentry jobs. He worked on houses in Henderson, in Riverhead, and once out past Tuakau towards the Waikato Heads, where he had to be away from home all week. On one of these jobs a big Irishman, Jack Maher, was giving him a hard time. They settled it after work, at the back of the house, and Len claimed he flattened Jack Maher, even though he arrived home with a damaged face.

SEVEN

In spite of the tail end of the slump, in spite of the war, with the difficulties and troubles it brought on the 'home front', the twelve years they spent in Newington Road were the happiest of Lyn and Len's married life. They soon managed to put a down payment on the house and Len was able to begin his improvements. First he enclosed the front porch to make a bedroom for Junior. Then he extended the living room by pushing a sunroom out the side. He concreted the back yard, put in new washing lines, built steps from the bottom of the path down to the road, and all the time kept a vegetable garden stretching from the back lawn to the line of macrocarpa trees cutting off the section from the grounds of the Catholic school. By the late thirties he was able to buy a car, a second-hand Chrysler convertible. He bought the empty section next door and put up a small workshop where he made joinery. One of the first things he built was a writing desk for Lyndahl. The Southern Cross and a crescent moon were inlaid on the writing surface.

Lyndahl was writing in snatches of time during the day. She sat up at night on a kitchen chair, with her feet in the range oven for the last of the warmth, and worked on stories and poems. A handwritten note on 'Tiger Town' says: 'I wrote this story when I was a mother, a wife, and my husband was on relief.' 'The Meek' was also written in those years.

Len was not a reader and it's doubtful that he read his wife's stories, even when they were published. But it seems he was sympathetic and proud of her cleverness. He approved of her involvement in politics too. Both were Labour supporters and Lyndahl, always needing to believe, was devoted to Michael Joseph Savage. 'Like many thousands of women, mainly mothers,' she wrote, 'I looked on Michael Joseph as almost a saviour.' There was rejoicing in the Gee house, and in the Chapple house in Millbrook Road, when Labour won the 1935 election. But although she stayed a Labour voter all her life, Lyndahl's interest in politics waned. Writing in the 1940s she says: 'Long ago when Michael Joseph Savage was prime minister I was political minded to the extent that I was elected President of our local (Women's) Labour Party branch . . .' Like her father, she could argue and speak to an audience. She came home from one meeting and said she had met a marvellous young woman, visiting from down south, who was eloquent and fiery and full of conviction. Her name was Elsie Freeman (better known later as Elsie Locke). Lyndahl would have liked to be like Elsie Freeman. But politics, with its compromises and dishonesties, was not for her. She went to an Auckland meeting and came home disturbed and disillusioned. Several things had been decided that delegates were instructed not to reveal to their branches. She did not stand for president again, and only five years later wrote: 'In those dear dead days I was very sure of myself – dogmatic almost. Now in these dire-living days I am unsure and, politically, "maze-o-doubts".'

But in the mid-thirties there were few doubts. She argued. She wrote, sitting at her desk, sitting by the kitchen range while her husband and children slept. In those days there were few outlets for stories and poems. She sent them to newspapers and women's magazines; they would not have found a place in literary magazines had they existed. They were unpolished, sentimental, angry sometimes, but full of good feeling and close observation. 'Mother Callahan' was published in a women's magazine called the *Mirror*. Complete short story by Lyndahl Chapple-Gee, the author statement says. Alongside the title is a pen and ink drawing, signed 'Chapple', of a woman leaning on a farm gate. This is Mother Callahan, waiting for her son and his bride. Instead she gets her son keeping a baby warm under his coat.

A second *Mirror* story, 'The Parting of the Ways', describes the friendship between a Pākehā boy, Carlyle Bent, and a Māori boy, Tou Tou. They lie talking beside the Kaituna River. It's the last day of school. Tou Tou will be heading north to Ninety Mile Beach. "'Py corry, Carlai, ninety miles of pipis should be plenty, eh?'" Carlyle will be going on to other, bigger schools. Wailing begins at the nearby pā and Tou Tou runs off to the 'ole fella's tangi'. Carlyle thinks of his friend eating fish, kūmara, pipis. Then he remembers it's steam-pudding night at home. He starts to run.

These stories are fresh and interesting. They mark an apprenticeship in writing for Lyndahl. It seems likely that fiction rather than verse would have been her way. She published several more stories later in the thirties, but wrote verse almost compulsively, some of it, one suspects, aimed at pleasing her father and her sister Dora. A book from her library, R.M. Bucke's *Cosmic Consciousness*, has the inscription: 'Given to Lyndahl provided she gets a poem accepted and published. Father 5/Oct/1937.' Dora, still in California and much published by now, arranged for the poem to be printed in a paper called *The Carmel Pine Cone*. Lyndahl pasted it opposite the inscription.

To My Mother

Little mother melancholy
I suspect your heart
Of holding grievous converse
In which I have no part;

For I have heard your lips belie
The trouble in your eyes
And I have known your inner tears
For love has made me wise.

And oh! The times I've prayed for words
To quiet all your fears
As you hushed mine with lullabies
When I was young in years!

Yes, little mother melancholy
I have found you out!
But not for love nor pity
Would I tell you of my doubt,

For well I know the part you play
As old as it is new;
Have you forgotten, little one,
That I am 'mother' too?
                                        Lyndahl Chapple

There were to be many poems of this sort. One must read Dora Hagemeyer's verse to see where the tone and language come from. Dora was probably the better poet, but her circumstances now were easier than Lyndahl's were ever to be. After her first husband's death in a motor accident she married a banker, Hurd Comstock. The couple and the two Hagemeyer sons visited New Zealand in the mid-thirties, an event that renewed Lyndahl's devotion to her sister.

Important though writing was, it came second to family – to her parents, her brothers and sisters, her husband, and especially her sons. Junior started at Henderson School in 1934, Maurice in

1936, and Gareth in 1938. They went off along Newington Road, down View Road and over the wooden bridge across Henderson Creek, up the hill to Station Road, past the jam factory (a small brick building) and along through the township to the Great North Road. From there they crossed the creek again and climbed the hill to the school.

One day they were caught in a sudden storm. Lyndahl knew they would arrive at school soaked, so she crossed the road to the Scott house (Scott the chemist) and persuaded Jean Scott, also a pupil at the school, to take a bag of dry clothes for them to change into. The headmaster called the boys, 'the Gee boys', out at assembly on the school forecourt and sent them inside to change. They were deeply humiliated, and let their mother know when they got home. She understood, apologised – but she had kept them dry.

They also instructed her that when she passed the school, which she did frequently to visit her sister Joyce, who lived close by, she must not call hello if she saw them in the playground. She could smile if no one was looking, that was all.

Lyndahl took enormous pleasure in her sons. She wrote about them often, sometimes disguised in stories, but more naturally in an exercise book with 'inviting clean pages' her eldest boy left lying about. She reflects on the difference between herself and her friend Molly, who has three daughters; how there's never a doll or ribbon to be seen in her back yard, rather fist fights and patched pants and rowdy conversations. 'It is not unusual for me to step outside and find bunches of boys arguing on the lawn, sunning themselves on the roof or clinging to the water tanks watching miniature yacht races.'

'Our youngest child is our wit,' she writes, 'our middle boy our scholar and our oldest son our handiest, working with his hands more than his head. At meals it is our youngest who takes charge of the table talk. He was recently late home for tea. When at seven o'clock he still wasn't home I began to worry and walked several times down the darkening road; returning to the house after the last anxious walk I found him at the table eating! He had come in the back way through the hedge. I suffered the usual reaction to overstrained love and was immediately scolding him soundly. He listened till my final "You remember the time in future my boy!" and then with open indignation said, "YOU wouldn't remember the time either if you were playing in an orchard with grass THAT high!"' Lyndahl is 'somehow put in the wrong' but also 'pushed pell-mell back into the past by his words. Grass THAT high!' She remembers 'making rooms and passages in long grass in a corner paddock' with her friend Madge. When boys threw stones at them Madge pretended to be knocked unconscious and the boys ran away, terrified. A man from a nearby house 'came weaving through the paddock with water and bandages' and found the two girls laughing gleefully in grass 'THAT high'. 'Trust my youngest to remind me that I was a child once too!'

She took the boys to watch a calf being born on Kellys' farm. 'The cow kindly delivered it by our fence.' (She could not, though, take the next step, and fell back on seeds being planted.) She told them about her childhood year in California, the snakes rustling the dry leaves in the gutters, a tarantula spider 'brown and furry as a bear, looking at me'. And if, in California, the Chapple children got wet on the way to school there were drying grates where they could stand in their steaming clothes. The boys loved these stories. They were hugely proud of their mother for having been to America.

She defied conventions in bringing them up. She believed in physical freedoms. 'To me wet days are only depressing while I am in the house. Out in the rain I revive . . . splashing along with wet face and wet feet . . . I enjoy it as a child does and catch drips with my tongue . . . I hope my boys take their shoes off coming home today; there is health in bare feet. I believe in known and unknown currents from the earth being good medicine for young and old alike . . .' She does her housework in bare feet and puts on shoes only when she goes out shopping. 'I'd love to go out barefoot today while the gutters are running! One hot brazen day in the big city a water pipe burst and an old Maori woman in from the country promptly peeled off her stockings and shoes and paddled in the cool running water. I wonder how many hot-footed onlookers envied her? I know I did.'

There were mental freedoms too. She excused her sons from religious teaching at school, although she was firm in forbidding exclamations like 'God strike me pink!' and 'Jesus wept!' She took pleasure in anarchic boy-things. One summer day rain started to fall, heavy and warm. She called the boys in but saw how much they wanted to be out, so she told them to put on their bathing togs, and for half an hour they ran and slid and wrestled on the muddy lawn. Then they washed themselves with buckets of water from the tanks.

On another morning her eldest son arrived home with a train cinder in his eye. She took the cinder out, then saw no reason to send him back to school. 'It is proving an education to have my son home unexpectedly. He has just shown me the action of water on carbide; he dropped a piece of carbide in a sauce bottle of water; it smelled and bubbled like witch's brew! And furthermore he struck a match and lit the gas escaping from the bottle top. I admit I was startled and wonder struck! Now he has cleaned my copper of verdigris; over the cleaning we came to the conclusion that verdigris was the French for green grease? Also he has fixed my wringer so that it doesn't sway with every wring; he showed me what was wrong with the screws. "See here Tiny," he said (he is already head and shoulders above me), "all it needs is the screws tightening!" Now he is whistling away in his father's workshop. I hope it's not another witch's brew! A week ago he blew up some carrots from the garden with home made gunpowder. It's nice but a little nerve-wracking having him around. It's not a witch's brew! He has just brought me in a teapot stand he made from a piece of three-ply. It calls for a brew of another kind so we are going to have a cup of tea and eat his school lunch with it. My good resolutions for the day are being broken one by one; I haven't sanded the back porch yet! Still it isn't every day my son gets a cinder in his eye and I get a teapot stand.'

*

Friends and neighbours appear in her jottings, which she keeps going through the late thirties and into the war years. She puts off cleaning the flour and sugar bins and telephones Molly: 'It's her birthday and she tells me she has just had her first present – a pair of gumboots! Precious, unprocurable gumboots! She was just off down the farm when I rang. She will be manuring all day she says – and then going with her three little daughters and her husband to a birthday tea at her parents' place. Molly is one in a million – attractive without make-up, brown-skinned and clear brained; she ploughs and digs and plants and picks – and keeps bees. I have just ordered a tin of honey from her. Yes Molly is good medicine; she puts me on my mettle. I must get those bins done now! Or else! as these Americans say.'

The neighbours on the left were the Pinckneys. They were cut off behind a high hedge and never became friends. On the other side, beyond two empty sections, were the Lisks, and Lyndahl became friendly with Ivy Lisk – although, for the whole twelve years, they remained 'Mrs Gee' and 'Mrs Lisk'. Mrs Lisk appears in the jottings as 'my neighbour'. 'She is like a piece of caustic soda, my neighbour – very cleansing and a little bit anti-man . . . She has an admirable straight left! . . . To another woman (forty, with no children and good furniture), who has an insatiable interest in the details of child-bearing, she says, "Have one and find out for yourself before it's too late. You can keep it off your new carpet." The woman stammered, "I'd like to but my husband . . ." "Damn the husbands! They're street angels and house devils! Don't listen to him.'"

Ivy Lisk kept a close eye on Lyndahl's housekeeping, which was erratic. 'My cheerful and resigned husband is fond of saying that my house is tidy up to my eye-level.' She could not bear to kill things, especially daddy long legs spiders. 'To have long legs broken must be more painful than to have short ones . . . My neighbour says sarcastically that all the moths and spiders I carefully sweep outside come over to her place.'

The Newington Road neighbours were fascinating: the Lisks; the Pinckneys, who grew orchids and sewed canvas goods on machines set up in their sunroom; the Flynns, with three wild boys like the Gee boys; the Kays, who replaced the Flynns (Mrs Kay believed in something called Radiant Living); the Scotts (Mr Scott kept a huge cage of budgies and made giant kites that never managed to fly); the Greenhoughs, in the railway house opposite (Stan Greenhough, a signalman, grew flowers in a glasshouse and invented new ones by wiring the heart of one into the petals of another – which Lyndahl condemned as unnatural); Mr Saunders, grumpy, monosyllabic, who built a house over the years, all by himself, in the draught-horse paddock; the Harts – old Ben with his lace-capped wife, his collection of Victorian novels and his stories of being a Captain's batman in the Great War; Mrs Harvey, who recited a poem called 'Damson Wine' at parties, growing progressively drunker with great artistry; the Scanlans – Jean, whom Lyndahl found 'hard', Laurie, who killed himself by drinking poison in the bathroom, and Murray, their son, a playmate of the Gee boys (his grief for his father affected Lyndahl deeply). There were also the Yelaviches, with daughters Nada and Nivenka. Lyndahl became friendly with several Dalmatian families and stood up for them when they were accused during the war of 'stealing our land while the boys are fighting overseas'.

Neighbours though, friends too, came second in her interest to Chapples. She could hardly help thinking of her father as a special person; his history demanded it. Her beliefs, her opinions took much of their colour and shape from his. Her mother too was special. Her life of devotion to her husband and family, her years of back-breaking work, her suffering for causes that began as her husband's but became her own made her, in Lyndahl's eyes, a kind of saint. One of the Chapple boys worked out the number of sacks of potatoes his mother had peeled in her life – a vast number that Lyndahl, sadly, failed to record. But she could not help raising her parents above all other people. The annoying thing, or amusing thing, to non-Chapples was that the whole family was raised too, and although several of the fourteen made some mark in life (school principal, poet) the rest were nothing out of the ordinary. Some achieved happy lives, some did not. Most were generous, several were mean, one was a snob. A couple of the girls were downright silly. Yet all were Chapples, and Lyndahl could not help herself; the name carried an almost mystical cachet.

During the thirties and forties numbers of her brothers and sisters lived in Henderson or close by. In the earlier part of that time Aynsley was still at Peacehaven. Dick was there, off and on, until he married in 1940. Joyce married a local man, Phil Reanney, the son of a German woman who kept a grocery store on the Great North Road. They lived by Falls Park, where Henderson Creek turns tidal. Flo (the pretty, complaining one in 'The Change') and her husband Jim Hollis were nearby. Bernice lived in Arkles Bay on the Whangaparāoa Peninsula. Deorwyn and her husband Ray, the commercial traveller of 'The Change', were in Titirangi. And

Geoff, a favourite among her brothers (he's John in 'The Change'), came to Henderson with his new wife Dawn early in the war years. Lyndahl immediately loved Dawn. Of all those who married into the Chapple family, Dawn was the one she shared most with – ideas, books, sympathies – and was happiest with. Joyce, close to Lyndahl too in those years, was a little jealous.

In the early thirties the slump closed the teachers' training colleges, leaving the youngest Chapple, Aynsley, with no prospects of a job. After working for a short while as a gardener, he left for the United States. A newspaper clipping tells the story:

> Bound for residence in California
>
> Aynsley Chapple, son of the Rev. and Mrs. J.H.G. Chapple of Henderson, left by the Mariposa last week, and at San Francisco will be met by his three sisters, Mrs George Whitcombe, Mrs Dudley Kell Jones, whose husband represents a well-known tractor firm, and Mrs Hurd Comstock who by her pen-name of 'Dora Hagemeyer' will be remembered by many as a poetess of no little merit. Her husband is a retired banker, and with their two sons they paid a visit to the family home at Henderson a year or so ago. Brother Aynsley will take up his abode with his talented sister in Carmel, California, after he has visited his grandmother who has lived in Los Angeles for fifty years.
>
> A very cheery party was staged at 'Peace-haven', the Chapple home, to farewell the popular lad.

The grandmother mentioned in the piece was James Chapple's remarried mother, Mrs Law. She seems to have played no part in James's life after he and Florence shifted from Australia to New Zealand. As for the 'cheery party', it could not have been cheery for Florence Chapple, who was losing her youngest and favourite child. A photograph taken as Aynsley left tells the story. The old couple

stand at the top of steps leading down from the garden terrace at
Peacehaven. James looks thoughtful; Florence is sad and already
grieving; Aynsley, handsome, curly haired, smartly dressed, ready
for travel and a new life, is serious. The only other person in the
photograph is Lyndahl, who poses (a habit of hers) and wears a
smile. But she too must have been unhappy. She was deeply fond
of Aynsley.

It is doubtful if his parents understood that their youngest son
was homosexual in his nature (although perhaps not in practice,
then or ever). Lyndahl and Len almost certainly knew. It made no
difference to Lyndahl. She enjoyed Aynsley for what he was – an
affectionate and cheerful brother, a person with an interest in politics
and social justice, a gifted pianist. Her acceptance of homosexuals,
or gays as they have come to be called, was unusual in those times
of deep-seated homophobia. Two other friends of the old couple,
John Watson and Jim Leaney, became frequent visitors to the Gee
house in Newington Road. They were a gay couple and John was
an even better pianist than Aynsley. Lyndahl had persuaded Len
to buy a piano so that her sons could learn to play. When John and
Jim visited, she and the boys gathered round to watch John's fingers
fly over the keys. The boys' taste was for loud and fast, Lyndahl's
for melodious and sweet. Len was not comfortable with the visitors
or the music. He always found a reason to go out.

Lyndahl went two or three times a week to Peacehaven, taking
her sons in the weekend. Although retired from church work James
Chapple kept busy. In 1924, while still in Christchurch, he had
published two books, *A Rebel's Vision Splendid* and *The Divine Need
of the Rebel*. The first was a collection of lectures with titles like 'The
Wider Bible of Literature', 'Cradles and Cannons', 'The Twilight of
Kings'. The second contained essays written in Grasmere in the
Lake District while James, after visiting his English aunts, was
waiting for a berth on a ship back to New Zealand. (Titles: 'A

Vision of Man the Creator', 'A Vision of the Revival of Art Under Socialism', 'The Vision of a Progressive Religion', 'Militarism, the Assassin of Demos'.) He was a true rebel, eloquent and angry; and was a great finder of quotations to support his arguments.

From A.C. Swinburne:

> We have done with the kisses that sting,
> With the thief's mouth red from the feast,
> With the blood on the hands of the king,
> And the lie on the lips of the priest.

From Edward Tregear:

> The stalwart troopers rode at ease,
>   In scarlet, gold and steel;
> Within the park the worker crept
>   To eat his scanty meal;
> Alas! the workers' meals have paid
> For sword and horse and golden braid.

Although old age slowed him, he kept busy. The study at Peacehaven was the best room in the house. It was lined with books on three sides, floor to ceiling, and had a wide desk where James worked. A brass Buddha sat on a shelf, with occasionally a stick of incense smoking in its mouth. A further smell in the room came from the medicated cigarettes the old man smoked for his asthma. His bakelite hearing trumpet sat on one side of the desk.

James read. He wrote. Among his papers when he died was the manuscript of a third book, *The Growing Point of Truth*. He wrote for newspapers – appreciations of poets like Wordsworth and Browning and Emerson, essays on social and religious matters. He gave public lectures and spoke at election rallies, usually in support of communist candidates. He either did not know or refused to know of Stalin's 1930s atrocities. He kept the faith, as Lyndahl did too. She went to hear him as often as she could. Her devotion to him never faltered. But an even greater love was saved for Florence. The old lady, in her kitchen, out in her garden picking fruit, tending her roses – a practical woman, although deeply emotional, with all her thoughts centred on her family – became an almost idealised figure for her daughter. Lyndahl would have said that she embodied love.

Len liked her too and she enjoyed his company. He was less impressed with James and avoided him, which wasn't hard: the old man lived mostly in his study. The Chapple mystique never made any headway with Len. Another son-in-law, Phil Reanney, was equally immune. They joked about Chapples, sent grins at each other, mostly good-natured. 'Chapples!' they would say – and sometimes 'Bloody Chapples'. The pair spent two weekends digging out and re-laying the Peacehaven drains. James gave them half a crown each. 'Bloody old Jimmy, mean as mud,' Len said. Lyndahl was sometimes able to share his point of view where her brothers and sisters were concerned, but not when the subject was her father. 'Bloody old Jimmy' was said out of her hearing.

Chapple life sometimes encroached too much on Len's. The family assembled at Peacehaven to celebrate Christmas. Dick set up a tree on the terrace, and the Chapple girls – Bernice, Deorwyn, Flo, Joyce, Lyndahl – decorated it. Each family put its presents under the tree, and Bernice called the children up one by one and handed them wrapped gifts. It took a long time. Then the food was eaten. 'What did you get, Mossie?' an aunt asked the middle Gee boy. 'Auntie Bernie gave me a scooter,' Maurice replied. Len overheard. 'I gave you a scooter,' he said angrily.

If Len had problems with Chapples, Lyndahl had them with Gees and Gee relatives. She liked her mother-in-law, called Marmee in the family. Helen Davidson had displeased her family by marrying Harry Gee, a carpenter. The Davidsons had social pretensions. But Marmee was a kind and gentle woman, with few pretensions of her own. She had a difficult life with Harry Gee but was loved by her children. When she died in 1938 after an operation for goitre, Len was distressed. No one had seen the death coming. He travelled down to Christchurch, where his parents had returned, for the funeral. There he renewed his acquaintance with his mother's sister, Nancy, and a few months later Nancy paid a week-long visit to the Gees in Newington Road. The family picked her up at Auckland Railway Station, Len driving his Chrysler convertible. Auntie Nancy – ladylike, beautifully accented in her voice – sat in the front beside him as they drove back to Henderson. Lyndahl was in the back with her boys. She had not much to say. At one point Nancy turned round and looked at them one by one, Aynsley, Maurice, Gareth, and they stared back, large eyed. Nancy shook her head and patted Len's arm. 'Poor Len,' she said.

Maurice and Gary were turned out of their room and slept in the sitting room while Nancy took one of their beds. It was a hard week for Lyndahl, who never measured up. Auntie Nancy had her breakfast in bed. The boys, walking carefully, carried in her toast and tea. Once she sent the toast back – not brown enough. Grimly, Lyndahl made a second piece. The visitor had food fads too. Linseed was part of her diet. She boiled small pots of it on the range, smelling out the house. But she was soon gone. Len drove her back to the station alone. Lyndahl could relax, although not for long. A harder time was coming with Len's father.

He arrived in 1939, with his Border Collie, Kep, and stayed for eighteen months. The whole family loved the dog but found it less easy to love the old man, who filled the house with his presence – his opinions, his demands, his likes and dislikes. He took Junior's bed in the closed-in front porch, and the three boys shared a room again. Even from there, with the sitting room in between, they could hear him snoring. Lyndahl, in the closer bedroom, was woken by the sound night after night. It wore her down, made her short-tempered in the day, but there was nothing to be done. She tried her best to insulate her sons from her father-in-law's coarseness in language and opinions. Her preference for men who sweated and worked with their hands, declared in her story 'Tiger Town', did not extend to Harry Gee. A concern must have been that the boys would see Grandpa Gee as equal in importance to Grandpa Chapple. She would not allow it, and looked for a name to keep them separate. Pater, she decided, she decreed, and for the rest of his life Pater was Harry Gee's name to her and the boys. He seemed to like it.

The old man spent much of his day in the workshop, making joinery for Len's jobs. He had brought his tools with him, a mortising machine the most spectacular. He also brought his Dodge truck, which he sold to Len. But first he built a kennel for his dog and set it up by a peach tree, against the Pinckneys' hedge. The boys played with the dog endlessly, throwing a tennis ball for him to leap and catch, or throwing it deep into the scrub that covered most of the section where the workshop was built. Kep never failed to find and return it. But the dog's real love was for Harry Gee. When the old man was out he spent his time lying by the steps down to the road, waiting for him to come home.

Kep died late in Harry Gee's stay at his son's house. The old man cried. The boys cried. Together the four dug a grave beside the path to the workshop. They covered it with a slab and printed the name 'Kep' while the concrete was wet. Shortly after that Harry Gee shifted to a house he had bought in nearby Glen Eden, ending one of the more difficult times in Len and Lyndahl's married life. The old man continued to be Pater.

EIGHT

Len's influence on his sons varied from each to each. For Maurice, at least, Lyndahl's importance was greater. Yet Len was an affectionate masculine presence for all three. The boys copied him, admired him, loved him. He was tougher, stronger, faster, a better fighter than anyone else's father. He taught them to swim in Henderson Creek. He cut them a Christmas tree from a pine growing at the edge of the section, and pretended to fall when he saw them watching from the bedroom window. They all rushed out, Lyndahl rushed out, and found him lying on the lawn beside the cut pine, laughing in delight at having fooled them. He took them to his jobs and let them punch the nails in the floor boards. He won the nail-driving contest at the Labour Party picnic. (Lyndahl tucked up her skirt and won the ladies' dash.) In his workshop he hammered and sawed and planed – long sweeps of the plane, with the shavings curling out like ribbons and bouncing on the floor. When he sharpened his chisels on the emery wheel white sparks streamed up his arm as high as the elbow. He was a hero. He had knocked men out. The boys never tired of the stories. He had dived all day at a Tauranga wharf, bringing up hardwood planks from a tipped barge, and that night had knocked out Jack Bishara in the Town Hall. He taught them to fight. There were only two punches they needed to know: a straight left to stand your opponent up, then a right cross to flatten him. When Maurice tried the punches against Ernie Lisk, setting himself up carefully, right cocked, left extended (while Len watched), Ernie thumped him in the face with three roundhouse swings. Len led Maurice inside, bleeding and crying, and Lyndahl told Len off furiously. So it didn't work, but belief in their father never wavered for the boys. They were just as sure of him and happy with him as with their mother.

When they needed to be punished, both would do it, Lyndahl by sending them to the bathroom to wait, Len by giving them a couple of smacks with his razor strop. As most adults did back then, they believed misbehaving children should be physically punished, but Len hated doing it, and Lyndahl, preparing to smack one of the boys on his bared bottom with the back of her hearth-brush for refusing to go to school, could not do it but sat down and cried. The boy had a happy day at home.

Once or twice a more severe punishment was called for. Len cut a willow switch from the tree in front of the dunny and whipped the boys about the legs. Lyndahl put iodine on the welts. But no one else was allowed to punish the boys. Lyndahl persuaded Len to let her buy an old upright piano so one of her sons could learn to play. Aynsley, the oldest, was chosen. She sent him to the nuns at the Catholic school for lessons. It lasted only a few months. Aynsley showed her marks where the teaching nun punished his mistakes by hitting his knuckles with a ruler. Lyndahl angrily withdrew him.

On the whole the Gees made a happy family. The boys enjoyed a mixture of discipline and freedom. There were happy meals at the kitchen table and happy evenings by the open fire in the sitting room. Lyndahl insisted on good manners. Everyone must be at the table before the others could start eating. The boys must not eat too fast or chew with their mouths open, or stretch over the table for things, but must ask politely. They must not say they were full but that they had had sufficient thank you. They must not discuss certain things – dog poo, kids being sick at school or wetting their pants. 'That's not a table topic,' Lyndahl would say. Their language must be clean – no swear words, not even 'darn'. They must eat everything on their plates, even cabbage, even curly kale, or no pudding. And if one of them happened to fart silently, as children do, she would say, 'Who made an odour?' No one owned up. They were scared of being sent out to the dunny in the dark.

The words for pee and poo were a problem. Lyndahl found the answer from her days teaching 'Maori kids' in Te Puke. 'Tiko', meaning excreta, was what she was looking for, and throughout their childhood the boys spoke of big and little tiko, pronouncing it 'tikoo'. They took the terms to school, thinking they were general, but soon learned better.

Several years later, another of her words embarrassed them even more. 'You boys should show some spunk,' she would say when they were bored or moping about. She had brought 'spunk' back from America and used it freely, sometimes in front of their friends, and no one ever found a way of telling her its meaning in New Zealand.

Lyndahl kept up a steady, unobtrusive propaganda for cleanliness and purity in word and thought and action. The boys went along with it in varying degrees. One, Maurice, was affected badly. It confused and tormented him through his adolescence and young manhood. But the fault was more his than his mother's. The other two boys came through with no trouble.

*

Lyndahl read and wrote. Len studied horse-racing form and went to meetings as often as he could. He soon became addicted to racing. On Saturdays he would come in from the garden or the workshop every half hour to listen to race commentaries on the radio. He went to meetings at Avondale and Ellerslie, at Whāngārei and Pukekohe, with two new friends – his best friends for the next fifteen years – Bob Norcross and Alan Place. Bob was the owner of the biggest grocery shop in town. He was the son of Henry Norcross, who had had the shop in the worst days of the slump. Lyndahl always spoke warmly of Henry – a cheerful old Englishman (she never placed his accent closer than that) who gave his customers credit when they could not pay and never chased them to settle up. Bob, his son, was equally friendly and generous, and Lyndahl grew fond of him. She liked Alan Place a good deal less – a tough little man who usually had a drooping fag stuck to his lower lip. They, Bob and Alan, were the Henderson bookies. Len phoned his bets to Bob every Saturday morning.

In the late thirties and early forties Joe Louis was world heavyweight boxing champion. Bout descriptions were broadcast from America, and Len and the boys listened avidly as the Brown Bomber won fight after fight – against Buddy Baer, against the German Max Schmeling (although Schmeling had beaten him in an earlier fight), against Two Ton Tony Galento. They were filled with pride when the British champion, Tommy Farr (a Welshman), went the full distance with Joe Louis. Wrestling came from the Auckland Town Hall, where Gordon Hutter described the matches in his over-excited style and discussed them between rounds with Blind Peter, who sat beside him. The boys were allowed to sit up and listen and try simple holds on each other – the Body Scissors, the Hammerlock – and sometimes harder ones on Len – the Indian Deathlock, the Octopus Clamp.

He was a tough, practical and gregarious man, enjoying the company of men like himself. He smoked, rolling his own from a Greys Fine Cut tin. Lyndahl smoked too, rolling her own. Tailor-mades were a treat they could rarely afford. They both drank a little, Len beer, which had to be brought home, as Henderson had no pub. Lyndahl preferred wine, a taste she acquired gradually, helped along by her harder-drinking sister Joyce. By wine she and Joyce meant sherry or port, which they bought in flagons from

Corbans vineyard or from Dalmatian growers in Henderson and Oratia. Unfortified (and unsugared) red wine was 'sour'; they pulled a face at it. Several times Lyndahl sent the two older boys along Millbrook Road and up a side road to Ivicevich's vineyard for a flagon of sherry, which they carried home between them in a shopping bag, but she stopped this when she discovered that the old Dally in the shed gave them each a glass of watered-down wine. After that she and Len bought any wine they wanted from Fredatovich's winery in Lincoln Road. Mrs Fredatovich, who was a friend and poker companion of Joyce, became a frequent visitor at Newington Road. Lyndahl too learned to play poker.

She and Len got on well most of the time. If Len found Lyndahl's interests outside his range and some of her behaviour 'stuck-up', she was stopped short by temperament, by a simple lack of interest, at the edge of the places where he was happiest. But they tried, they made allowances, they got on. Len had built Lyn a writing desk after all. And Lyndahl chose a horse from *Best Bets* now and then, and let Len put on half a crown with Bob Norcross. They had many happy times. There were picnics at French Bay and Titirangi Beach, and holidays too: the best for everyone (except Gary, who caught the mumps) was in the late thirties, just before the war, at Stanmore Bay on the Whangaparāoa Peninsula, where the old farmhouse they rented was just up from the beach and there was not another house in sight. A photograph shows them on the veranda, Gary in pyjamas and dressing gown, with a swollen face, the other two boys in bathing togs, Lyndahl in a sailor suit, Len grinning. A happy family in spite of the mumps.

Back in Newington Road there were arguments now and then. Once during the evening meal Len had had enough of some disagreement between them. He stood up, took Lyndahl by the shoulders, marched her to the sitting room, put her in and closed the door. Back at the table he found three pairs of alarmed eyes fixed on him. Again he stood up, marched Aynsley to the sitting room, then Maurice, then Gary; closed the door and went on with his meal alone. 'Poor Len.' The boys found Lyndahl sitting on the sofa, smoking a cigarette. She told them not to worry. She had a little smile on her face. Lyndahl was calm in crises. After a while Len opened the door and they all went back and carried on with their meal.

Lyndahl did not record arguments in her writing. Although there were sometimes worries, especially about the war that was coming, she was more concerned with other people's troubles than her own. She grows angry over 'a family of fourteen, drastically poor. Until a few months ago they rented one of our suburb's shabbiest houses. A new baby had just arrived, bring the total of children to twelve raggedy-Anns. The last was just a few weeks old when the council cut the water off because the landlord hadn't paid the water rates. He wanted to get rid of his tenants so he could renovate the house and rent it at a greater profit – which he has since done. The town's poorest and largest family has moved on – no one seems to know or care where.'

She tells of her youngest boy having a sleepless night because the school dental nurse has put pieces of rubber between his front teeth to prepare them for fillings – 'six fillings!' Lyndahl can't believe it. She has always taken care of her sons' teeth. She takes the pieces of rubber out. 'I think I will see the dental nurse before allowing her to drill.'

She treats domestic troubles humorously. With Len off at the Pukekohe races, she decides to make Christmas puddings. She ties them in cloth and puts them to boil in the preserving pan, but they emerge misshapen and half cooked. Len, arriving home, takes a hand. He jams the puddings into the new pressure cooker, which Lyndahl hates and will not use. After a while there's a hideous rush of water and steam. The safety valve has blown out of the cooker.

A length of cloth 'rises from the hole, dancing like a dervish'. Then comes pudding mixture, spouting as high as the ceiling. Len carries the cooker outside to let it cool down. They give the boys sixpence each and send them to the pictures in the Town Hall, then spend the rest of the evening scraping and washing the ceiling and walls. But at the end of it Lyndahl has one lop-sided pudding, which she stores proudly in a cupboard.

She tells of the clothes line collapsing, not once but twice, on Monday morning. (Washing was done on Monday, an unwritten rule.) After the second collapse she sits on the back step smoking a cigarette and looking at her sheets and towels spread across the muddy lawn. Mrs Lisk finds her and after a while, laughing, they rinse the washing clean, hang it on the tied-up line, then go inside for a cup of tea.

Sometimes she speculates about the role of women, about the meaning of life and the existence of God. She's sure he's there but is not the Christian God. She's no theist, and not even properly a deist. God is love. As for Jesus, he is the ultimate good man.

All this time she is writing poems and stories. Some of the poems are published in the literary pages of local newspapers, and several in California, where Dora submits them. One drew a fan letter from a woman called Mary Schindler. Lyndahl kept up a correspondence with her for many years. She wanted a mental life but it would not arrive properly. Her writing had few admirers outside her close friends and one or two family members, James and Florence Chapple in particular. Late in the thirties she found an outlet for the stories in *Woman To-day, A Monthly Magazine for Women. For Peace, Freedom and Progress.* Elsie Locke was the secretary, and the advisory board included several writers, the best known being Iris Wilkinson (Robin Hyde), Dorothea Turner and Isabel M. Cluett. Lyndahl's best story for *Woman To-day*, 'Mother's Holiday', appeared in February 1939. The author's name is now hyphenated: Chapple-Gee. It's the story of Anna Worth giving birth to her fifth child. It's not an easy birth. At one point the matron slaps Anna's buttock 'the way a farmer slaps the rump of a cow' and tells her she's not trying. Lyndahl had been slapped like that, giving birth. Anna vows she will not forget. Her husband, John Worth, is in the story at the beginning and the end. He's tender and clumsy. Anna feels sorry for him.

'Mother's Holiday' has moments that are literary rather than felt but there are episodes that show the sort of writer Lyndahl might have become. A girl in the next bed has lost her baby and, Anna suspects, has no husband:

'Suddenly the squeak of a man's boots sent a thrill of anticipation through the ward. Three pairs of eyes turned hopefully towards the door. Through it a thick-set man was peering short-sightedly, discomfort and doubt reddening his heavy face. In one hand he was gripping a bunch of wilted mixed flowers.

"'Is Jesse McDoo in here?' he asked, catching Anna's friendly eye.

'There was a sudden movement in the bed on Anna's right.

"'Dad!" the fat girl was crying. "Dad! Oh, Dad!"

'Presently, from behind the screen that the man adjusted round his daughter's bed, Anna heard his first whisper: "Your Mum don't know I'm here."'

NINE

Although there were other stories and many poems, most of Lyndahl's energy during these years went into a novel for children. The original title was *The Little Colonial* but when she tried to find a publisher several years later she renamed it *Tane and George*. Tane is a six-year-old Pākehā boy. His full name is Tane Carlyle Emerson Gough. He lives with his mother, Annie Rae, who had been a teacher but now, in the slump, is the cook on a back-blocks sheep station. Tane's only playmate is George Paeroa, a Māori boy from a nearby pā. A shepherd, Big Steve, is in love with Annie Rae. Early in the story a swagger appears in the station kitchen. He wears a lady's felt hat without the trimmings. His face is 'as bristly as a nail brush and what were left of his teeth were the colour of tan nugget'. Annie Rae heats up some fried scones. The swagger, sitting on the doorstep, eats them whole, with butter running down his chin. 'Scat!' he says to Tane, stamping his unlaced boot. Then he steps into the kitchen and slams the door. Tane rides for Steve. They find Annie Rae holding the swagger off with a bottle of vanilla essence, which she tells him is acid. Steve hauls the man outside and knocks him down three times. Tane asks him to stop, because 'it isn't fair. He's so dirty and you're so clean. Make him have a wash and perhaps he won't frighten ladies anymore.'

In an earlier episode the boys build a hut, George using a three-bladed pocket knife that Tane would never be allowed to have. George is a Huckleberry Finn figure, wearing 'man-sized denim trousers that didn't fit him anywhere' and a ragged straw hat with hair poking through a hole. His Māoriness is underlined by frequent mentions of brown eyes and skin. He loves the condensed milk that Annie Rae doles out in the kitchen.

In the third chapter Steve saves a woman and her daughter, Rosemary, from a stuck car. The girl wears a pretty bonnet and has auburn curls, but when her no-nonsense mother makes her take off the bonnet the child's shorn head is revealed. Rosemary, in tears, runs out of the room. She has had scarlet fever and her curls are sewn into her bonnet. Tane decides the mother is stupid and cruel, and Annie Rae agrees, looking at Tane with sorry eyes.

In chapter four George dies. We're not told what of but it seems to be pneumonia. His father, Piri Paeroa, calls for Tane and they ride, 'a small pakeha boy on a big grey horse and a big Maori man on a small brown horse', over the hills to a packing-case house, where Tane finds George lying on a bed, covered by a Māori mat. He has 'a small friendly goodbye kind of smile' on his face. So Tane smiles back and 'without a single tear, says goodbye'. George's mother gives Tane a greenstone tiki to wear for George. The chapter ends with Annie Rae talking to her son about 'kinship' and death.

In chapter five Annie Rae tells Tane about his father, who is 'locked away where he can't be cruel to anyone again'. A stranger with a black gun arrives at Tane's hut.

"'I'm a hungry man and I must have food . . . go to the house and bring me bread and meat and cheese and I'll be watching you every step . . . if you talk to anyone or tell a soul I'm here, I'll use this see! And you'll be dead before you've got time to be sorry . . ." The stranger stroked the black gun as gently as if it were a black kitten he was cradling in his hand.'

Tane fetches food from the kitchen and while he's away the stranger reads his diary. He is, of course, Tane's father. Tane brings back food and watches the hungry man eat the bread and butter and meat in great lumps that he breaks between his hands.

'"Get me some water from the creek," ordered the man, giving Tane a mug. When he had drunk deeply he said rather surprisingly, "Thank you, Tane." Then picking up the green diary again the stranger began to write in it with a stubby pencil of his own. When he had finished he handed the book to Tane.' He tells Tane he has written a message to his mother but not to show it to her until tonight or he might be sorry.

'"Goodbye and I'm sorry if I frightened you son."

'Before Tane could believe it the tall stranger was gone out of sight the way he had come.'

Annie Rae reads the message: 'I came looking for you but I met the boy and read his diary about Big Steve and you and I've decided to give you all a break . . . I won't be bothering you again. I'm going to get out of the country.'

Annie Rae never tells Tane that the tall stranger was his father.

In the final chapter Annie Rae and Big Steve get married, and two years later there's a baby girl. Tane had wanted a brother to call George. Steve says they'll call the baby Georgina.

'All the disappointment went out of Tane. "Oh!" he said breathlessly, "now George will be happy too."'

Tane and George was a brave attempt to write a New Zealand children's novel at a time when very few existed. The background, the landscape, the places are well drawn, the slump is a presence, and the observation of small things – kitchen, hut, clothing, moments of behaviour – is exact and sometimes revelatory. The characters are less successful. Big Steve especially is unreal. And the story itself is constructed as a series of lessons that Annie Rae underlines as she talks to Tane. Lyndahl could not get away from her habits of moralising and sentimentality (or curb her use of exclamation marks). But a good editor might have shown her ways of writing to her strengths, which were considerable. With time and opportunity she might have found the ways herself. She must have been deeply disappointed when *Tane and George* failed to find a publisher.

She had great energy in those years. When *The Little Colonial* (as it was then) was finished and rejected she started on a narrative poem for children. It kept her busy for several years. There were additions and revisions. She read the poem – the story – to her sons, who enjoyed it and learned to recite large chunks:

> This is a tale, a peculiar tale,
>   That has never been told of yore;
> It started to grow, a long time ago,
>   When Mihi was only four.
> To begin where it started, one warm summer night,
>   New Zealand was Maoriland then,
> No white man had come, with his musket and drum,
>   To fight with the brown-skinned men. . .

The title is *Mihi and the Last of the Moas*; the subtitle *The Adventures of Mihi, a little Maori Boy with the Very Last of the Moas*.

The poem is in sections, with headings: 'Alone in the watchtower'; 'Mihi is found by the birds'; 'Morepork goes to the Moa for help'; 'The Tuatara tells a secret'; and so on. At the end of the story the moa falls ill deep in a cave, and Mihi builds a raft and floats him into the sunshine:

> No doubt you will guess that the sun's warm caress
>   Made the Moa quite magically well!
> And indeed if it did, as 'tis right to suppose
>   The bird might be living still,
> And the Maori boy too, since he also knew
>   The secret that we never will!

The poem ends several verses later, advising the reader walking by the sea or 'over far headland and range' to always 'look twice, or possibly thrice,/ And you might see the end of this tale . . . for all that you see is not all that can be/ In the Land of the Long White Cloud!'

Lyndahl submitted the poem to publishers with five watercolour paintings and a number of pen and ink drawings attached. She dedicated it to 'The Family Tree and all its Branches'. Oswald-Sealy Ltd accepted it and brought it out in 1943 in a hardcover edition of thirty-five pages, with one of Lyndahl's paintings, Mihi running through a dark cave holding a glow-worm lantern, used as the cover illustration, and the rest, along with the drawings, illustrating the text.

A researcher has suggested that Lyndahl paid to have the book published but in fact she received a small payment, probably in the region of ten pounds (or guineas), and was very pleased with herself. The book though created little interest. A short review appeared in the *Herald*: 'Young readers will love "Mihi and the Last of the Moas" by Lyndahl Chapple Gee. It is the story of a little Maori boy who suddenly finds himself alone in the bush when his tribe desert the pa after a fierce battle. How the wild creatures of the bush, the morepork, the tui and tuatara, befriend him, and how he goes adventuring with the very last of the moas, is beautifully told in verse. The book is illustrated with line drawings and colour plates by the author.' *National Education* said it was a tale '. . . sure to appeal to the child in the junior section of the school . . . the language is simple and the rhythm is attractive while the illustrations by the author are very pleasing.'

When the story was broadcast on 2ZB in Lady Gay's Young New Zealand Radio Journal the *Herald* praised it again, calling it 'a delightful poem . . . a charming fantasy . . . prettily told . . .' Lyndahl waited for more praise, but was crushed by a one-sentence acknowledgement in the *Listener*: 'The printers have done their work well.' And when she gave her brother Kingsley a copy, he read a few lines and tossed it aside. 'Doggerel,' he said. Lyndahl recovered from that. Kingsley had always been her least favourite brother. But she never attempted children's narrative verse again. These were the war years and while she was open to all sorts of disappointments and worries something hardened in her, as her next story was to show.

At the same time a light seemed to go out in Len.

TEN

He had got through the slump. He had kept his family together and kept them fed. The combination of a Labour victory in the 1935 election and the Depression coming to an end seemed to open up a happier future. Len knew how to work. He was also sharp-minded and adventurous. He had hated being on relief and hated the sort of jobs he had managed to find. In his and Lyndahl's first stay in Auckland in 1929 he had worked on the Civic Theatre building just being completed in Auckland's main street. The contractors were the Fletcher brothers, already well started on the career that would make them New Zealand's biggest construction company. Len had no time for them. There was plenty of labour, men were competing for jobs. The Fletchers and their foremen were 'hard bastards, mean buggers', he said. 'One word out of place and you were down the road.' While he could tolerate 'hard bastards', he hated 'mean buggers' all his life.

As the slump wound down he found work around Henderson. He teamed up with others at various times and they built a number of houses, several locally, two as far away as Riverhead and Tuakau. He bought his first car and then his father's Dodge truck; bought the next-door section, dug a driveway through the clay bank and put up a workshop. He kept on with building work through the first year of the war. If he had thoughts of enlisting, Lyndahl talked him out of it. But soon he was caught in another way. He was manpowered and sent ten miles up the road from Henderson to work on shelters and gun emplacements at Whenuapai Airport. He stayed on manpower for most of the war.

The army commandeered his Chrysler car and, in the words of one of his sons, 'the old man nearly cried'. He had put it up on blocks for the duration. They came and towed it away. Along with this went something greater: over the war years Len lost his sure sense of himself. He was thirty-five when New Zealand declared war on Germany. Men of his age began enlisting, and when conscription started two of his brothers-in-law, Dick Chapple and Phil Reanney, were called up. Both served in the desert and Italy. Dick, now married, had a child, and so did Phil. Len was older than both. He had three children and was in a protected trade. Also, he had a wife who was horrified by the war, sickened by it. He may have felt her health would collapse if he went away. And indeed, early in the forties she suffered some sort of nervous collapse, and went for a recuperative break, taking the boys, to the boarding house at Piha beach. It was meant to last a week, but after two days her worry about Len, alone in the house, drove her back to Newington Road, where she found him happy enough. So Len had reasons for not going to the war. Yet he felt he was shirking and would be taken for a coward. His sister Kathleen, a nurse, passed through Auckland on her way overseas. For his children, Len became sterner in those years, more remote, and although he still wrestled with them (three boys against one man on the living-room floor, a tangle of limbs), boxed with them, took them swimming in the creek, showed them how to build canoes out of sheets of old corrugated iron, supervised the building of an underground hut, and might, when Lyndahl told slump stories, chime in with one of his own, they could feel his unhappiness.

He became more impatient and aggressive. One day when the family was out, the neighbour, Lionel Pinckney, topped the pine tree growing in the back corner of the Gee section. Len was furious. He told Lyndahl he was going next door to give Pinckney a piece of his mind. The Pinckneys must have heard through the hedge. When the boys followed Len down the front steps they saw Mrs Pinckney running down the road to her father Ben Hart's house. They listened through the hedge as Len told Mr Pinckney off – loud angry voices. Mr Pinckney said the tree shaded his back yard. But he had not asked permission and he had trespassed. Len won the argument and came home feeling better. It did not last. His temper stayed on edge all through those years.

In 1945 he was directed to take a contract renovating and extending the Australasian Battery Factory in Henderson. The war in Europe was over and the Pacific war nearing its end. Len could feel he was working for himself. The existing building stood beside the old jam factory in Station Road. Len and the two men he employed for the job renewed the cladding, then extended the building another sixty feet and around the corner into View Road. It was no more than a stucco-clad lean-to but it marked the beginning of Len Gee's career as a builder. Henderson boomed in the postwar years. The centre of town shifted to the Great North Road. Rows of shops went up. Len built most of them and for the next ten years was Henderson's biggest builder. Sadly, though, he did not become a happier man.

*

In 1939 James and Florence Chapple sold their house and land in Millbrook Road. With Dick married and gone, they could not manage the property. They shifted to a bungalow in Verona Avenue, Mt Albert. Lyndahl had called on them almost daily but now was restricted to occasional visits by train. Her sister Joyce, living in a state house in a street at the back of Henderson School, helped fill the gap. They began to spend a lot of time together. And Peacehaven was not entirely lost. A family called Parker bought it and Lyndahl became friendly with them: the mother, Mrs Parker, the son, Jack, and especially the daughter, Muriel, who was to remain a friend for the rest of Lyndahl's life. Muriel, an intense, talkative, lively-minded woman in her thirties, seemed to be on a perpetual quest for enlightenment, for a teacher to unravel for her the mysteries of life and show its meaning. At times she was too much for Lyndahl, too enthusiastic, too unremitting in her search. She was exhausting. Lyndahl came to like Jack just as much. Jack tagged along.

The two women read the same books and discussed them whenever they had the chance. They read Lin Yutang, Gerald Heard, R.M. Bucke's *Cosmic Consciousness* and Alexis Carrell's *Man the Unknown*. They looked at the teachings of Frank Buchman's Oxford Group but were not captured, and then dabbled in theosophy. For a while they were devoted to Krishnamurti, for his teachings and his beauty equally. Muriel also read James Chapple's books and became an admirer. Soon she was enamoured of him, which alarmed Lyndahl, who was protective of her mother. She need not have worried. The old man also found Muriel alarming, especially when she told him what a wonderful child they could have together; and in any case his love for his wife never wavered. She was his ideal of womanhood and his loving companion, both.

Lyndahl could not keep up with Muriel in her perpetual searching. She had another life: her husband, her sons, a house to run, her writing to do. As well as this, her seriousness had a sentimental side that prevented her from becoming as eager and intense as her friend. She read fiction, which Muriel did not. She wanted to be moved by examples of unselfish love, unspoken love, sacrifice, happiness and fulfilment. Maurice Hewlett's *The Forest Lovers* and Margaret Kennedy's *The Constant Nymph* moved her deeply. She kept them in her library for many years. And Dora sent her a copy of *A Well Full of Leaves* by Elizabeth Myers, and Lyndahl read it several times, marking passages of 'nature mysticism' that especially pleased her. But chief among her small number of novels was Mary Webb's *Precious Bane*. At the end Kester Woodseaves kisses Prue Sarn on her 'hare-shotten lip'. That became Lyndahl's touchstone for love.

Another new friend was Marilyn Tomkies, an Englishwoman who lived with her husband Otto in a house downriver from the Tui Glen picnic ground. Marilyn equalled Muriel in talkativeness but was less intense. She enjoyed the same books as Lyndahl, including – after the war – the scandalous *Forever Amber*, and she too wrote. In 1948 the Tomkies left for California, where Otto was to take up a management job with an American 'millionaire' he had met (Len was sure the job existed only in Otto's imagination) and Marilyn hoped to interest a Hollywood studio in her screenplay, *Moonflower*. The Tomkies sailed bravely away and Lyndahl and Len never heard from them again. No movie called *Moonflower* was ever made.

Lyndahl wrote poetry but read very little of it. If asked to name a great poem she would have said Joyce Kilmer's 'Trees'. She wrote a poem to Joyce Kilmer, an American killed in the First World War:

> Oh! Wealth we lost of which your poem was part!
> A sprig of beauty plucked from out your heart,
> And given with young hands to a careless world,
> Oh! Wealth we lost when flags of war unfurled . . .

She had not read the writers her oldest and youngest sons had their second names from. She did not read Robert Browning and William Wordsworth, two of her father's favourite poets, but enjoyed a third, Walt Whitman:

Let me glide noiselessly forth;
With the key of softness unlock the locks – with a whisper,
Set ope the doors, O Soul!

Lines like these were very much to her taste.

She was moved by music, which did not come to her live, except when John Watson visited, but from the radio. She could recognise 'classical' and say names like Chopin and Beethoven with the beginnings of knowledge, and respond to the singing of performers like Lily Pons and Beniamino Gigli (Len turned a deaf ear; he preferred brass bands), but her real liking was for music that moved her easily – the singing of the duettists Nelson Eddy and Jeanette MacDonald, the tenor Richard Tauber and the baritone John Charles Thomas. Her favourite singer was Paul Robeson, and of his songs the best was 'Lindy Lou'. Everyone must be quiet when it came on the radio. Paul Robeson was singing to her:

Lindy, I'd lay right down and die
If I could sing like dat bird sings to you-u,
Ma little Lindy Lou-u.

One day at school a relieving teacher asked Maurice's class to name the world's greatest singer. Maurice's hand shot up. 'Paul Robeson,' he said.

'Flat as a pancake,' the teacher replied.

Lyndahl was outraged. The teacher was young and ignorant, she told Maurice, who was entirely on his mother's side. Lyndahl was only a little mollified to learn that the greatest singer was Beniamino Gigli.

'When flags of war unfurled'. Lyndahl blamed men, and much of her writing in the late thirties and early forties attacked their

Double Unit

blindness and greed. Women, she felt, especially mothers, should run the world. In a story called 'Mary', published in *Woman To-day* in 1938, she expressed her horror about the war that was coming, and made it plain where the hope for a peaceful future lay:

'Headlines jigged in slack and grotesque abandon before Mary's closed eyes. She tried to waken.

'"War!" screamed the Peoples of the Earth.

'"War!" sobbed Mary in her sleep. "God where are you?" She struggled again valiantly against the dream, only to find herself shouting to a milling host of khaki clad men.

'"Wake up! Wake up!" she commanded desperately. The men at last and with one accord stood still – they faced her; they would listen; then Mary saw with cold horror that they had the faces of sheep! "God! What shall I do?" she cried, her sleep-held form shrinking beneath the blankets.

'"Try the women," God answered clearly in a voice of healing. Mary's horror subsided. She sobbed "Yes, God," and hastened to do His bidding.

'The dream held. Mary found herself possessed of a steadily burning courage that drew mothers, wives, and sweethearts from their bereft homes as the Pied Piper's tune drew little children. They gathered; they formed behind her in silent steadfast lines, reaching as far as the eye could see. And Mary led them down a broad straight road to the sea, where transport ships lay waiting for their cargoes.

'Here more khaki clad figures came forward to frame the dream. Like a calm and crestless wave the women came on and on. The men spoke not, but suffered themselves to be put aside while the women took possession of ships and seafront.

'And now high on the bow of the ship Mary stood gazing down upon a mutely waiting host. Women, as far as her vision carried, and men with the faces of men; Mary smiled.

"'Go back to your tasks. Produce and provide and live in Peace!" she called, and to the farthest in their ranks they heard, and caught up her last word with one voice "Peace!"'

It's significant that this story is not by Lyndahl Chapple Gee but by Lyndahl Chapple.

As war began again, she was in equal states of anger and grief. But as it went on she began to be afraid. In 1942, when Japanese planes bombed Pearl Harbor, she became frightened for her family. Would the Japanese get to New Zealand? And even if they did not, how long would the fighting last? Aynsley was thirteen. Would he and then his brothers have to go? The thought filled her with dread. Len was at home, and largely at her insistence he stayed. She was disappointed in her brother Dick, who went when he was called. With his father's example to follow, he should have been a conscientious objector. Later in the war, one of her brother Hollis's sons, a fighter pilot, died when his aircraft was shot down.

Then there were the soldiers who came here, the Americans. They seemed so young and innocent. Joyce, with her open nature, got to know several of them (and was watched closely by neighbours who suspected her of 'playing around with the Yanks while her husband was overseas'). She brought two young soldiers, Bob and Red, to visit Lyndahl and Len. Red, loud and full of jokes, got down on the floor with the younger boys and played 'Sink the Nazi Navy'. Bob talked with Lyndahl. Over several visits she grew fond of him, in a motherly way. He believed the war had to be fought but was afraid of dying. Unlike Red, he made no show of wanting to go back. She worried about him when he left and wondered all her life if he had died.

Jim Jameson, a Henderson friend (Lyndahl's rather than Len's), was another who went to the war. Lyndahl's copy of *The Story of an African Farm*, the book she had her name from, was a gift from him. In 1973 she wrote on the fly leaf: 'Given to me by Jim Jameson, a temptation who came my way in Henderson during the slump days . . .' One day he and Lyndahl met by chance in an Auckland street. Jim was in uniform. He invited her to a tearoom, where they had a cup of tea and a scone. Then he asked her to come to a hotel, where he would take a room. He was going to the war, he said, and might be killed. Lyndahl said no. She and Jim, her note ends, 'were never more than brother and sister'. (She saw Jim Jameson only once again, years later. He came drunk out of a pub. They looked at each other 'with dead eyes' and went off in opposite directions.)

Another friend, Bert Chambers, became a conscientious objector, on political not religious grounds, and spent the war years in various North Island camps.

As the Allied forces stopped the Japanese and began to force them back, attention shifted again to the war in North Africa and Europe, where most of the New Zealand servicemen were fighting. 'The News From London' came each night on the radio. The *Herald* printed lists of dead and wounded and missing, overwhelming Lyndahl with pity and sadness. She felt 'helplessly unhappy' and submerged 'in an engulfing tide of pity', and she turned again to the God in whom she could not all the time believe.

'I pray God to confuse and confound the war guilty – to visit them in their dreams with the mangled baby bombed in its cot, the old mother buried beneath bricks, the war widow weeping on her bed . . . What is there to do but helplessly pray to God, to pray that there is a God . . . I sense almost physically the uneasy milling of the great human flock which waits patiently and pitifully for a good shepherd . . . I can only say that to meditate too long upon the war would send me mad – and I do not intend to become a mad mother!' Later in the same notes (a continuation of 'Potato Peelings') she says: 'I have moments of peace beyond telling in spite of the war. One rare whisper from God quiets for me the endless shouting of leaders and led alike. I feel unshakeable then and sure that when the sounding brass shall have died away the old eternal truth will be found still standing unalterable, "God is Love".' And again: 'I have reduced my politics to this – that any government that would equalise men's and women's importance in their naturally different spheres of work, eliminate poverty and restrict wealth, educate all, de-commercialise religion and revitalise Christianity by practising it, would be worth working and living for; but I hesitate to say worth fighting and dying for, I am too much a mother.'

If she had been asked to name heroes she would have said the mothers at home raising their children, the men in the objectors' camps, and the common soldiers pushed forward into the guns. Never the leaders, never the generals or the politicians. Especially not Winston Churchill. Lyndahl followed the family line on him. He was 'a warmonger'. Her mother especially detested Churchill: 'that fat old sausage with his fat cigar'. His aristocratic connections, too, did not go down well with the old lady, who would close a book with a snap and not read any more if she found a lord or lady in the pages. James Chapple remembered Churchill's ruthlessness in helping break the 1926 General Strike. They gave him no marks as war leader, and neither did Lyndahl.

There was, however, one leader they admired, perhaps revered – Joseph Stalin. One of the lectures that had landed James Chapple in prison in 1918 was 'The Glorious Bolsheviks of Russia'. He had said then that he hoped to see a revolution like the Russian one in New Zealand some day, and perhaps he still waited for it. None of the events of the thirties – show trials, failed five-year plans, mass starvation – appeared to shake the old man's belief, and Lyndahl's, that the Russian leaders, Stalin especially, were devoted to 'the people, the common man'. The Hitler–Stalin pact and the Russian invasion of Finland must have worried them. They avoid them in their writings. But when Hitler sent his armies into Russia, everything was right again, in spite of Russian defeats.

Stalin could be raised up. On Lyndahl's bench of heroes he sat beside Michael Joseph Savage. She presented him to her sons as 'kind old Uncle Joe', sometimes 'dear old Uncle Joe'. They grew up believing in his benevolence and had difficult adjustments to make later on. Lyndahl never made any. Stalin remained in her pantheon for the rest of her life. She never believed in his crimes; they were 'American propaganda and politicians' lies'.

ELEVEN

Mihi and the Last of the Moas came out in 1943. It was not quite the last of Lyndahl's publications. In October 1945, only a month after the Hiroshima and Nagasaki bombs brought the Pacific War to an end, the Caxton Press published an anthology of New Zealand short stories called *Speaking for Ourselves*. The editor was Frank Sargeson. He included a story called 'Double Unit', by Lyndahl Chapple Gee. She was in good company, listed on the contents page between Roderick Finlayson and A.P. Gaskell. Others in the volume included D.W. Ballantyne, John Reece Cole, Greville Texidor, Maurice Duggan and Sargeson himself.

'Double Unit' is a successful story. It's organised well, although perhaps is over-schematic. Two women, Louise and Millie, live side by side in a double-unit state house, as Lyndahl's sister Joyce and a pretty young woman called Maisie Cole did. Each has a five-year-old son and, like Joyce and Maisie, a husband at the war. Louise, quiet and faithful, longs for Joel's return; 'she is lonely for the company of one man'. Millie 'was lonely for the company of men in general'. They react to this loneliness according to type, 'Louise romantically, Millie remedially'. By the end of the story the husbands are home. Louise's Joel has coarsened in appearance, manners and speech. He drinks and tells crude jokes. He is rough in his love-making. Millie's Rodney 'had no fun left in him and he wouldn't drink. He looked and behaved like a middle-aged man, and his love-making had no warmth in it; she supposed he had worn himself out.' Louise finds 'her own love of peace and quiet being eaten away by Joel's corroding habit of restlessness'. Millie copes with the new Rodney by leaving him at home minding Jackie while she goes to a Saturday night show. Dressing, she hums 'The Blond Sailor'.

Louise finds photos of Joel kissing an Egyptian girl (a Wog, as he calls Egyptians), of the girl sitting on his knee in a negligée and swimming with him 'in her birthday suit'. On the boat coming home 'bunches of soldiers turned out their kits for snapshots, letters and cabaret programmes to destroy'. They called it 'evidence day or E day'. 'Joel had forgotten to toss all his evidence into the sea.' Louise, 'with the past despoiled and the future soiled', vows to live her life for her son and never to have another child with Joel. Rodney learns of Millie's unfaithfulness from a neighbour. He wonders what leftovers his life has to offer him. His gardening, his hobby of writing – he has roughed out his war experiences and is on to his political beliefs: '. . . both subjects tended to turn red under his pen'. And he has his son, although he decides, 'It's a bloody world and no fit place to bring children into.'

The story ends with the boys swapping souvenirs their fathers have brought home: a collection of Egyptian coins for a commando knife.

"'Hot diggety!" Jackie said, unsheathing the knife. "I wish we could swap fathers too."'

It's plain that the husbands and wives should swap, but Lyndahl does not take things that far. For most of 'Double Unit' she stays free of sentimentality. Louise and her son, Sunny-Jim, are the least real of the characters. The others though, especially Millie, are convincing and the writing has a new sharp edge. It also has sly turnings and reversals and touches of humour. The lives of the women are neatly and economically filled in. One wonders how much influence Frank Sargeson had on the story. In the euphoria of having it accepted, Lyndahl began to refer to him as Sarge. She hadn't met him, wasn't to meet him for a number of years, but she plainly felt familiar with him (concealing that she had never enjoyed his stories, finding them drab and dry and without a spiritual dimension). She must have sent him other stories with 'Double Unit'. In a letter, now lost, he advised her that it would be better to change 'the distracted rodent' into 'the rat'. The phrase occurs in her *Mirror* story, 'The Parting of the Ways'. It's likely he suggested a change or two in 'Double Unit', but the story is Lyndahl's own – her observations, her experience, her view of life and how it is and how it should be, all arranged, dramatised and phrased convincingly. It presents a new Lyndahl and should have been her new beginning. But 'Double Unit' is the last of her publications.

TWELVE

It was Len's turn to sit working while everyone else was asleep. He wrote building specifications and drew plans, sitting at the kitchen table late into the night. He had a talent for mathematics and technical drawing. His sons looked on his productions – floor plan, roof plan, front elevation, side elevation – as works of art, and marvelled at his precision and the pages he filled in his bold handwriting. It seemed an equal accomplishment to Lyndahl's story-writing.

One of the first houses he built was opposite the Holy Cross Church in View Road. The priest would live there. It must have been forgotten that several years earlier the Gee boys had vandalised the Catholic school. The battery factory job came soon after, followed by two blocks of shops in the new town centre on the Great North Road, a building for the Bank of New Zealand, and dozens of houses, most for clients but some for sale on completion – spec houses. He never employed more than six men and he remained a hands-on carpenter himself.

There's a sense in which Len left his family during these years. He was grabbing at fulfilments that had almost eluded him. He wanted to use the energies that had been frustrated in the slump and war years. He knew his abilities and wanted the things he felt they entitled him to – money, comforts, a house that fitted him, a position, recognition, enjoyments. He wanted a wife who would be admired for attractiveness and a good dress sense and social skills. Lyndahl could not play the part. She stayed the same and saw Len grow away from her. Like Louise in her story, she became 'lonely for one man'.

She had, a little earlier, resumed her almost daily visits to her parents. James and Florence could not settle down in Mt Albert. They returned to Henderson, to a small house in Lincoln Road several hundred yards along from its junction with the Great North Road. A huge oak tree grew on the adjoining section, which they also owned. The garden was well established; and Dick, back from the war, built a new tea-tree summerhouse on the front lawn. So that somebody would be close to the old couple, he and his wife Christine bought the section on the other side and put up a house. (The builder: Len Gee.) Dick screwed the name of James and Florence's final home on their gate: Journey's End.

Millbrook Road had been closer for Lyndahl. Now she made a much longer walk. Newington Road, no longer blind, cut through paddocks to the Great North Road. She went that way, and down the hill past Henderson School, where only her youngest son remained as a pupil, through the town, where her husband was building shops, up the hill past Corbans vineyard and winery, with its little shop on the eastern side of the railway line so liquor could be sold legally (the western side was 'dry'), and along Lincoln Road to her waiting parents. They, as much as her sons, were her emotional anchor. She spent an hour with them, talked with her mother, shouted into her father's ear trumpet, drank tea, then walked back home, doing her shopping on the way. A part of her life was full, while another part was, like Louise's, 'being eaten away'. And Len? He too was being eaten away.

He was decisive, energetic, tough, determined. He put in long hours and he needed relaxation and entertainment. His interest in horse racing grew. He kept up his friendship with Bob Norcross and Alan Place, phoned his bets to Bob, won and lost, and went to meetings as far away as Thames and Te Rapa. He made new friends, among them Richie Wilkinson, the owner of the battery factory, and his wife Frances, and half a dozen other couples who liked to drink and party. Lyndahl tried to keep him company. She tried to be the wife he wanted, but her heart was not in 'good times'. She drank a little, and then a little more, and tried to be talkative and cheerful, but the talk was not about things that interested her. She embarrassed Len when, leaning forward, cigarette in hand, she argued fiercely about politics. They had never had more in common than their children, their hard times and hard work and endurance, their disappointments and their making-do and their hopes for the future. That was plenty to keep them close. But their interests beyond these things never overlapped and now, in better times, the differences began to show.

Sometimes, in that small house, the boys overheard arguments. Lyndahl was nearly forty and must have dreaded getting pregnant at that age. Len accused her of no longer 'wanting him' in bed. She replied that she was too old for that sort of thing.

In the family much of Len's good humour seemed lost, but socially he was full of stories and jokes. His hair was still dark, his eyes had kept their piercing blue, he was straight-standing – a handsome man. Among his and Lyndahl's new friends there were women who liked him. One, Frances Wilkinson, liked him too much. She was an attractive woman and responsive to men; blond and pretty and full-bodied. She made herself up with care and dressed expensively. The Wilkinson marriage, everyone knew, was running downhill. Early in their acquaintance, while Len was still building the battery factory, she made it plain to him that she liked him sexually.

Lyndahl saw what was happening and did not seem to mind. She let Len know that she knew what he was up to, and he admitted to liking Frances more than he should but said that he didn't know how to get away from her. The Wilkinson house was behind the jam factory. Frances invited him in for cups of tea, sat him on the sofa and asked him to excuse her for a moment, she'd just put on something more comfortable. Then, he said, she would run back through the room wearing only her panties – 'Excuse me Len, I just have to do something in the kitchen.'

'What am I supposed to do?' he said (although he knew).

Lyndahl seemed amused. She did not dislike Frances, who was always friendly and chatty. Perhaps she felt that Len deserved some fun; she went to Frances and told her she could have him for a while but she must do it without breaking up his family. Frances had not thought that far. Perhaps even the possibility that Len's family might be broken up alarmed her – or perhaps she did not want him handed to her as a gift. Whatever the reason, she stopped inviting him in for 'cups of tea'. The battery factory job finished and the affair, or non-affair, came to its end – or seemed to come. Many years later, talking about those times with one of his sons, Len said that nothing had happened between Frances and him, they had not gone to bed. But he also said, with a touch of satisfaction, that some years later, when the Wilkinson marriage was over and Richie Wilkinson had a new wife, he had bumped into Frances in Auckland and she had invited him to her flat for a drink. There, Len said, it happened. But not again, he said. That was the first and last time. So ended what seems to have been the only affair Len had. Lyndahl never found out about the final encounter.

Back in the mid-forties, she continued to be amused, and let it show. She would have claimed she was being broad-minded. (How much pain it concealed can never be known.) Len still took bets for her on horses. In 1948 a mare called Frances was a starter in the Auckland Cup. Lyndahl knew nothing about the horse's breeding or form but she said innocently that she liked the name and please would Len put on a ten-shilling bet for her? Playing her game, he complied, after telling her the horse 'didn't have a bolter's'. Frances won and Lyndahl made a nice little sum of money. Len managed a small grin of approval. They went on in this way, mostly good-humoured, with give and take, but their closeness was gone. And Lyndahl's health was going too.

By 1948 a number of things had changed. In Lincoln Road James Chapple had grown frail. There was no more writing, no more 'orating'. He read, he walked in his garden, he sat with his wife and enjoyed visits from his children and grandchildren; and in 1947 he died, following a prostate operation. He was eighty-one.

The family gathered. After a funeral service written by himself and full of quotations from his favourite writers, James was cremated. His sons and daughters scattered his ashes around a tree in the Waitākere Ranges.

So his remarkable life came to an end, but he was to live on for many years in the memories and lives of his family and friends. For some he's still alive. But the loss of her father struck Lyndahl hard. As a child and young woman she had taken her direction from him. In most of the things she believed, in her attitudes, interests, prejudices, in almost everything, he had been her guide, whether he had meant to be or not. Her mother was still there but her mother was simply loving and loved. James Chapple had been Lyndahl's intellectual support, her constant reference in most of the things touching on her life of the spirit and the mind. (Both of them would have called it that.) Muriel Parker believed that Lyndahl never recovered from the death of her father.

Several years earlier, after a conversation in which she seems to have said he deserved a halo, and he had replied, 'No halo for Dad,' she attempted a poem, 'To Dad'. It's plain from the handwritten copy that she couldn't get it right, but several of the lines show how she felt:

> To those of your children who cherish the bond
> You have pointed one way; it leads up and beyond,

You have given one gift, an unquenchable thirst
For the Truth in whose lap we were tenderly nursed.

And later:

Love for our father, a pure solid gold,
Has gleamed through the layers of life's every fold.

Lyndahl's love continued to gleam for the rest of her life. Whether he deserved it or not, she granted him a halo.

Another death came in the following year. Lyndahl's brother Geoff died from a heart attack at the age of forty-four, leaving a daughter aged five and a son aged three. Lyndahl's grief for him seemed different from that she felt for her father. Geoff was one of the younger Chapple brothers, one of those she had grown up with. He had been the family jokester; it was Geoff who kept them laughing. And he kept a knowing eye on his younger sisters. He appears in 'The Change' as John, the brother who tries to spoil Lynda's romance with Simon – for which Lyndahl had long forgiven him. He was athletic. As a boy he had been able to walk up and down stairs on his hands. Lyndahl believed it was this that weakened his heart.

In some ways Geoff's death struck her more deeply than her father's. It was too early, it was wrong and cruel. She grieved for Geoff's widow Dawn and for the children. She had grown to like Dawn more than any friend she had – enjoyed her humour, her enthusiasm for new and interesting things, her intelligence. She did all she could to help Dawn through the weeks and months following Geoff's death. But for Lyndahl herself, life now seemed to have a hole at its centre. For years she wrote nothing. Her God had been elusive but now her faith in him seemed entirely lost.

Len too was having his troubles. One day, driving the old

Dodge truck down Henderson Valley Road, and perhaps with personal and business worries on his mind, he failed to see a train approaching the crossing. The engine hit the truck behind the cab and carried it a hundred yards along the line. A railway gang heaved the wreckage up and pulled Len out. He was lucky – cuts and abrasions but no broken bones and no injury to his head. He spent only one night in hospital. The truck that had been with the Gees for so long was a write-off. And Len was fined ten pounds for careless driving.

It was more than time to get away from the house in Newington Road. Over the years there had been improvements – an electric stove, a flush toilet, connection to the town water supply, a telephone – but meat and butter and milk were still kept in a safe on the back porch (James Chapple, five foot three, had gashed his forehead on an edge of it); the wash was still done in the copper and tubs; and the house, with only a makeshift third bedroom, was too small. For the year Harry Gee had spent with them it had been almost impossible to live in. And later, for six months, they had given a home to Joy Hollis, the daughter of Lyndahl's sister Flo. Now with the boys older – Aynsley apprenticed to Len, Maurice and Gary at secondary school – the house had started to bulge. They could afford something bigger and more comfortable. Len began to keep his eye out. No one knew Henderson and its houses better than him and it did not take him long to find what he was looking for.

THIRTEEN

The house was in Tirimoana Road, just down from Te Atatu Corner. Lyndahl more than liked it, she was thrilled with it. The section was a full quarter acre. It sloped down from the road, widening as it went, with the house, a stucco bungalow, set towards the back. There were neighbours on only one side, behind a high hedge, and the view from the living room was almost as wide as the Waitākere Ranges view from Newington Road: paddocks falling away to a mangrove reach of the upper harbour, stretches of sea beyond, some distant slopes of Auckland city, and Rangitoto Island rising behind the headlands of Birkenhead.

The house had three bedrooms, the main one with a sunroom attached, a large living room opening through glass doors to a covered porch, a dining room (at last the Gees did not have to eat in the kitchen), and a modern kitchen with space for that ultimate luxury, a refrigerator. The bathroom was small but Len built a laundry ('washhouse' was left behind in Newington Road) on the side of the house, beyond the back door. A second toilet went in there. And Lyndahl got her first washing machine.

As well as the house, Len bought five acres of land at the side and back. The paddocks ran down to a narrow creek enclosed in scrub. He cut an entrance road to the back of the house and built a workshop to make joinery and store his timber. Several of his men worked there each day. Len was satisfied. He had good tradesmen working for him and new machines in his workshop. There were shops and houses to build, plenty of jobs: the Bank of New Zealand building, a butcher shop for George and Harry

Holborow, a house for his friend Bob Norcross, and a large two-storeyed one for Dr Friedlander, a local dentist. He built houses in Titirangi for two families who had left Malaya when the civil war started. He sponsored a Dutch bricklayer, Bill Verryt. But it was a grim sort of satisfaction. Things were not right. He and Lyndahl were not happy, and she was not well.

There were many things about the new house she liked: the space, the carpets (the one in the sitting room at Newington Road had been threadbare), new furniture, kitchen appliances, the new laundry; the view over the harbour, where she could watch the tide come and go in the mangroves. She left a billy on a fence post in a corner of the section and a man who ran cows nearby filled it each morning with creamy milk. She loved picking ripe figs from the large tree at the back of the house. What else? The neighbours over the hedge, an old couple, the Waterhouses, were friendly. Vladimir Loncar, a young man from down the street, dropped in and talked with her about theosophy and all things spiritual. (Her sons were not interested in theosophy.) She claimed, only half joking, that Vladimir looked like Jesus Christ.

Dawn Chapple was a quarter-hour walk away. Joyce was twenty minutes. The walk to Lincoln Road, where the old lady sat by the window waiting for Lyndahl, was longer now. It took three-quarters of an hour. Lyndahl managed it two or three times a week, submitting to the unconscious tyranny. Her mother took such pleasure in her company. Lyndahl came in the gate. 'Ah, here's Lindy.' She stayed for an hour, then walked home or caught the bus to Te Atatu Corner, where there was a grocery store for the shopping. This was Lyndahl's routine, when her health allowed, for the next ten years.

The problem of daily care for the old lady was solved when Dick and Christine sold their next-door house and moved in with her. The sale caused trouble. When the house was going up Dick had promised that, if he ever sold it, his friend Clearwater could have it at the price it had cost to build. In the postwar boom, house prices increased by at least half. But for Dick a promise was a promise, the price had been agreed and that was that. His wife raged at him; his relatives, even Lyndahl, tried to persuade; Len explained market realities patiently, then contemptuously – 'Bloody Chapples.' Dick smoked his pipe and kept quiet and would not budge. His friend kept quiet too, and out of the way, and Dick let him have the house for not much more than half of what it was worth. A few months later Clearwater sold it again for its market value.

Lyndahl was the only one who saw some virtue in what Dick had done. She admired his honesty and simplicity. He was the one, she said, who should have been called Clearwater.

She was up and down. Her doctor called her illness a nervous breakdown. A difficult menopause began, and went on for several years. The doctor treated her with phenobarbitone, which calmed her and made her drowsy. She liked the drug. 'I need some of my phenobarb,' she would say. Len hired an ex-nurse, Mrs Riley, to look after her in the mornings and help around the house. The two women got on well, although Mrs Riley, like Ivy Lisk, remained 'Mrs'. She was on hand, and calm and competent, when Len, alone in the workshop, ran his hand into the planing machine (the 'buzzer') and chopped off the top joint of his ring finger. She got him to the doctor, brought him home and put him to bed. For a while he and Lyndahl were immobilised together.

There were times when Lyndahl was up and busy. She visited her mother, did her shopping, cooked the meals. And once, when compulsory military training was introduced, she returned to her political and fiery earlier days, heckling a pro-conscription speaker at a meeting in the Henderson Town Hall. She was disappointed at the National victory in the 1949 election and sickened, as many New Zealanders were, by the emergency regulations the government brought in during the 1951 waterfront dispute. She came to despise the prime minister, Sid Holland. Len kept quiet about politics. The new friends he was making leaned mainly to the right.

He joined the Masonic Lodge, but 'the mumbo jumbo' made him impatient and he soon stopped going. He preferred the company of his racing cobbers. He still found time for race meetings. He went to parties, sometimes taking Lyndahl, and organised several at home. Two of his new friends were musical. A man called Armishaw (the brother of Eric Armishaw, who had beaten Len in the 1928 New Zealand welterweight final) played the piano. Ramon Opie was a tenor, well known in Auckland amateur operatic circles. They came several times and played and sang. Lyndahl loved it and Len was pleased to see her animated. He was animated himself; he was a good host. Lit up a little by alcohol, he was cheery and jokey, almost jolly. Women still liked him and fell for him, but he never responded in any serious way. One, the wife of a new friend, seemed almost sick with love. He kept clear of her, and Lyndahl was kind, patting her with friendship. It kept on for a year or two, until the couple left Henderson.

So the years went by and Lyndahl was as well again as she would ever be. One can picture her wandering on the sloping lawns, looking at the long view, stopping at the white picket fence to admire Len's horses in the paddock, picking a ripe fig and eating it, and wondering what had become of her life. Inside, in the sunroom, she lay dozing on the sofa. The writing desk Len had built almost twenty years before sat unused in a corner.

Their generosity to their sons was ungrudging. Len expected help from them – the lawns, the garden – but he made no demands; he gave his support freely in everything connected with their education and futures. Only Maurice carried on to university. Gary, after working for a year in an advertising agency, became a junior in the Henderson branch of the Bank of New Zealand, where the manager was a friend of Len's. Aynsley worked through a full apprenticeship. Len was pleased with him. He had the aptitudes and energy for carpentry. Len also employed his father, and he put the boy and his grandfather together, hoping the old man would pass his knowledge on. It didn't work. Aynsley came to him one day: 'If you don't get that old bastard off my back I'll hit him with a lump of four-by-two.' Len knew his father. He kept him and Aynsley working on different jobs after that.

He was puzzled, impatient now and then, that Maurice sat reading so much of the time. He did not understand an arts degree, would have preferred engineering or science or law. But the boy pleased him by taking manual jobs in his holidays, once as a brickie's labourer on one of Len's jobs.

Unlike Lyndahl, he was untroubled by Aynsley's buying and riding an old motorbike (too fast) and buying a .22 rifle for rabbit shooting, and borrowing a .303 and heading off with mates to the Ureweras after deer. He watched the two younger boys play rugby, but his hope that they might become good boxers soon faded. In 1949 he had turned up at Avondale College to watch Maurice and Gary fight in the school boxing championships. Both had managed to get into finals. The referee was late and Bill Martin, the teacher running the tournament, knowing from Maurice that Len had boxed, asked him to fill in. Len took one bout, then the real referee turned up: Eric Armishaw, who also had sons at the school. The two men shook hands without warmth. Gary won his bout. Maurice's arrived. He was in the blue corner; his opponent, a boy known as 'Killer' Morrison, in the red. With his father watching, Maurice got his left jab working well, but could not find an opening for his right. He managed not to take any punches. Len told him later he had won. Maurice thought so too and even 'Killer' Morrison agreed. But Eric Armishaw said, 'Red the winner.'

Gary was the toughest of the boys and the best fighter. One night Len came home late from having a few drinks after work. He and Lyndahl quarrelled in the kitchen, until Gary, in the bathroom, sprucing himself up to go out, could take their bickering (more than bickering) no longer. He opened the door and said, 'Why don't the pair of you stop acting like children?' Len was enraged. He ran into the bathroom and aimed a punch at Gary, who, not bothering with a straight left and right cross, knocked his father down with a short right hook. Then he ran. Len was groggy for a moment. Then he too went outside and prowled the section looking for his son. Lyndahl – calm in the crisis – went into Aynsley's bedroom and hid his .22 rifle under the bed.

Gary had got away to a friend's place up the road. He did not come home that night, but turned up after work next day and nothing was said. It had blown over, or else Len had buried it deep. It's possible he was pleased at the perfect punch his son had thrown.

FOURTEEN

When James Chapple died, his bookman sons, Leonard and Kingsley, took most of his books – 'all the valuable ones,' Lyndahl said crossly. Still, she got several valuable to her, chief among them Robert Browning's *Poems* (a selection) and Walt Whitman's *Leaves of Grass*. She opened them to see his underlinings and exclamations. From Browning's 'Paracelsus':

> Blind opposition – brutal prejudice –
> Bald ignorance – what wonder if I sunk
> To humour men the way they most approved?

James Chapple wrote in the margin: 'I have not! I will not!' And when Whitman wrote of 'many an arrogant lord . . . klinking wine-glasses together over their victory', the old man could not restrain himself. 'The asses!' he declared in the margin. Lyndahl was pleased to have all this without any need to read the poems.

Two other books that came to her were the old man's Bible and his Cruden's Concordance. He had written 'For Lyndahl' in the Bible. It's the copy he used while studying for ordination, and his multitude of annotations and comments, written in a minute hand in red or purple or blue ink, show his orthodox thinking at that time, but also his gift for preaching and finding words to point a way. The comments, underlining, overwriting, lines darting across the pages, linking one passage to another, rarely let up. The first comment comes in Genesis 1.3: And God said, Let there be light: and there was light. James Chapple underlines it, then underlines 'Let' again.

Not satisfied, he overwrites 'Let' and 'light' and the second 'light'. In a balloon in the margin he gives references to Job 38.19, Jno. 8.12 and II Cor. 4.6. A ruled line heads to another balloon: '"Let." Sinners have the power to prevent the LIGHT.' James carries on in this way throughout the volume, ending with another balloon at Revelation 22.20: 'I come quickly; Amen. Even so, come, Lord Jesus.' James, referring to an underlining above (Rev. 22.17), says: 'What a beautiful echo this is. See also Psa. 27.8.' Some pages are so densely ruled, ballooned and overwritten they're hard to read. For example, on the second page, from Genesis 2.5 to Genesis 3.19, there are twenty balloons in the margins, most containing dozens of words in tiny handwriting, with lines linking them to underlined passages; and there's also a spiderweb of lines linking passages and words to each other. Throughout the book there are dozens of tipped-in pages with James's handwritten comments in his various inks. It's a fascinating volume, and although Lyndahl was delighted to have it she probably did little more than turn the pages and admire her father's cleverness. He had soon got past this sort of Bible religion.

Her illness left her without energy. She did not write. It's not certain she even wanted to. Her reading was more restricted than it had been – the 'heavy' books she had once managed seemed beyond her now, although their ideas, filtered to her by people like Muriel Parker, continued to interest her. She was excited for a time by Aldous Huxley's 1954 book, *The Doors of Perception*, and would happily have tried the magic mushrooms he recommended if she had been able to get them.

She picked up some of the books Maurice was reading for his university course; was puzzled by James Joyce's *Ulysses*, loved D.H. Lawrence's *The Rainbow*. Several of the poets pleased her too – John Donne, W.B. Yeats – but, Yeats aside, she was resistant to modernist verse and would have agreed with her father who, coming across a poem by T.S. Eliot in an anthology, wrote 'Not poetry!' in large letters in the margin.

Len, meanwhile, continued his generosity to his sons, giving Maurice bed and board while he sat reading and trying to write short stories and novels. Lyndahl encouraged the writing; Len stayed patient, hoping his son would grow out of it. When Aynsley met a young woman, Margaret Bowen, at ballroom-dancing classes, and married her, Len gave the couple a section as a wedding present and arranged a loan so they could build a house. He himself was building spec houses on adjacent land. Aynsley built his own house, and he and Margaret moved in, a mile or two down Te Atatu Road from Lyndahl and Len. Lyndahl was pleased with her daughter-in-law, liked her friendliness and good humour, and also found her background interesting. Margaret was born in India and had lived there until 1947, when she was sixteen. The Bowen family came to New Zealand after India gained its independence and the troubles of partition began. Lyndahl especially enjoyed Margaret's mother, Hazel Bowen, a marvellous talker with endless (sometimes unending) tales to tell.

Soon there was a child, Angela. A new generation of Gees had begun.

As her health improved Lyndahl talked several times of getting a job. She had been a hard worker, running a house and raising children in times when food and clothing had to be scraped up almost from nothing, while writing in the moments of time she could spare, but apart from serving in a shop when she was a girl and her several years as an untrained teacher she had never worked out in the world. Now she found she did not want to, although she talked wistfully about it. She wanted to be discouraged and Len obliged. 'My wife doesn't need to work.' She was keener to get a driver's licence. With a little car of her own she would be able to visit her mother and friends more easily. Len arranged lessons, arranged them more than once, but she failed each time. She could not get the hang of it, seemed unable to understand gears and accelerator and brakes. She began with little confidence and steadily got worse. So driving failed and Lyndahl kept up her walking.

Gary was posted to a bank job in Kaikohe. Maurice, his teacher training done, went south to Paeroa on the Hauraki Plains. Len and Lyndahl were alone. Sadly, no new companionship developed between them. They lived together in reasonable friendliness. While Len worked hard at his business and used his five acres to run horses, Lyndahl took up clay modelling. She made the head of a land girl, strong-featured, with a scarf around her hair, then a bust of her father that captured the old man's strength and intelligence. Slowly she turned to writing again. She still seemed to have publication in mind but there's no record of her sending poems or stories away. 'The Change', her long account of her childhood and girlhood, was written at this time. She also wrote, not for publication, a short piece that shows how things stood between Len and her. It too is called 'The Change', suggesting that her menopause had still not ended. It's dated Friday Sept. 30th, 1955.

'Yesterday was a sore day; it should have been a happy day; I went to the City with my husband; I very seldom go into the City now, there is so little I need. How boring can a faithful wife be to her husband? I have lately wondered that and after yesterday I am wondering it again. I wanted to see some antiques but by the time my husband had done the things he wanted the sale was over. I had time only to buy a shopping bag at Woolworths before all the shops were shut; that was my day's shopping; an empty bag.

'He had told me where the car would be parked and feeling as empty as an old bag myself I hurried back to it; I felt that he was watching me as I came along the busy pavement aswirl with high stepping office and shop girls. I had on flat shoes and the nearer I got to the car the more clumsy and ordinary and old I felt. I hated him watching me. "What are you looking so damned mournful about?" he said as I got in the car. I have learned not to answer these sort of questions. I know they are not meant to hurt as much as they do. I sat back and let the warmth of the car soothe me; at least the car was warm.

'Before we pulled away from the curb a young brunette with hair piled high on her head and rippling with youth and sex consciousness stepped past us and my husband's eyes followed her. Apparently I react all wrong; I felt suddenly sorry for him; I usually do when I sense he is feeling old and out of it himself. As we drove out of the City I had several long secret looks at my husband. He is a pleasing looking man still; his skin is a healthy brown and his features are regular; when he smiles there is a touch of the satyr about him; I know that women like his smile. His hair is almost white; his fifty years show up most at the back of his neck. I've noticed repeatedly that age grips a man by the back of the neck and a woman by the throat muscles. When we got home and after tea I went into the bedroom while my husband was out attending to his horses, and took a long look at myself in the mirror. I have shapely legs and a shapely body still; in fact from the shoulders down I could pass for a woman of thirty; I am small made and muscular and olive skinned. It's above the neck line that the fade is showing, two tightening lines under the chin, tiny lines under the eyes, and two wings of greying hair at the temples.

'"So be it," I said to my image, "if it wasn't for my husband I wouldn't look at you."'

It would be interesting to have a companion piece from Len. It would, perhaps, have mentioned Lyndahl's appearance: hair cut short and fluffed up a little, face without make-up, no attempt to soften the signs of advancing age, dress plain and serviceable, a stillness of expression that sometimes slipped into wistfulness or a frowning thoughtfulness. Perhaps he would have mentioned her intelligence and interest in people and ideas, her sense of humour, her snort of amusement, followed by an uninhibited laugh – which he heard infrequently these days. He might have indicated that although he was loyal to her and loved her in his way she was no longer the wife he needed.

Still, for all their disagreements and their failure to overlap in tastes and in notions of what was desirable and good, they looked after each other and tried to be kind.

Gary married Ngaire Studd, a lively young woman he had known since his schooldays. Len made the same gifts to them he had made to Aynsley and Margaret: a section and help with a loan. The couple built behind Len and Lyndahl's house in Tirimoana Road.

At this time Len was immersing himself more and more in the world of horse racing, and towards the middle of the decade he bought a filly at the National Yearling Sales. He was, by now, friendly with a trainer, George Carmont, and George said the little horse was a bargain, especially as she was related to the champion filly Yahabeebe. Len paid six hundred pounds. As time ran out for naming the horse and getting her registered for the season (all the names were taken, Len's practical and Lyndahl's poetic ones), George, with only an hour left, recalled how he had first described the horse, and wrote on the form: Little Beauty. Lyndahl wasn't pleased. Len could live with the name as long as the horse ran fast. Little Beauty went into training at George Carmont's Avondale stables. Len drove in to see her several times a week and paid the training fees without a murmur, but Little Beauty was not fast enough. In two seasons she never won a race, although once she finished third. Len sold her at a loss. But he had had a lot of fun in spite of the cost and his Saturday disappointments. He kept up his friendship with George Carmont, and Lyndahl enjoyed him too: a gabby little ex-jockey with a fund of racing stories that he told with a great sense of comic timing, although his accounts of the shady side of racing could be horrifying.

Several years later Len bought a hurdler called My Sun. He was a better horse. After finishing well in several races, he won the Mangere Hurdles at Ellerslie. The race was supposed to be a pointer to the horses that had a chance in the Great Northern Hurdles, the top New Zealand race of its kind. Len believed his horse could win but was disappointed again. My Sun finished out of a place. Still, with the Mangere Hurdles, Len had fulfilled an ambition to lead a winner back to the birdcage. It was the only time. He never owned another horse that came in first.

Lyndahl continued her quiet life, visiting friends now and then, and her mother often. Len played his part by driving her to places she could not walk to. The Parkers had shifted to Titirangi; the Millbrook Road Peacehaven was now only part of Chapple history. Although Len found Muriel a bit of a joke, he liked her brother Jack and he drove Lyndahl to Titirangi frequently. On his side of the family, his sisters Kay and Rona made visits, and he and Lyndahl called on his father in Glen Eden now and then. Harry Gee had a housekeeper and was more amiable. He had taken up photography, joined a camera club, where he made himself unpopular by jeering at 'arty' shots and those who took them. He worked on his invention, a machine for making concrete blocks, but it failed to interest the big concrete makers, Winstones and Humes, and the machine lay rusting in the back yard.

Auntie Nancy made another appearance. She was Mrs Petherick-Blinkhorn now, a name everyone enjoyed, and had turned into a garrulous and dotty old lady. Lyndahl found her much easier. Auntie Nancy was besotted with the new queen, Elizabeth, who had just toured New Zealand. A film had been released, *The Flight of the White Heron*. The old lady could not stop talking about

The Flight of the Red Herring, which Lyndahl chuckled about for months afterwards.

Aynsley and Gary and their wives were close by. Maurice came up from Paeroa now and then, and Lyndahl took an interest in various nieces and nephews. Her favourite among them was Rex Hollis, Flo's son. He had been a visitor in the Newington Road days, when Jean Scott from over the road had been his girlfriend for a while. Lyndahl watched his career with more than interest, with fascination. He was clever, witty, articulate and deeply serious. Partway through his training for the Anglican ministry he had a change of heart – of mind – and became a communist. He trained as a journalist and spent his working life with the communist newspaper *People's Voice*. Lyndahl approved, although his hard line, his dogmatism worried her. She was certain he would get into trouble. Len liked him too; they had bantering arguments, insulting each other good-humouredly. Rex was serious about Len being a capitalist exploiter but couldn't stop joking: 'When the revolution comes we'll put you up against a wall and shoot you.' 'Like hell,' Len said. 'I'll have the contract building them.'

Joan Chapple, King and Winnie's daughter, visited often and seemed for a while to take the place of a daughter in Lyndahl's life. She went on to become a surgeon, an innovator in her field. Malcolm Fergus, Deorwyn's younger son, turned up from time to time. He was writing a novel, which turned out to contain more philosophical argument than story. (Lyndahl and Maurice both read it in manuscript.) When Deorwyn's marriage ended and she left for California, Malcolm vanished to Australia and no one, not even his mother, heard from him again. His older brother Ray had gone to California earlier, hoping to make his living as a jazz clarinetist. He died there from a stroke before he was thirty.

Lyndahl and Dawn kept their friendship going, and Lyndahl

took an interest in Dawn's children, Bronwyn and Geoffrey. She kept in touch with Geoffrey, or Geoff, for the rest of her life as his career in journalism began to take shape.

Another who interested her was Joyce's son, Darryl Reanney. In the mid-fifties he was in his mid-teens and the most promising of the Chapple grandchildren, a brilliant boy. He was to have a career as a microbiologist and biochemist, a university teacher (Canterbury University and La Trobe), a TV presenter (the seven-part *Genesis* for the ABC), and the author of two books about human consciousness and the interface between science and mysticism. Of all James Chapple's grandchildren, he would have pleased the old man most. But before his career could start he and the other Chapples had to endure 'another shake of the kaleidoscope'.

FIFTEEN

The events of 1956 to 1960 are difficult to get into chronological order. For Lyndahl and Len there were more grandchildren. By 1960 they had seven. There were visits from American relatives. Aynsley (senior) came several times, to his mother's delight. Mercy, a sister Lyndahl had hardly known (she was one of the two girls who stayed behind in California in 1918), made a visit with her husband. Deorwyn, sweet, docile, put-upon Deorwyn, came with her new husband, Roy Cunliffe, an Australian American. Everyone loathed Roy. Three adjectives for him too: loud, bumptious, arrogant, domineering (that's four). Make it five: racist. Roy would have been at home in a Ku Klux Klan hood. He was also, Deorwyn told Lyndahl, sexually voracious and demanding. The visit Lyndahl really loved was Dora's. She had been widowed a second time and made a third marriage in 1957, to ninety-year-old Louis Mayer, a well-known sculptor and a friend of Albert Schweitzer. Schweitzer married them. The New Zealand Chapples liked Louis Mayer as much as they had loathed Roy Cunliffe. He and Dora spent some of their short stay with Lyndahl. The bond between the sisters was as strong as ever. Louis made a bas-relief profile of Lyndahl and sent her a bronze casting after returning home.

There were changes among the Gees – the birth of children, the reappearance of Maurice, who had given up his teaching job and was trying again to write a novel. He behaved as if he had a right to bed and board and handouts. Lyndahl's patience, like Len's, had worn thin, but they let him stay six months before seeing him off to Wellington. There was a death. Old Harry Gee fell ill, spent time in hospital, and died in 1957. Len's brother Alf had died several years earlier, in his forties. Apart from his sisters, Rona in Christchurch and Kay, married and living in Australia, Len had no close relatives left. Lyndahl had them in abundance, but she quickly lost two more.

Jean, another sister Lyndahl had scarcely known (like Mercy, she had stayed in California), died at the age of fifty-nine. The story that came back from America was that she had collapsed while dealing a hand at bridge. Another version: in the middle of telling a joke. She was, from several accounts, a woman who loved good times. In this she was like Joyce.

Joyce died from a stroke in 1958. She was forty-nine. A shock of disbelief ran through the family. Poker-playing, hard-drinking, soft-hearted Joyce had been a fixture. She had been going on her careless way for years and had seemed set for many more. The old lady in Lincoln Road was unable to take it in. Joycie was gone. Florence could not understand why she kept on while her youngest daughter died. As for Lyndahl, part of her own life was removed. 'The Change', written just a few years earlier, shows how close she and Joyce had been (Rae with the brilliant smile and the way with boys, Lynda with the crooked teeth and cow-like eyes). There was less than eighteen months between them; they had slept in the same bed and quarrelled over stockings and lipstick. Then, through the slump and war years, Joyce was only two or three streets away, always bouncing back, it seemed – worried, cynical, sour about this and that, but coming out of it with a what-the-hell remark and another glass of Dally plonk. The Gee boys had loved her, and she had been a refuge for Lyndahl even when she and Phil moved from Henderson to Owairaka after the war. Lyndahl and Len were frequent visitors. Now Joyce, Joycie, was dead. The tranquillity and acceptance Lyndahl had learned from Dora was knocked aside. Her grief for

Joyce was more personal, it seemed, even than the grief she had felt at her father's death.

Not long afterwards, Dick's wife Christine left him and set up house with her newly widowed brother-in-law, Phil Reanney. Dick stayed on for a while with his mother, then took jobs out of Henderson, and very little was seen of him anymore. Phil and Christine kept the house in Owairaka but, not surprisingly, had little contact with the family again. How Darryl felt can only be guessed.

Florence Chapple, unhappy and unsteady, could not be left alone. It was time for another daughter to help out. Bernice, fourth-born child, second girl, now in her sixties, and her husband, Andrew Kydd, were persuaded to give up their home in Arkles Bay and come to Lincoln Road. Andrew was in his eighties. As a young man he had been a friend and supporter of James Chapple, one of those who had seen the family off to California and welcomed them back and helped look after Florence and her children while James was in prison. Now he had to give up his 'little bit of heaven', as he called the Arkles Bay house, and come to Henderson. It made him cross. The arrangement was never a happy one. But Florence Chapple was starting to fade. Lyndahl went almost every day to help Bernie and sit with their mother. The old lady's death could not be far away.

It was not the only thing troubling Lyndahl at this time. Maurice, who had been living in Wellington and, for a short time, in Dunedin, turned up for a few nights in August 1959, saying he was on his way to Melbourne. Travel was the only reason he would give. Flights to Australia left from Whenuapai Airport. Len drove him there, said goodbye, but returned from the car park long enough to see that his son was travelling with a pregnant young woman. Len was not one to jump about and wave his arms. A grim-faced expression of I-could-have-told-you-so was more his way. Lyndahl wasn't noisy about things either. She probably had a glass of wine and a cigarette. But it worried them both – a son who could not find his way now sinking into deeper trouble. News soon came from Melbourne that another grandson was born. His name was Nigel.

They got through the months. The Waterhouses were gone from next door and Lyndahl got on well with the young new neighbours, Gerrard and Marti Friedlander. Aynsley (junior) had given up carpentry and was running a farm Len had bought near Waimauku, and Gary was managing a menswear shop in New Lynn, so two sons were nearby. In Lincoln Road Florence Chapple sank into dementia. Caring for her became a problem. Bernice had an elderly husband and was not young herself. Lyndahl was the only daughter close enough to help. Between them they managed until relief came, for a short while, from an unexpected direction. Maurice and his partner, Hera Smith, turned up from Melbourne, bringing their baby, nearly three months old. One of the good things that came from this was that Len and Lyndahl loved Nigel at once. Len in particular formed a bond with the child that helped sustain him for the rest of his life, and became equally important for Nigel. The other piece of good fortune: Hera was a highly qualified nurse and was willing, even eager, to help with Florence Chapple, sponge her, change her clothing and bedding, perform the personal care that Bernice and Lyndahl, although they were daughters, found difficult. The arrangement lasted until, in the new year, Hera started a radiography course and shifted to accommodation in Auckland, and Maurice and the baby went to Wellington to live with friends who had a new baby of their own, almost Nigel's age.

The concern in Henderson was now entirely for the old lady. She was able to sit in the garden, in a wicker chair under a peach tree, wearing one of the long Edwardian dresses she had never given up and clasping the head of her walking stick with one hand on top of the other, but she recognised no one, not even Lyndahl. She did not speak. Perhaps shadowy figures – perhaps coloured ones – moved in her mind: a young red-headed man reading aloud from the Bible; herself laughing as he carried her over a stream; and laughing as he pulled her, wearing a pink flannelette nightdress, up a ladder to a bed made of sacks filled with straw . . .

Florence Chapple died in May, aged ninety. The family – those who could be mustered – scattered her ashes alongside her husband's in the Waitākere Ranges.

If the couple had a headstone it should read no more than Flo and Jim.

SIXTEEN

Len and Lyndahl's time in Henderson was coming to an end. They had been there for thirty years while the little town grew into a suburb of Auckland. Len had built more houses than he could remember, had built shops and office buildings, a bank and a factory. He must have felt that in some ways Henderson was his. He was friendly with most of the shopkeepers and businessmen – Bob Norcross, the Holborow brothers (butchers), Max Wiltshire who owned a shoe shop, Sel Peacock, a men's outfitter, Steve Ozich, the developer he had built two rows of shops for, Roy Smith the banker, Bill Roberts the town clerk, and many more. He was well enough established to be summonsed to a charity mock court in the Town Hall, where a bewigged 'lawyer' charged him with leaving the cement out of his concrete. Len played along and was fined five pounds but found the charge insulting rather than funny.

By the end of the fifties he was tired of the worry and the work, the tax problems, the regulations, the fourteen-hour days. He ran his jobs on the job, not from an office; he needed to know everything that happened and be on hand to fix mistakes, and although he had good tradesmen his temper was short. He ordered a subcontractor to get rid of a workman using 'dirty' language that passers-by could hear. He sacked another, a brickie, for building a substandard fireplace. His own men seemed to like him, they knew where they stood. He held on for another few years, but then had had enough. He judged himself not rich but well-off. He would try something new. In the early sixties he packaged up L.W. Gee, Building Contractor and sold it to his foreman, Jack Gill.

Lyndahl was ready for a move. To her the hard years of the thirties had been the good ones. She and Len had been together and their troubles were manageable. She had been writing and in a small way making a name. Her daily walks to visit her parents and to do her shopping had made her a well-known figure in the town. Now, although she had friends left, many were gone. She had memories. During the war she had often called on an old German woman, Mrs Rendt, who would otherwise have been almost completely isolated. A neighbour, a railwayman, intrigued by her hairstyle, stopped her in the street one day and asked, apologetically, if she wore her hair like that because she had something wrong with her ears. Lyndahl lifted one of the buns to show him her ears were normal. And people remembered her. An elderly woman who had been a girl in the thirties wrote to Maurice many years later saying that one of her most enduring memories of Henderson in those times was of Mrs Gee walking home with a load of groceries in her shopping bag and changing it from one hand to the other, after pulling her fingers straight.

The war and ill-health and Len's success in building changed it all. The deaths – her father, Geoff, Joyce – changed it in another way. They cut the safe ground of family from under her. With her mother gone and Dora, the sister she loved most, living on the other side of the world, there were only fragments of family left. Her sister-in-law, Dawn, had shifted further off. Bernice, in the Lincoln Road house, was the only sibling in walking distance. Her sons and their families scattered and came back and scattered again. Aynsley had given up farming and was in Hamilton, working for a company that made interior partitions; Gary was in Taumarunui, managing a menswear shop; and Maurice, still a worry, was in London. In 1962 he needed a handout to get home.

In that year they sold the house in Tirimoana Road and bought a modern brick bungalow on five acres of land a few miles south of Kumeu. Len soon had a couple of horses grazing in the paddocks. He had a new car in the garage, the lawns trimmed, the grounds looking like a park. Lyndahl enjoyed the house, with all its conveniences and gadgets. For a few months the shift seemed to work. Len subdivided the land he still owned in Tirimoana Road. He bought five acres on the Hobsonville road, across the tidal reach from the place Paremoremo prison was built later on. For him the change in their lives seemed a good one. He was busy, he did some business, he had a bit of land, ran a few horses. He had his racing friends. He was out a lot.

Lyndahl, at home, with no way of getting out until Len had the time, began to feel she was in a prison. Kumeu village was two miles away, along a busy highway with no footpaths. Few of her friends made the trip north. They were not car-driving people. Len saw her isolation and realised the move was not going to work. He sold up again and they shifted to a house on the Hobsonville land. It was an old bungalow. Lyndahl did not mind that. But her isolation continued. So again Len sold – again too soon to make the profit he had wanted. They crossed the harbour to the North Shore, to a house on the southern headland above Torbay beach, a beautiful site with a steep drop down cliffs to the sea and a view over the Hauraki Gulf. Here, one would have said, they could be happy; and they managed to stay a while. But Lyndahl was still dependent on Len, still could not get out, and Len himself, without a piece of land, felt isolated and out of things. He had nothing to do. He needed to be closer in, closer to his friends. Again they moved.

This time it was to Takapuna, and there they stayed, although three short moves were still to come. The first house, off a right-of-way from the main shopping street, Hurstmere Road, was too small. They shifted to a larger one two back from the beach but found it too small as well. When, after a few months, the chance came to buy the beachfront house, Len took it. The picking-up and leaving, the rushing from place to place, came to an end. They stayed for six years.

SEVENTEEN

From the wide windows of dining room and living room the lawn sloped down to an open fence above a stone wall. Five steps led to the beach. With a wind behind it, the high tide lapped the wall. At low tide the water was more than a hundred yards away. Rangitoto Island stood in the centre of the view. Lyndahl painted it on brown hardboard: a black three-peaked sprawl across the horizon. The red sky fades behind it. A pale-blue early-morning sea crawls on the sand, where three black-backed gulls, dimly seen, stand side-on to their shadows. A lighthouse – a single white stroke of paint – breaks the island's shoreline. Lyndahl never painted another picture so simple and pure and full of sadness.

Little remains of the writing she attempted in these years. She was still unwell, with nothing she or anyone else could put a name to except nerves – but looked at from a later time with loss and sadness and incomprehension. She could not understand how her life had reduced itself to a business of getting through the days.

She was active, she seemed busy, running the house, doing her shopping in the busy streets, but she must have turned about at times looking for someone not there, the person she might have become. Now and then she ran into Frank Sargeson, doing his own shopping, and she returned lit up from these encounters, as though she was part of something again. But there was little writing to show for it. An uncompleted poem describes a visit from Hera's mother, Lydia (Riria) Smith, who stayed for several days. She and Lyndahl had grief and disappointment in common. Lyndahl wrote that she knelt at the old Māori woman's knee and 'woman to woman' they wept together.

Another painting she did at this time shows how she thought of herself, how little self-worth she felt. An ageing woman, recognisably Lyndahl, sits in an armchair – a skinny armchair, matching the skinny legs and arms of the woman. One hand holds a cigarette, the other a glass of wine. She looks at the viewer with an almost sad defiance. It's a caricature and yet it says, This is me. One of her sons has the Rangitoto painting, another the self-portrait, if that's what it is. Few of her other paintings survive.

She enjoyed the beach and so did Len. They went for walks up and down. Lyndahl liked the summers and winters equally – the swimmers, the yachts, the family groups spreading out their towels; then the cold grey sea, the waves bursting at the foot of the wall, the black island. Being comfortable, being comfortably off in this beautiful spot, pleased her. She felt that their early struggles entitled Len and her to a life of ease; yet she never lost her left-leaning beliefs. She called her husband's solicitor Inch-worm (his name was Inch). She retained her contempt for those who measured everything in terms of money and gave their lives to the making of it. She might have said that the best thing about Len was that he was endlessly generous.

There were Chapples nearby. King and Winnie lived five or six houses along the beach. Lyndahl enjoyed having them close but Len never got on with them. One morning Winnie rang Len and asked if he would help her mount a set of cupboards on the wall. He walked along the beach with his tools and spent the morning on the job, no easy one. Winnie was not much help and would not call one of her sons working (brain work) in another part of the house. Len got the cupboards up, Winnie said thank you and he went home. The next day, in his workshop in the double garage, he found himself short of a couple of screws and remembered he'd used that sort at Winnie's the previous day, so back along the beach he went and asked for two. Winnie counted them into his hand. 'There you are, Len. They'll be sixpence each,' she said.

Len enjoyed telling the story. Lyndahl laughed at it too. It was mainly her father and mother, and selected brothers and sisters, who pleased her now – and Winnie, after all, was only someone who had married into the family.

The beach house was marvellous for children. Aynsley and Margaret had been living in Hamilton but shifted to Auckland in the early sixties and bought a house on the North Shore. They and their four children came often. Lyndahl loved to see the boys, Stephen and Terry, wrestling on the lawn the way her sons had wrestled in Newington Road. In the summer they were there almost every weekend. Gary and Ngaire still lived in Taumarunui but visited as often as they were able to. There were two boys in that family, with two girls still to come. Maurice was the one causing problems.

After getting back from London he had gone to Rotorua to renovate a house belonging to Hera's mother. Hera and Nigel would join him when the job was done. Len had been seeing a lot of Nigel, both at the beach house and earlier at Torbay. He stayed for long periods, and Len and he became more like father and son than grandfather and grandson. Nigel had some preschooling at St Anne's School, a girls' private school along Takapuna beach. Winnie helped arrange it. Len walked him along each morning and picked him up after his half-day, and Nigel seemed to take no harm from being the only boy in a class of girls. The two drove down to visit Maurice in Rotorua. Len took his toolkit and dismantled a wall between two small rooms to make a large one – a job beyond Maurice's skills. Soon the house was finished and Nigel shifted down with Hera. His loss left a gap in Len's life, and Lyndahl's, but Nigel's coming and going had only begun. He was to remain a large part of their lives.

Len dabbled a bit in property. He kept up his interest in horse racing, the trots now as much as the gallops. He and Lyndahl rarely went out Henderson way, although Len kept his friendships there and Lyndahl kept in touch with Muriel Parker in Titirangi. Takapuna and the beach seemed to satisfy her. Her granddaughters, Angela and Carolyn, older than their brothers, were a source of pride, interest and love as they grew. They filled the place of the daughters she had never had. The boys came often, bringing their dog, and the beach house became a part of all four children's lives. Gary and Ngaire and their boys continued to visit from Taumarunui, and Len and Lyndahl drove down to visit them there. It has the appearance of a full and happy life and what was missing from it they managed to keep to themselves. Len shouted himself a trip to the 1964 Tokyo Olympic Games, travelling on a cruise ship. He made friends quickly, as he was always able to do. A group of younger men, he said, elected him mascot and he was rarely out of company.

There were upsets. Maurice, having finally parted from Hera, was staying at the beach house with Nigel when Hera turned up and, after a nasty argument, took the boy away. Lyndahl, still with 'nerves', cried, 'Len, they're killing me.' This time Nigel was gone for only a few months. He stayed again when Maurice left for Wellington to begin a librarian's course, then, with Lyndahl not coping with a small boy, went down to Taumarunui to live for a while with Gary and his family. Later in that year he shifted to Wellington, to his father, an arrangement that lasted more than a year before Hera took him again, a kidnapping swoop, and vanished into Australia for several years. Len and Lyndahl worried about the boy, and Len had his solicitor Laurie Inch attempt a search. Maurice hunted too but nothing was heard of Nigel until 1970.

A year earlier they had lost a grandson. Stephen, Aynsley and Margaret's older boy, had been Lyndahl's favourite among her nine grandchildren – although she would have denied favouritism. Yet his quiet nature, his earnestness, his way of sometimes falling into dreams and wandering by himself, had a special appeal for her and she loved him deeply. He was the one among the boys who would come and sit with her and talk in his earnest way. He was, too, a strong quick boy. She loved watching him and his younger but sturdier brother Terry wrestle on the lawn then dash off in their togs down the beach for a swim.

Stephen was clever, but not clever enough in his schoolteachers' judgement to keep his place in the accelerated class where he had spent two terms. They told him that at the beginning of term three they were dropping him back to an ordinary class. He must have been devastated by this, and must have brooded about it for the whole of the term holiday. No one picked up on the depth of his misery. The day before school was to start he went into his father's garden shed and drank weed killer. Perhaps it was a cry for someone to understand. Perhaps he did not mean to die.

I do not know how his mother and father managed to go on after Stephen's death, nor how Len managed. But Lyndahl, in her grief, seemed almost to lose her mind, and never established a proper balance in her life again.

There's more that could be said but it has the sound of guesswork, so – Stephen died, his parents and sisters and brother kept on. They moved house closer to Takapuna. And Lyndahl, as she recovered slowly, came out of her bedroom and tried to pick up the activities of her former life. But she could no longer live in the beach house where Stephen had sat and talked with her in the sunroom and he and his brother had wrestled on the lawn. She and Len had been settled and had found a life that suited them better than any they had known since their first years together – but the fact was,

Lyndahl could not stay. Len too was ready for a move and once again he went house-hunting.

EIGHTEEN

The shift was their last, to a double-unit townhouse on the corner of Gibbons Road and Blomfield Spa. Len bought both units, rented out then sold the corner one, and he and Lyndahl settled down in the other. One of his first acts was to chop down a large pōhutukawa tree in the front yard, upsetting several neighbours – but that was his way: the tree filled the gutters with dead leaves so it had to go. The house itself was less convenient than the one they had left. Downstairs was taken up by a garage and workshop and a small self-contained flat. The living areas were upstairs: sitting room, kitchen, bathroom, two bedrooms. There was a restricted view of the sea. It wasn't ideal but it would do.

They were still close to the Takapuna shopping centre, while the beach was only a hundred yards away. When she walked there, as she began to do again, Lyndahl went south, away from the house she had lived in before.

Their days were filled with bits and pieces, this and that – there seems no other way of describing it. Sons and daughters-in-law came, grandchildren came. The downstairs flat, really just a large room with a kitchenette and bathroom attached, was in frequent use. For a while their lives went evenly as they learned to deal with the tragedy. In the summers Len spent a lot of time at the beach, sunbathing and swimming. Lyndahl rarely swam but she walked the half mile to the southern headland and sometimes spent an hour smoking and thinking, or pondering, sitting with her back to the sea wall. Slowly she began to write poems again. She looked at her childhood:

I remember, I remember –
(How young was I?)
Lifted out of my bed
To stare at the sky
From a wash house window;
My feet in a wooden tub,
I did as I was bid;
In bewilderment
At all this hub-bub
About and about.
Something outside they said,
What could I do but stare?
With my cold feet
I was neither here nor there.
But this I remember well –
My father said to me
'When Halley's Comet comes back this way
I will be long dead.'
Now I am old and do not care
If I never see that light again.
My feet are still cold and bare.

She looked at herself as a young wife:

      Was it?

That was me,
Once upon a time,
That new born mother
Of three sons
Visiting a farmer's wife
Up in the foothills

Of the Waitakeres –
Feeling on top of the world
Fulfilled,
Smelling the grass
Of the orchard
Where the kids shouted.
That was my primrose path,
A moment of ecstasy
When I flung myself
Into a patch of oxalis
Green as a velvet cushion –
Buried my head there,
Nuzzled the earth,
Slept a moment –
Deliriously free,
Bone tired.

But most of her writing was about where she found herself now:

There is no anywhere,
Inside or out –
Neither here nor there.
No one but me
Alone in the universe
At midnight . . .

*

Three years went by until the next change. Hera and Nigel were living in Whakatāne. As always, Len worried about the boy and the life he was forced to lead – from place to place, from school to school – so he drove to Whakatāne and asked Hera if he could take Nigel to live with him and Lyndahl in Takapuna. He would give his grandson good care, steady schooling, a permanent home. Hera agreed, and Len and Nigel drove back to Auckland, where grandfather and grandmother became, in effect, the thirteen-year-old boy's parents. The arrangement lasted for the rest of Len and Lyn's lives.

Len was happy in his relationship with Nigel, and proud of him. In his first day at Takapuna Grammar the boy was introduced to his class: Nigel Gee from Australia. He took his seat, and every few minutes heard the boy behind him whisper, 'Abo. Abo.' Nigel endured it for a while. Then he turned round and knocked his tormenter out of his seat with a single punch. So, half an hour after enrolling, Nigel was back in the headmaster's office being caned. But Len was pleased with him: he had acted like a man. Nigel and the boy he had hit became good friends.

Dawn Chapple came to live in Takapuna, in a small house behind the shopping centre and only two hundred yards from Len and Lyndahl. Having a good friend close helped bring Lyndahl back to better health. She wrote, and began to paint again. The painting was for herself, for enjoyment; and the writing, which survives only in scraps, seems to be for herself too. Very little is typed, most is handwritten on pages torn from cheap writing pads. There's only one typed story, 'The Ancestor Dig', about a couple, very like her and Len, searching for the husband's great-aunt deep in the country, where 'bald-headed hills . . . were humped all around'. There's tension between the pair. They walk between 'hefty gate posts spaced wide apart and bleached of paint. One had a large wooden ball for its head, the other was beheaded . . . the sore red eye of the lowering sun stared down at us . . . a clay track led upwards, with gorse in bloom on the slope ahead.' The wife, Lillian, wants to go back. The husband, Arthur, says, 'Like bloody hell we will.' He thumps one of the gate posts 'with determined pride'. 'Solid Kauri.' The couple have the sound of Len and Lyndahl. The story, though, doesn't go anywhere. It's main interest is in the observation: '. . . three rusty rainwater tanks huddled together on an out of plumb tank stand . . . the only sound was our breathing and the munching of some animal in the orchard . . . a fairy tale door, lead-lighted from top to bottom in blues and reds, yellows and greens . . . I knew I had run in and out of just such a beautiful doorway back in my childhood. Arthur raised a fist to knock. Locked doors meant nothing to him.'

No one answers. They go into a kitchen: 'one small window offered a shred of light to a bare deal table with a black iron pot on it . . . a bentwood chair with a twisted back looking as if it had always been sat on sideways . . . a horse saddle hung on a wall . . .' There's a coal range with no oven door and a black cat curled up inside, and 'on the drying rack, four roosting white hens eyeing me sideways on'.

A woman comes. She 'looked like a child's drawing of a woman, box-shaped with spiky hair and thin long arms and legs . . . she moved silently on bare feet . . . eyeing us from one eye . . . a profile like one of her hens.' The woman and Arthur agree they might be related. Lillian watches: '. . . the leather apron: did she shoe her own horses? . . . on her engagement finger the biggest solitaire diamond I had ever seen . . .' She is suddenly sickened by herself, sick of Arthur and of 'the smelly situation'. She runs back to the car and the story dies.

There's a lot going on between the lines. There's a fair bit stated. Three times Lillian says she needs a drink, and at the end complains that she lacks a smoke and a tranquilliser. Did Lyndahl and Len make a visit of that sort and find an old woman like 'Miss Maddern'? Lyndahl writes in anger and disgust that is never explained. But Len did have relatives, if not 'ancestors'. In a short non-fiction piece, 'Bitches I Have Met', written at about the same time, his 'nicely hatted and gloved' cousin, met at the races, asks Lyndahl, 'How is your brilliant son getting on?' – meaning Maurice, who had published two novels by this time. 'Which one?' Lyndahl replies. 'I've got three brilliant sons.' She adds: And I meant it.

She's more spirited; a little of the old Lyndahl is coming back. In February 1973 she wrote, on brown scratch paper, a list of the Chapple family. It's as if she's trying to settle them in her mind:

For the genetic record of a family of fifteen – the quick and the dead.
Those gone – 1973
1. My father died at 81 of bladder complications etc. etc.
2. My mother died of a stroke, aged 91. Most of all missed and beloved.
3. Their first loss was Nina, a baby daughter, who caught a disease from an unhygienic midwife.
4. Came sister Jean, who died laughing, telling a joke, of a heart attack in the USA.
5. Then brother Geoff, of angina pectoris. He, like a clown, walked on his hands too early, and lived to be fifty.
6. And sister Joyce, unnerved by life and loving, broke down at 'the change'.
7. Kingsley, another brother, died of cancer I think, in his sixties. He was kind too.
Those still quick
8. My brother Dick, 'gone bush' after a marriage break up.
9. And while I think about it, there's me, still kicking against the pricks at 65.
10. First born sister, in California. Over eighty, is writing poetry, our 'second mother.'
11. Last born Aynsley, a brother and a homosexual, 'well

heeled' but still searching for something, frantically.

12. Another sister, gentle Bernie, 73, lives for her garden, all alone.
13. Poor Flo, a widow, cantankerous, but who can still laugh at herself – bless her for that.
14. Then Deorwyn, domesticated, most like our mother to look at, a yes woman to her boss husband.
15. Mercy, mis-named? I think not. She kept those parcels coming to me through the years of the slump.
16. Holl, on Waiheke Island, an early 'drop-out', is coming into his own painting in 'dinkum' oils.
17. Leonard, first-born brother, I scarcely know, or ever did – yet do I love him too in spite of his being a teacher once.

It's a curious list, with judgements suggested here and there, and sometimes withdrawn. She's seeing clearly as well as affectionately, and things get blurred. Most significant is the note on her father. She had always written of him in an almost worshipful way, had almost, but not quite, awarded him a halo. Here she finishes him off with a couple of etceteras and it's her mother who is 'most of all missed and beloved'.

She wrote about her childhood again, in a poem called 'The Dreaming Time', already quoted from. It includes memories used in 'The Change'. Then there's a piece called 'The Worst Storm of My Half-Remembered Childhood' – L.C.G. 1973.

'We were living in Thousand Oaks, a suburb of Berkeley, San Francisco, a New Zealand family a long way from home and the big old house in Timaru where we played under pine trees and in the orchard . . . I was asleep when the big thump came, as were my sisters, two to a bed; we scrambled over one another to get to our

Mother first; she was frightened of storms too, but not our Father, who liked to explain them to us, how to count between flashes of lightning and bangs of thunder and guess how far away they were . . . My sisters and I were allowed to sit on the end of the double bed with our feet tucked under the blankets; the blinds were down but the lightning came right through them. After each flash my stretched eyes couldn't see anything at all, not even my Mother and Father; then when my eyes were just coming right the thunder made the whole house jump as if a giant had hit it with something . . . the world outside seemed to have turned upside down; water was running from everywhere, off the roof and down pipes; was that sucking singing noise the gutter outside the gate coming into our garden? Something was laughing out there too, chuckling its head off. One of my older brothers was going round downstairs banging windows shut; the whole night was full of noise, and nobody said a word. The last eye-popping, brighter than light striped black and white flash sent me under the blankets feeling for my mother's feet – anything to hang on to in the blacker than black nothingness that followed it; the thunder shook even the over-loaded bed. "I want to go home to New Zealand." I knew that was what my Mother was praying for us all.

'I woke up in my own bed to the tinkle of cups in the kitchen; but it wasn't morning yet! It was still dark outside, I could see that much again. And I could hear the silence now. I went to sleep happy beside my warm older sister who was braver than me.'

By May 1975 the memories are much the same but the tone has changed:

'And I remember the kitchens; the outside safe with its inside door over the sink bench; and the iron stove and my mother's back as she stirred the meat and dumpling stew we were all waiting at table for. Dad was in his study writing about wars and the world, and he was a man and special. About that time I think I realised the difference between men and women; my father in his study and my mother setting his tray, even with a serviette ring, and serving him his meal first, while we all waited. And I remember my mother scraping out the stewpot when we had all finished and had had enough, and seeing the dishes in the sink for washing up. I think I began hating the opposite sex early in life because my mother always catered for their needs first; I and my seven sisters were somehow expected to wait upon ourselves last, no tray in a quiet place for us, no serviette rings and first servings, no time to think while "they" waited to be waited on . . .

'To be allowed into our father's study was really something; I can still see it, the fire burning, making the only sound in the room; books all round the walls; it was a strange room but fascinating, especially for a girl; on a table near the fireplace was a big terrestrial globe, green like a pumpkin and marked all over; if my father gave his benign nod you could spin it around and find New Zealand where we lived; it was scary to know I lived down there in an ocean away from the rest of the world. I was glad to get back to the kitchen, the old black stove, the smell of stew, and the noise of my brothers and sisters; somehow I felt sorry for my father in his study with all his books, and without Mum. "Mum". She was always there in the kitchen, brown-eyed and ready to listen; telling me to go and wash my face and I would feel better; sometimes I did feel better wiping the tears and scowl off my face with a wet cloth. Temper and shouting didn't pay off; it only ended by my standing in front of our Father in his study, being threatened by the leather strap if I didn't control myself and try and help Mother more.

'And yet, and yet, there were the bright bright times when the family was happily happy and, close together, we were all floating around in a beautiful multi-coloured bubble which no one could burst. And our Dad was in this bubble too, and telling us a rude rhyme about "the little dog who lifted his little leg and peed against the wall". This was the Father we all waited for, the Dad with the vulgar streak and a sense of humour, who sometimes played hide and seek with us out on the shadowy lawn amongst the black bushes and tall trees at red sunset . . .'

That is the last of Lyndahl's pieces about her childhood. Her memories have undergone revision and, while no longer 'golden', some happiness remains.

She wrote about her present life, sometimes in a bitter, unhappy way:

'Memo of a day ill-spent

'Tomorrow could be different; but as yet I am stuck in a sick indolence of spirit which began with the silly birds waking me up from being a non-being, forcing me to become mobile again. I didn't want to get out of bed and begin it all over again – make a cup of tea, read the paper (what rot, what rottenness), set the table, stand at the stove, boil the eggs, make the toast, serve breakfast with a smile behind which my face is a gargoyle of disillusionment. "Easy girl, you'll frighten yourself." They don't hear me so I can say what I'm thinking; they have stopped hearing my voice unless I lose my temper and shout; I am someone in the kitchen; a noise moving about in their dreams waking them gently with the promise of food. Who I am has never crossed their minds in all the years of my service as a wife and mother. "And who am I?" I wonder sourly.'

At other times she had less trouble finding an identity. She watches the rubbish being collected, and writes: 'They are indeed beautiful people . . . bare-backed and brown, dusty and cheerful, banging the rubbish tins. They brighten my day . . . as they carry our beer tins and bottles away. I envy them from behind my curtains, lonely as hell . . .' She remembers her 'beautiful grandson, part Maori and full of love . . .' and thinks of herself as 'an old pakeha, whose only sin was not to love wisely in a Maori pa'. It's not possible to work out what the last comment means. Sometimes pieces of the past slide out and slide away before she can hold them – or perhaps she has no wish to hold them but just to let them come and go. 'It's funny,' she says, 'how one thing leads to another in a hop-skip-jump sort of way.'

'Those Dunnies' begins with a knock on the door when she's not in the mood for company but wants to put her 'bunioned feet' up. She's irritated that there's no beer in the house to go with the tomato sandwich she will make. The visitor is Alicia, 'a solo mother of two kids, she is quite beautiful'. In spite of the age gap she and Lyndahl 'click'. Alicia tells her how halfway through secondary school she became pregnant to 'a young cow cocky', and how her mother took over and arranged the wedding. This leads, through several steps, to Len leaving that morning for the Whāngārei races – 'in his retirement he has reverted to the company of "the boys" . . . he feels he has done his duty by me . . . to think we married for love – or was it because we had to? . . . still, I'd rather die than be left alone here without him. But I meander, I talk to myself.'

She describes how she paints in oils, 'best when I am a bit drunk'. Her last effort hangs on the wall, 'the old homestead of an early settler's family, brick chimneys still catching the first and last light of the sun'. Alicia likes the painting, especially the tin-roofed dunny. It reminds her of one her grandmother used to have 'with two holes to sit on, one built low for the little ones at the side of the hole for the grown-ups'. So the piece ends, and Lyndahl has filled in the morning enjoyably with a friend Len never knew she had.

She watches an old house being demolished, possibly the one she painted. It stands behind a hedge that crowds her off the footpath as she passes. One day, after a drink at the Mon Desir, 'feeling as tipsy as the old place looked', she ignores the Keep Out notice and goes in to talk to the demolition man. He lets her look around – 'the vandals cleaned her out weeks ago'. The old rooms are mildewed. Wallpaper hangs off the walls. In a bedroom 'that must have been bright and beautiful once, the rose pattern had faded to a brown pressed-flower colour'. The 'bachelor man' finishes his lunch with a bottle of beer. As he wrenches off weatherboards, she asks him when the house was built. He tells her 1843 – "'by a ground shark who bought this area down to the beach from the Maoris. He built the house to rent to a surveyor and his missus, or something; wanted to stake out his claim I reckon; been told this land was tea-tree right down to the mean tide then; some Pom with a plum in his mouth got in early I reckon eh?" "Yeah," I reckoned too.'

A hot humid New Year passes. 'I'm not so young. My feet give me hell. I can't even get down to the beach to paddle and cool off.' So she watches the old house, where everything is down except the brick chimney. She puts an iced beer in her bag for 'the bachelor' and crosses the road. He is raking odds and ends that 'skulked about'. The chimney 'with a rope round its neck is ready to be pulled down'. She gives the man the beer – 'He was a nice bloke' – and he says if she's interested in old wooden what-nots he'll bring her something one day. 'I get around these old dumps. I won't forget.' He waves her goodbye with the beer bottle.

'Well, all is quiet behind the hedge now,' Lyndahl writes. 'I never saw or heard the brick chimney fall.' But several weeks later, coming home 'with a bottle of wine in my bag', she goes in past the Keep Out sign. 'Nothing was left on the section except the brick hearth surround, the skeleton of the small Shacklock stove, and the cabbage trees and wild rose bushes enjoying themselves in the sun . . . I saw the oven door lying flat on its face but intact. It was heavy to lug home but I made it, hanging on to its handle knob. I felt comforted.'

So Lyndahl wrote and painted and found things to interest her while Len enjoyed himself at the races. If 'the bachelor man' brought her a wooden what-not, she keeps it to herself.

As well as prose pieces, on scrap paper, she attempted poems. There's a bundle of them, handwritten, beginning in February 1953 and running through to 1975. They're simple pieces – deliberately simple – and many are unfinished. Some are written out of loneliness and bitterness, others mix in small amounts of happiness. Often she can't find the words she wants, or else she forces a rhyme and loses what she means to say. They're memorable – at least to those who knew her – for single verses, single lines, and sometimes single images and phrases.

Her son Aynsley's children had a dog that trotted several miles through the streets to visit her:

> Golden Sam, old man –
> The only dog
> I ever came to know
> And not be afraid of.
>
> You don't come to see me
> Any more?
> I think I understand –
> But I miss your bark . . .
>
> Don't ever crawl
> Dog; don't howl
> Like me, nervous in the night . . .
>
> Grown old, I am
> Mercifully
> Loved as you are . . .

Loved but lonely, and 'lonely', in the end, seems to drive out 'loved':

An old battery hen –
What am I to him –
Immobilised –
When he is off to the Trots
With his racing cobbers.
I sit here alone;
No meal but my own
To prepare – an egg and a lettuce leaf.
Poor cocks, for an evening free!
Odd to know I am going mad
With no one to blame . . .
I hope he backs a winner tonight;
He didn't when he backed me.
We have never met each other yet.

She starts a poem called 'Gentle Idiot':

I've turned the other cheek so often
My face is numb;
My mind between the opposites
Struck dumb.

Myself in hiding,
Waiting what might come
I am as a little child
Sucking an adult thumb.

She fails to carry on. There are four attempts at the next verse, all
scratched out. Three lines recur – 'Dark as my day is', 'I live by my
own light' and 'I am not what they think they see'.

Much of what she wrote is dated February 1973. A few things are earlier, a few later. Her middle son Maurice arrived in Auckland late in 1972, with his wife Margareta and two small daughters, Emily and Abigail. Lyndahl and Len now had all three sons and their families in the same city. Perhaps their proximity led to the poem 'To My Daughters-in-law':

> If I keep away from you
> It is because I do not know
> How to say, I understand,
> And pray my sons prove gentle men.

She wrote a poem to Abigail, her newborn granddaughter:

> Youngest seedling yet;
> My old arms
>   Loved you . . .

Len's help was practical. He had visited Maurice and Margareta in 1970, when they lived in Napier, bringing Nigel, new-found, for a short visit (Lyndahl paid his fare from Australia). He gave advice about buying houses and showed his son how to hang a door. In Auckland he gave the family rent-free use of a Takapuna house he had bought for resale. They stayed for three months before shifting to Mt Eden.

Lyndahl wrote a happy piece (prose or verse, impossible to tell) about walking on the beach in a storm. The wind wakes her from a 'day-sleep', out of 'a nowhere dream into a world of noise'. She ties on a headscarf, leaves her 'creaking, complaining house' and walks to the beach, nearly losing her footing as the gusts jog her into a run. She watches 'the slow lashing struggle' of the pōhutukawa trees, the waves riding high, 'mounting each other' as she stands

secure with her back to the sea wall. The waves outshout the wind.
She watches until the storm dies as suddenly as it has risen.

It's the last piece of that sort she wrote. More typically, she
looks into herself:

The Ice Age

God, are you playing a game with me –
Turning me into a stone?
Stones can cry out under pressure
So please God leave me alone.

I cannot tell light from darkness
My eyes are sleepless with fear
From seeing so much and so little
From staring too far and too near.

Empty my mind is a tom-tom
Bloodless my heart misses beat
Frozen my hands hang idle
I stumble on skeleton feet.

Was my loving as sick as my pity
My passion and prayers a joke?
I have no breath left for praying;
Lord, I throw down your yoke.

If only I could stop caring
Would this ice break into a thaw
The earth spring back into colour,
Might I even laugh once more?

And she looks at Len:

> When we are 'out of speaks',
> I look at the back of your head –
> Silver threads – and long to touch
> Your heart, before we both are dead.

Her longing was, in a sad and roundabout way, fulfilled.

After 1976 there are no more poems. There is no more writing of any sort. The chronology of Lyndahl's last four years is hard to sort out. Each part dissolves into an after and before. Perhaps that is how her days seemed to her. About halfway through – 1978 or '79 – Len was unwell and his doctor, who was also a friend, made a visit. (Len was, in fact, tired, worn out.) After the examination – blood pressure, stethoscope – he asked the doctor to have a look at Lyndahl before he left. She was resting in her bedroom. The doctor agreed and, after twenty minutes in the room, came out and said, in a tone more wondering than matter-of-fact, 'Len, your wife's an alcoholic.'

'Yes, I know,' Len said.

NINETEEN

Everybody knew. Everybody saw how it had happened and yet had somehow missed the step that took her there. She had always enjoyed a drink, a 'little glass of vino'. She and her sister Joyce had developed a taste for flagon sherry during the war, and 'vino', a word their brother Dick brought back from Italy, became part of their lives. It lifted their worries away, it made them happy and they saw no harm in it. But over the years sherry, and beer too, became entangled with Lyndahl's shocks and disappointments. In her writing she frequently mentions her need for a drink. She comes home tipsy from the Mon Desir. She gets cross because there's no beer in the house. So it goes on. The happy young wife of the 1930s becomes the shrunken woman of the late 1970s, sitting all day on the sofa in her dressing-gown, smoking a cigarette and sipping her glass of 'vino'.

Len had already seen that her drinking could not be stopped without causing her even greater pain and confusion. It's possible the doctor agreed. The best that could be done was to try reducing her intake of sherry without her noticing it. Lyndahl seems to have been unaware of her condition. 'Would you get me another little glass of vino,' she would say. And sometimes: 'I don't drink too much, do I? It helps me relax.' Cigarettes were also an addiction. She still rolled her own. Nigel remembers sitting on the sofa with her and rolling a whole day's supply, while she sipped her drink. At times like that, he says, she loved being cuddled – 'she was like a cat that wanted to lean into someone'.

She ate very little – nibbled a sandwich or a lettuce leaf for lunch. Len or Nigel would bring her things to eat. Her daughters-in-law, Margaret and Ngaire, helped with food and company. Their children came in often to see 'Nana', and her delight in seeing them was plain. (Maurice and Margareta and their girls had shifted to Nelson in 1975.) She ate a bite of dinner at the table, but for most of the day she sat on the sofa and seemed to think, or dream perhaps, with her glass in one hand and her cigarette in the other, and a faraway look in her eyes. Happy? Unhappy? It's impossible to know. She had a wispy sadness in her last years, with now and then a hint of disappointment underneath, and perhaps of anger too.

She attempted small cleaning jobs, but soon gave up. She wiped down the benches, she tried to straighten beds. Len did the vacuuming and the rest of the housework. He cooked the evening meal for himself and Nigel, with a small helping for Lyndahl. Sometimes Nigel cooked or they had takeaways. They tried to sit down together, but sometimes Lyndahl had gone to sleep on the sofa or in her room. If not, they might watch some television until, early, she went off to bed. So the days went by.

Once or twice a week Len walked to the liquor store and bought a flagon of sherry. His first job on getting home was to pour half of it into an empty flagon. He topped them up with water, and Lyndahl took her weakened drink and never seemed to notice. Len felt he was doing something to help. He hated buying the sherry, partly, he said, because the woman in the liquor store started looking at him as if he was an old soak.

From time to time someone would say, 'You should put her in a hospital, Len.' He would not. He knew how unhappy she would be, not only because the staff would stop her drinking. 'She's my wife and I'll look after her.' He exhausted himself, physically and emotionally, with the looking after. Once he lost his temper and Nigel had to stand between him and Lyndahl. His two Auckland sons and their wives helped. Nigel helped. But most of it fell on Len. He tried to see that she ate. He helped her to bathe and helped her to bed. He restricted her drinking as well as he could. So, in this way, her longing that she would touch his heart before they both were dead was realised.

Twice Lyndahl spent two weeks in a North Shore rest home. Len had to have a break or he would fall ill. She hated it there and pleaded to come home. 'I don't cause any trouble. I look after myself.' She believed she did. It was plain that things could not go on as they were – but still Len insisted that he would look after her. The end, though, was closer than anyone realised.

Len was away, not at the races this time but for a short break with friends up north. Lyndahl had waved him off from the upstairs window. Margaret was staying for a few nights to look after her. Early in the evening Lyndahl was on the sofa with her drink and cigarette when she fell into a coughing fit that brought on a stroke. She fell sideways on the sofa and never moved again, never regained consciousness, but died in hospital that night. She was seventy-three.

Lyndahl's funeral service was non-religious. Rex Hollis, the nephew she had spent so much time laughing and joking with in her Henderson days, spoke the eulogy. The family and a few friends gathered in the Gibbons Road house for a quiet celebration of Lyndahl's life. Those who had known her early had the happiest memories. They dispersed then to their homes, leaving Len and Nigel to carry on their supportive lives. Len tipped the last flagon of sherry down the sink.

A short time later Aynsley and Gary scattered Lyndahl's ashes around a tree in the Waitākere Ranges.

Her sons' strongest memories of Lyndahl are of the active, loving mother of the 1930s and early 1940s. That life fulfilled her, as her poem 'Was it?' shows. She was both 'deliriously free' and 'bone-tired'. But she was also at the beginning of something else, was on the verge of becoming a writer. She had much to learn, and things to unlearn, but would have gone on if events beyond her strength to combat had not pushed in from outside. She sank under them, and under ill-health and personal tragedy, and down there, beneath a weight that crushed her, lost the voice she had worked for, and could only make thin cries, and write them down, asking to be heard and recognised by those who saw her daily but did not see. At the end her only way out was 'another little glass of vino', brought to her by the husband who had bewitched her as a young man, and made her happy for a time, and himself too, and who still loved her in his way.

Rest in peace, Lyndahl.

TWENTY

From her living-room window Lyndahl had enjoyed a view of the sea. As the years went by a neighbour's tree narrowed then obscured it. Len asked him to take a few branches off so Lyndahl – he didn't care so much himself – would have her view back. The man refused. After Lyndahl's death it continued to annoy Len. Nigel was annoyed too. One day he and his cousin Carl, Gary and Ngaire's son, took Carl's chainsaw next door (like Lionel Pinckney in Newington Road) and lopped off the offending branches, an action that would have alarmed Lyndahl but pleased Len very much. He believed in direct action. The view was open again. There were no repercussions.

Len stayed active in his last years, within a narrow range. He kept his interest in horse racing but only occasionally, immaculate in his double-breasted suit, went off to a meeting. In the summer he spent a lot of time sunbathing on the beach. He liked, Nigel says, watching the pretty girls. He mowed the lawns, cleaned the house, did most of the cooking. Curried sausages became his specialty. For breakfast he liked bacon and eggs; wouldn't touch muesli. 'Fowl mash,' he said.

For several years he had been a member of a club with rooms a hundred yards away near Takapuna's main street. He went there almost every afternoon to play snooker and indoor bowls. He had a talent for friendship and the knack of popularity with younger men. So he had happy times. His one wider journey was a three-month visit to his widowed sister Kay, who lived in Brisbane. She was a follower of the Indian guru Sai Baba ('a greater man than

Jesus') but must have known better than to try to interest Len. Kay was a lively woman, and Len enjoyed being with her and reliving old memories. He had not seen enough of her and his other sister Rona.

Back home, his life resumed its easy way. He was a gregarious old man. If he had periods of loneliness he never complained about them. Nigel kept him company much of the time. Len helped Nigel in a couple of teenage scrapes, saw off two dodgy older so-called friends (Len could be hard and direct), looked after him like a son. Nigel returned the affection. They took good care of each other – and sometimes not so good. When one of Nigel's friends, dropping him home at 2 a.m., drove through the garage door, taking it off its rails, Len came down in his pyjamas, 'looked at us all sitting in the car, completely out of it, shook his head and disappeared back to bed. The next day we beat the door back into shape, put it back on its tracks, dented and with the paint ruined. Pop never mentioned it once.' Everyone close to Len called him Pop.

A worry for Nigel was that several of Len's younger friends at the club were hard drinkers. Len tried to keep up – dangerous for a man approaching eighty. He never cared for wine but drank a little beer at home, and whisky at the club. Several times he arrived home with his brain fuzzy and his reactions slowed. Watching him come down the street, Nigel saw him shape up to a lamp-post and shadow box with it. Drink never changed his nature for the worse; he stayed happy, his friendliness increased. But there were dangers. One night, after climbing the stairs, he reached back to turn off the light, tangled his feet and stumbled backwards. He fell down the stairs, smashed through the landing window and fell another six feet into the covered porch, where a few potted cactuses sat on raised planks. The planks broke his fall. Nigel ran out from his room, down the stairs, put his head through the smashed window and saw Len lying in the debris on the concrete floor of the porch. He thought, Jesus, he's dead.

Len wasn't dead. He was scarcely damaged. Patched up, he was back at his club the following night, telling his friends how he had fallen at the centre of his house and ended up outside.

His drinking never got out of hand. He grew happy, then he came home – and managed not to fall down the stairs again.

In 1984 Nigel left for an overseas trip. He expected to be away for about three years. Len kept on in the house alone, although he had frequent visits from family and friends. Aynsley came in for lunch several days a week. The club became more central to his life. When a large extension was made to the building, he kept his eye on the work, making sure everything was done according to specifications, and the club responded by naming the new area the Len Gee Annexe. He made the short walk up the road daily, had his couple of whiskies and played a game of bowls or snooker – snooker he liked especially, he had the steady hand and sharp eye the game requires.

He had no business interests left and no property except the house. Money did not seem to worry him and he remained as generous as ever. When he sold his building business in the early sixties he had believed himself well off. His buying and selling of properties was meant to increase his wealth; but, for various reasons, he always sold too soon, so he didn't get rich. People believed he was. Aynsley Chapple said several times (and it annoyed Lyndahl), 'Len Gee must be a millionaire.' That was far from the truth. In his last years Len owned his house, he had his old-age pension, and he had a modest amount of money in the bank – a backstop if times ever got tough. He did not worry about money and seemed not even to want a lot of it.

His health stayed good, he kept active, kept daily contact with other people. After lunch he would take a nap on the sitting-room chaise longue that Lyndahl had sometimes used instead of the sofa, but if anyone came in he would spring to his feet and walk about, trying to make it seem he had not been snoozing. Perhaps he thought an afternoon sleep was giving in, or even unmanly.

At his eightieth birthday party he told jokes, danced with his daughters-in-law and his sisters Rona and Kay, who came from Christchurch and Brisbane. He drank too much whisky, and seemed robust and glowing (that was drink) and enduring. Yet in six months he was dead.

The impression of robustness was false. Len was running his constitution down – and yet, if he had been asked to balance the damage to his health from drinking and socialising against the enjoyment they gave him, there's little doubt he would have seen his time as well spent and the lost extra days as not worth having.

His illness wasn't painful, it simply weakened him progressively. He realised he was dying and adjusted to the knowledge – became quieter, slower, fonder, accepting his condition with a kind of ease. Although his stubbornness and mental strength remained, there was no fighting.

Nigel was in Indonesia with his Swiss girlfriend when he heard Len was ill. They abandoned their plans for further travel and flew back to New Zealand. Nigel spent all his spare time with Len who, over a six-week period, became weaker and weaker. Gary and Aynsley, Ngaire and Margaret shared the nursing, but in Len's last two weeks they hired a nurse to manage his bed care. He was never in any pain.

Len died on a September morning, with his three sons, two of his daughters-in-law and his grandson Nigel gathered round his bed. It was a peaceful death – a deep breath, almost a sigh, at lengthening intervals, and then no breathing at all. One of his sons tried to close his eyes but they seemed to want to stay open. Later in the day Nigel, putting his thoughts down, wrote: I've never felt so lonely in my life.

The funeral service was held in a North Shore church packed with friends. There were several old men from Henderson. One of the sons tried to put the family's feelings into words. Then a minister, who had not known Len, completed a service heavy with worms and corruption and the hope of eternal life. Some felt that Len didn't need that sort of thing. He had had no formal religious belief. As Nigel said later: 'That wasn't Pop.'

What he and Lyndahl were, I hope this memoir has shown. There's no summing up. Their lives went this way and that, were happy and unhappy; joined with each other early and grew apart and joined again. They achieved some of what they had hoped for, and missed a lot more. Those of us still alive remember them with love and gratitude and sorrow.

Len's Auckland family put his urn of ashes in his Gladstone bag and took them into the Waitākere Ranges. They scattered them around the tree where they had scattered Lyndahl's six years earlier.

'Some people came across us as we were sprinkling them,' his grandson wrote. 'They were very polite.'

BLIND ROAD

ONE

A friend of mine recently published a collection of linked stories called *Gravel Roads*. The title brought to mind the geography and times of my early life, waking memories of noises, smells, footsteps, journeys, dangers, and suggesting the generalisation – open to denial – that gravel roads run through all New Zealand childhoods. There's a macrocarpa hedge, dusty at the fringes, with glimpses of an orchard beyond, where apples lie bird-pecked and bees hum in the silence. There are blackberry jungles dropping into gullies and clay banks topped by broken fences, with dry paddocks beyond and bored cows munching. There are stone-bruised heels, too painful to stand on, and white dust blackening between our toes – the big one stubbed, with a flap of skin lifting from pink healing flesh. There are jagged stones the size of apple cores, and smooth ones like balls, to throw at the porcelain cups on telegraph poles. There's a car rolling dust clouds, forcing us into the gutter, and pine roots for climbing out of danger up the bank. There are fields of gorse, impenetrable, a corner where scrub stands like a wall, a culvert under the road leading to a pool where ferns hang low and eels nose up. Further along, a house with broken veranda posts and a sagging roof, where loose hay spills out of windows; another house, rusting, leaning, a girl on a trike in the yard – and proper houses now, the edge of town, footpaths to walk on, a horse trough, a two-storeyed house, a corner grocery, a football field with goalposts, a concrete cricket pitch. The gravel road is cut clean and turns into asphalt – the sealed main street of a little town.

I had three gravel roads. Two were blind – a word that sometimes brings a jolt of fear – while one went on, dipping and turning and meeting other roads, out of Henderson, over the railway line and up the valley into the Waitākere Ranges, then over and down to the wild beaches of the west coast. It was my road only as far as my grandparents' house and the swimming hole and the timber dam and the wooden box of Sunnyvale Station – the place, it always seemed to me, where Henderson Creek began. This was Millbrook Road. The other two gravel roads ran dead straight and ended in less than half a mile.

I lived first in Henry Street and then in Newington Road. Newington Road has too many memories. I was there from the age of three until sixteen. Everything is sharply defined as if the sun strikes down from straight overhead, leaving no shadows; and when I allow shadows they have sharp edges too. But Henry Street shifts and sometimes fades away and I wonder why the few things I remember have their place ahead of the thousands of others that must have filled my days. There's a dark room where sunlight falls on couch squabs dented with shiny buttons. There's brown lino, worn through, and an open door with wooden steps down to a yard, where a clothes line runs from the tank stand to a shed with flaking red paint. Tea towels are drying in the wind and a tea-tree prop lifts the line in the centre. In the room – which is kitchen and living room combined – a woman stands, wearing an apron. This is my mother. I have no other memory of her inside the Henry Street house, and no memory of my father at all. Why should that be? – the two most important people in my life – yet the man over the swing-bridge at the end of the blind road has a steady presence: his pipe, his moustache, his brick-red face and bald head and coarse brown jacket. The bridge bounces as I cross; the wires, like a fence on either side, tremble; the water is a long way down, its colour between black and green; but my mother lets me cross without holding my hand, although she has her fingers hooked in my trouser-straps. And now she's picking squishy persimmons from the tree in Pat Phillips' front yard. These things stand out like pictures lit by a candle in a dark room – and here's another: my older brother Aynsley carries in a parcel from the roadside letterbox. His face beams with happiness. It's a jersey knitted for his first day at school and comes from a woman called Marmee.

What I learned later fills out those earliest memories. Pat Phillips is the man with the moustache. He and my mother argue good-naturedly, almost merrily, about politics. He's an ex-soldier from the Indian Army. The friendship lasts for years, from Henry Street to Newington Road, until Pat Phillips dies. And Marmee, whom we never meet, is our grandmother in Christchurch. She dies too, following an operation for goitre. The name Marmee, we learned later on, comes from Louisa M. Alcott's *Little Women*.

My father rides a bike – at last I remember him. He wheels it round the side of the house and puts it in the woodshed. He has black hair with a spear-point in front called a widow's peak. His eyes are blue. They're the sharpest thing in that house where everything is black and brown, and the yard is dry and weedy and the paddocks stretch out white and brown and the tea-trees by the creek have flaking trunks and tops the same colour as the water.

There's a drain pipe with a curling lip at the blind end of the road. It goes down to the creek, where the swing-bridge sags into the dark.

Henry Street is unpeopled by time. I have stronger memories of it from later on when Harry Smith, my best friend at primary school, lived in our old house. His father was a railway blacksmith, a taciturn man who never once spoke to me on my weekend visits to play with Harry, and his mother a thin woman, sharp all over and aproned like my mother. She rarely came out of her kitchen.

There's memory and there's story, which takes me back to times before I was born. My parents shared the telling, my mother in a narrative, often humorous and always coloured, that filled in her childhood, then the slump and marriage and hard times, and my father, with fewer words, remembering events pleasing to boys – boxing matches, fishing trips, hard times too. He had knocked out men – that, I think, is the first big thing I knew about my father, outside all the things one learns in daily life. He had been a tough young man. Neither he nor my mother ever said how he, a carpenter, had met a parson's daughter and married her.

It happened in Tauranga in 1928 and '29. There can have been few worse times to start married life, with a new baby – born only five months after the wedding, as I discovered recently. Photos show a pretty young woman and a handsome man. They began their life together in Te Puke, boarding with Lyndahl's schoolteacher brother Kingsley and his wife. Lyndahl had earlier been a teacher in a 'Native School' and she kept a greenstone tiki given to her by a pupil when she left, showed it with pride to her sons, and kept a wooden patu, charred by fire, as well. But the young couple were not happy with Kingsley and his wife who, they felt, looked down on Len because he was a carpenter and not a 'brain worker' like them. The young couple soon left for Auckland, where their first son, Aynsley, was born. Then they made another move, to 'a smoky tin shack' on Ngāmotu beach in New Plymouth. Wharfies walked along the beach, sometimes deep in the night, on their way to and from work. My mother used Ngāmotu beach in a story called 'Tiger Town', written several years later. I mix up things she told my brothers and me with others she used in fiction. The wharfies are in 'Tiger Town' but our father going to watch boxing matches in a New Plymouth hall and standing in for an absent boxer and smiling at Mum, round the door, with a bloody mouth, when he came home, is one she didn't write but told. Dad added that he had won his fight. We boys were delighted by that, and saw that our mother only pretended to be cross and was pleased with Dad too. And we enjoyed the drama of their escape from the tin shack on Ngāmotu beach, where they could no longer pay the rent, and the service-car driver who smuggled them to Auckland. They stayed only a few months before, Dad hunting for work, shifting to Whakatāne in the Bay of Plenty. Bad luck came on the back of hardship. They rented a small cottage – not much more than a shack again – and Dad, after lighting a cigarette as he and Lyndahl went out one afternoon, leaned back inside and flicked the dead match at the waste basket by the stove. The match – Mum was good at drama – wasn't dead at all. Fire engulfed the house and burned it down, nearly trapping an old half-blind neighbour who felt his way in to rescue the baby from its cot. But Mum and Dad had taken Aynsley with them and the 'brave old man', after feeling in the blankets, managed to get out again.

These stories are like my Henry Street memories – they light up one after the other as though I'm passing with a candle through a dark room. They're pieces of furniture or paintings on the wall. Whakatāne has only the fire. The young couple left soon after that, but not before, on 22 August 1931, I was born. I don't know exactly where: my birth certificate simply lists the date, the town, my parents' ages, 25 and 24, my father's occupation, carpenter, and my mother's maiden name, Chapple.

TWO

Chapple: the name has the sound of a cracked bell. It rang through my childhood and I noticed the flaws only as I grew older. For my mother the note was always pure. In coming to Henderson, a small town west of Auckland, in 1931, she moved back to the source: her father, James Henry George Chapple, and her mother, Florence Eugenie Chapple (née Gough, which Mum gave me as my second name). They had shifted from Dove Cottage in Tauranga to Peacehaven in Henderson. The bungalow stood on a rise above Millbrook Road, half a mile along its course beside Oratia Stream (which we came to call Henderson Creek).

I have no memory of the first Henderson house Mum and Dad lived in, a short way down from the Catholic church in View Road. Again it was more shack than house. They stayed only a few months before shifting to Henry Street – a move that had the single drawback of moving Mum further from her parents. She had to walk a mile and a half through Henderson's tiny shopping centre and along beside the railway line past Mary Street, Thomas Street and Anne Street (named, like 'Henry', for the families of Thomas Henderson and Henry McFarlane, immigrant businessmen who had settled in the district in the 1840s and milled kauri logs from the Waitākere bush – there were George and Catherine Streets too). She went past the jam factory, a small brick building, turned into View Road, followed it down to the creek and over a one-way wooden bridge, then turned into Millbrook Road and walked along to her parents' house. I must have made this journey by pram, then pushchair (if Mum and Dad were able to afford them). There was no car, although Dad had a bicycle. Perhaps my mother went to Peacehaven less frequently than I imagine. When my brother Gareth was born early in 1933 she had three preschool children, and for several years must have been almost confined to the house. Even the short walk up Henry Street to the grocer's would have been made with difficulty. I remember my brother Aynsley on a trike; but don't remember pushchairs and prams, only bare feet on dusty footpaths and gravel roads.

The shift to Newington Road came in 1934, at about the time Aynsley started school. The slump was still going – how often we children heard that word. 'Slump' seemed to me like a slow heavy creature snuffling outside the back door in the night. But with their shift things began to get better for the Gee family. Worldwide, the Great Depression was losing its hold. A Labour government was elected in New Zealand (a new benevolent uncle, Michael Joseph Savage, came into our lives, his photo framed on the mantelpiece, his weak little treble on our radio) and my father found steady work. His days of being on relief were soon behind him, and his days of riding to the sawmill on his bike and following timber trucks coming out in the hope of getting a day's work stacking or carpentering on a job somewhere. Work, hard work, made up my parents' lives for the next few years, and the time was the happiest in their married lives (before a shadow, a tragedy even greater than the slump fell on them and everyone: Hitler's war, the Second World War). Dad was off to work, then came home to work in the garden. A quarter of the quarter-acre section was planted in potatoes and peas and beans, silver beet, beetroot, pumpkins, marrows, curly kale, cabbages, tomatoes – I can't think of a vegetable he didn't grow. Before long he began improving the house, enclosing the front porch for my brother Aynsley's bedroom, building a sunroom out one side, laying a concrete back yard, concreting the path to the dunny behind the hedge, putting in new steps down to the road;

and Mum worked in the kitchen and scullery and washhouse, blacking the stove, lifting the ring with a poker and dropping in lumps of firewood, sliding scones into the oven, stirring the stew, peeling potatoes, sweeping, beating mats on the washing line, carrying buckets of hot water from the copper to the bathroom for our weekly bath, hanging out the washing and running to bring it in when it rained.

There were jobs we boys could help with as we grew older: digging, hoeing, lawn-cutting, mounding earth over the full dump where empty cans and bottles went, and digging a new one. Often we had to be pushed and scolded into helping, but even small children could lessen their parents' load. From the time I was five or six I helped my older brother wash the dishes every night. My younger brother soon had to join in. One washed, one dried, one put away in the narrow scullery. Sometimes we helped Mum with the clothes washing which, breaking the unwritten rule, she would now and then do in the weekend instead of on Monday. It was heavy work, lifting boiled sheets and towels from the copper, using the copper-stick Dad had planed and shaped in his workshop, wringing them from the near tub into the further one for their final rinse, where one of us had blued the water to bring out the white of the sheets (bluebags were good for soothing beestings too), then doing the final wring, battling with the handle that did not want to turn, and helping carry the basket of damp washing out to the lines strung across the back lawn in a V. Mum flapped open shirts and blouses, tea towels, towels and sheets, pegged them up skilfully, both hands working and a peg between her teeth for the middle part of the sheets. (Sometimes we borrowed the wooden pegs, two each, and jammed them together to make six-shooters for quick draws. Destry and Tom Mix, the movie actor who played him, were the western heroes of that time.) When the water in the copper had cooled enough we scooped it out with a bucket, then a small enamelled chamber pot, and tipped it into the near tub to drain away. Standing in the tub, helping lift the bucket out, then pouring the warm dirty water over our feet was the best part of the job.

There was heavy use of water, but the tanks on their stand against the back wall of the house were replenished by the heavy Auckland rains. I can't remember them ever being less than half full. They were made of corrugated iron, like the house roof, and, like the roof, were painted red. The tops were open and mosquito larvae bred there in the season, flicking and darting well clear of the outlet to the house, which itself was clear of the silt that settled on the bottom. Later on, when Newington Road went on the town water supply, we were able to use the two tanks as swimming pools and for trying out the model yachts we built in Dad's workshop. 'Model yachts' sounds elaborate, but the ones we made were little more than flat pieces of board sharpened to a bow at one end. The single mast was a piece of dowel fitted in a bored hole; the sails were paper. Or we used pieces of flax stick halved lengthwise, with a bit of lead for a keel to keep them upright, and sharpened sticks for masts embedded in the soft wood. We made a superstructure by pinning on rear cabins and a forecastle, made two-masted sailing ships with square sails, and as we grew older we sailed these six-inch craft on pools and down rapids in the creek.

The house was on the south side of the road, above a clay bank and behind a narrow lawn. The section stretched out at the back to a macrocarpa hedge hiding the grounds of the Catholic school. Smaller hedges ran down both sides, one cutting us off from neighbours who were never more than 'the Pinckneys', and the other from a half acre of tea-tree scrub. There were lawns at the back of the house, the larger with the washing lines crossing it and the other bounded by the garden. A path led between them from the back door to the dunny, that feature of rural and suburban houses of the time. Ours was hidden by a scrawny growth of willow and eleagnus. Every few weeks we were woken from our sleep by sound of the night man running up the path with an empty can, then labouring down with the full one on his shoulder.

The house had the basic kitchen, living room and two bedrooms. A scullery ran off the kitchen, while the bathroom, with a wash basin and a claw-footed bath, opened off. The small back porch had a safe for meat and milk and butter; the washhouse, beside it, had its copper and tubs and two deep bins for firewood and coal. That was our house, a standard working-class family home, moderately comfortable, unremarkable, but to my mother it must have seemed palatial and full of comforts after the cramped sheds and shacks and poky cottages she had lived in – although no more, she would have said, than busy mothers and working men, whose 'honest sweat' kept the country going, deserved. 'Honest sweat' was a favourite term. For Dad, though, the shift meant opportunity.

I don't know whether he bought the house or rented for a while, but it seems no time before he was making improvements. He and Mum took the front bedroom, which left the side one for us three boys – Aynsley, Maurice, Gareth. It was wide enough for narrow beds placed either side of the window, leaving a gap of not much more than two feet between them. A built-in wardrobe stood behind the door and there was room for a small chest of drawers. Aynsley (called Junior now to distinguish him from the uncle he was named after) slept in one bed, I in the other. Gareth was in his cot at first, in our parents' bedroom, but joined me in my bed after a year. Top-and-tailing was no bother, the tangle in the middle of the bed seemed natural, and Gareth (soon to be irrevocably Gus, to Mum's horror) and I (Mossie or Moss), after some usually friendly kicking, slept easily.

THREE

We ate in the kitchen, which was warmed by the wood range where Mum did the cooking. Our food was plain: vegetables, bread, cheap cuts of meat, lots of mince stew and curried sausages, lots of potatoes. Eggs appeared now and then, and Mum served them to Dad and us boys. She loved eggs but ate them rarely; they were a treat she could not afford. There was usually pudding with the evening meal – rice pudding, sago or tapioca and, too often, bread pudding to use up the crusts and scraps and stale bread. We groaned about bread pudding but ate it to the last bite. We were hungry boys. In summer we had jelly and custard and stewed fruit, blancmange sometimes, or junket with grated nutmeg on top. Mum had a jelly mould shaped like a rabbit, which she used at Christmas, and it was Dad's joke to put a trail of currants or sultanas at the rabbit's rear end.

Much of our family life took place in the kitchen, but unlike some of the other families in the street we made full use of the living room or sitting room – the names were interchangeable. It was never a 'best room', as theirs was for the Lisks, who lived on the other side of the scrub sections. There the door out of the kitchen was always closed. On my one glimpse inside I saw closed curtains and the dim shapes of armchairs and sofas and the gleam of crockery in a china cabinet. None of us, Mum included, in thirteen years of knowing Mrs Lisk, was ever in that room. The polishing and darkening and closing off must have satisfied our neighbour in some way. But she had only a husband and a son. Our living room flowed on from the kitchen. It had a grey carpet that over the years became more and more worn, showing brown threads of hemp through the faded pattern. A sofa stood in front of the fireplace, with a second-hand armchair on one side and a sideboard between the bedroom doors. Soon Dad knocked a hole in the outside wall and built a sunroom. It had space for a couch and a writing desk. Before long the living room also housed an old upright piano. Mum could not play but was determined one of her sons would. It fitted under a rose in a stained-glass window set high in the wall between the living room and the front porch. Dad had this porch in his sights too. Before long he transformed it into a bedroom for Junior. Hammer and saw, chisel and plane, Dad was always busy. Junior shifted there eagerly and soon had the walls covered with pictures torn from magazines – cars, motorbikes, gunslingers. Gus moved to the empty bed, and our top-and-tailing was over.

Kitchen and living room have an equal place. The stove was always warm in the kitchen; there was coal in a bucket on the hearth and a pile of sawn tea-tree beside it. Dad's half-dozen boxing cups, some knocked about from travelling, stood on the mantelpiece. The couch under the window was long and comfortable and, best of all, the radio, a Philco shaped like church doorway, stood on a triangular shelf in a corner and, after Dad had put in a new valve, brought us popular songs, news about what was going on in the world, boxing and wrestling matches and the serials we boys were soon addicted to. It's strange that this addiction has left me only two names: 'The Green Hornet' and 'The Air Adventures of Jimmie Allen'. The Green Hornet captured crooks with his Japanese servant Kato, while Jimmie Allen and his friend Speed Robertson were also in the business of catching evil-doers.

The songs I remember best from this time are either sentimental or for children. The baritone John Charles Thomas was popular. Everyone thought he was a Negro (in the language of the day) but when he toured New Zealand years later he turned out to be white. The mistake amused him and he offered to blacken his face. His best-known song, and Mum's favourite after Paul Robeson's 'Lindy Lou', was the sentimental ballad 'I Will Take You Home Again, Kathleen'. He also sang, for children, 'The Green-eyed Dragon', who had thirteen tails and ate little boys and puppy dogs and big fat snails – 'so hurry upstairs and say your prayers and tuck your head, your pretty curly head, beneath the clothes . . .' We enjoyed this but soon grew out of it. We did not say prayers. We did not have upstairs either, but if I'd thought about it the advice would have solved a problem I had with another song, in which children 'climbed the wooden hill to Bedfordshire'. Where and what was Bedfordshire? In England probably, they had things called shires there – but why would they have wooden hills? I didn't work it out till years later.

I loved the kitchen. It was the warm safe place; my mother was there, food was there, I was allowed to lift the range ring – the centre one a plate, the outside one a real ring – with the poker and drop in more wood and coal. Sparks jumped out, or a tongue of flame, and after a while the chimney boomed. The damper should be turned then, but that was Mum's job. She made jam, mostly plum, in a preserving pan – we were not allowed near the seething brew, but while it was cooling picked out plum stones with spoons and put them in a saucer for sucking later on. She looked in pots, stirred them, shifted them on or off the heat, showed me the doughboy swelling on top of the stew or opened the oven door to see that the scones were browning. Best of all, she spooned hot syrup over my favourite pudding, date roll. Dad's work socks, sometimes his underpants and often my and my brothers' trousers dried on the rack above the stove. Now and then Mum took on the messy job of blacking it from a bottle, using a cloth. Later, when aluminium paint took over from blacking, I or Junior or Gus did the job, making the stove shine like a new shilling.

We carried out the ashes, but only when they were cold. Care had to be taken in the kitchen, where Dad was sometimes over-exuberant. I was wrestling on the floor with him one night when one of us jolted Mum passing with a pan of hot fat and sent it cascading over my chest. Hot, not boiling. I screamed as much from fright as pain and Mum, for a moment, thought she had killed me. Then she wrapped my red chest in a tea towel soaked in cold tea and I took no more harm than a few blisters. But both my parents were shaken. Wrestling, boxing, and what my mother called 'horseplay', were banned in the kitchen after that.

In winter the living room was our place. It wasn't large but with a fire going it was warm and comfortable. We could not listen to the radio from there but talked and read and played Snakes and Ladders and Pick-Up-Sticks and built things with our Meccano set until it was time for bed. Mum told us stories about her life. We learned about her pacifist father and mother taking their family to California to get away from the war. They stayed for a year and came home again, minus two older daughters who had found boyfriends, when America joined the fight against Germany. It was a story that filled me with excitement and pride: America, where they made the pictures we went to on Saturday nights, where there were snakes in the gutters and rich people had swimming pools in their back yards. My brothers and I began using words like 'cookie' that none of our playmates understood. We boasted of our mother who had been to America almost as much as of our father who had knocked men out. He told his tales too. And they both talked about the slump and their hard times and the fun they'd had.

I don't remember that Mum read us stories, but she must have because I grew up familiar with the fairy and folk tales of Andersen and the Grimms, as well as stories from the Arabian Nights. She read us the children's narrative poem she was writing and I learned to recite passages from it. I knew that she wrote stories too hard for me to read; I saw her working on them in the kitchen at night when I woke and wandered out in my pyjamas, and she showed them to me and my brothers in magazines like the *Mirror* – her name there strangely changed to Chapple-Gee. Sometimes she worked at the writing desk Dad had built for her. Its place in the sunroom allowed her to look across the Henderson Valley to the Waitākere Ranges – the Waitaks – making their wavy line along the horizon. The writing desk was as much a marvel as her name in magazines. How had Dad made it, made those legs with twists in them, and put the Southern Cross and a crescent moon on top? The word was 'inlaid'. It seemed just as clever to my brothers and me as writing stories. And anyway, Dad told stories too: fights he had won, camping on Mayor Island on weekend fishing trips. As Guy Fawkes Day approached he would say:

> Please to remember the fifth of November
> The gunpowder treason and plot.
> I see no reason why gunpowder treason
> Should ever be forgot . . .

which didn't make much sense to us boys. More interesting were lines from the only other poem he knew, which he would sometimes recite to amuse us:

> When caveman Ogg went out to woo
> He took his brontosaurus too . . .

When he reached the lines:

> And seizing on a slab of granite,
> He tapped her gently on the bonnet

203

Mum would cry out: 'Len, Len, that's enough.' We never found out how the poem ended.

Slump stories were favourites – the slump was still going on in our early days in Newington Road. I loved the story of their early-morning flight ('moonlight flit' hadn't come into use) from the shack on Ngāmotu beach; loved stories of friendship and generosity and sharing, hardship too and no-waste too. The next-door neighbour (Ngāmotu beach again) called Mum in to show her a mouse drowned in her billy of milk. She picked it out by its tail and threw it out the door, but did not throw the milk away. No waste. One day the same woman found flies drowned in the milk. She fished them out one by one and sucked off the cream.

FOUR

Mum's bookcase stood on the right-hand side of the sitting-room fireplace. Here the books were all too hard for me. Few of them were 'stories' and all were 'grown-up'. There were none that bridged the gap between my school readers and the simpler children's classics and adventure books. I soon stopped looking, and can recall only one title, which puzzled me for years: *The Maori Race*. It was by a man called Edward Tregear. The Maori Race? I hunted through it, trying to find out what sort of race it had been and who had won.

One day Dad brought home a *Chums Annual* he had found on one of his jobs. It was fat and heavy to lift, its cover was worn, the binding on the spine was loose and some of the pages torn, but it quickly became my favourite book. I read it for years, by the fire, in bed, on the kitchen sofa. Its year must have been 1917 or '18 because two of its serial stories were about the Great War: 'With Haig on the Somme' and a story about the crew of a British tank. Two brothers were at the centre of the Somme story. I followed them through the book, week by week, as shells exploded around them, as they led bayonet charges and advanced in the face of machine-gun fire. After one bayonet charge the younger brother finds his elder covered with blood. 'Don't worry,' says the elder, 'it's not my blood it's German gore.' Gore! It horrified and thrilled me. And the tank advanced in its story, week by week. 'You can see where we've been from the trail of squashed Huns.' It was strange reading for the grandson of a pacifist and son of a pacifist mother. I did not know how deeply the fear of another war affected her, or how that war, when it came, threatened her reason and eroded her good health, both physical and mental. She must have longed to take the *Chums Annual* away from me. 'Mum, listen. This British soldier throws a hand grenade and it says "Private Schmidt's head parted company from his shoulders".' 'Don't, oh don't,' Mum said, distressed; and horrified too, horrified at me. I read her no more bits from the *Chums Annual*.

It had other stories. I enjoyed them all – the third division soccer team whose star player and his friend, a fat goalkeeper, thwart an evil developer who wants to steal their ground. They lead their team, the Rovers (something Rovers), to victory in the FA Cup. The goalkeeper, Fatty, even scores a goal, dribbling from his goal-mouth through the opposing team, as the Rovers (maybe Wanderers) beat the top teams one by one: Blackpool, Chelsea (whose name, 'the Pensioners', puzzled me), Aston Villa (equally puzzling). Each week there were half a dozen ongoing stories: a racing car driver, Skid Kennedy; a detective, Sexton Blake. Sexton Blake's foe was a German spy called Zimmler the Wolf, a name that almost persuaded me to prefer him to sissy-named Sexton. Zimmler creeps into Sexton Blake's bedroom, quietly turns on the gas, and creeps out. But Sexton has been watching through hooded eyes and trails Zimmler to his lair . . . But hold on! Am I confusing *Chums* stories with those from *The Champion*, a boys' weekly that came my way (how?) in the Second World War? And maybe confusing Sexton Blake with Colwyn Dane, another 'tec with a sissy name. The only *Champion* 'hero' I'm sure of is Rockfist Rogan, a Spitfire pilot who each week shoots down some Messerschmidts and knocks out his opponent in a boxing match.

Nothing much had changed between the first war and the second, except that the *Champion* stories were less bloodthirsty.

I read books that troubled Mum less. At some point in my school career – probably Standard Four – I won a Temperance Essay prize with an entry, more story than essay, about a drunk old tramp who gets knocked down and killed by a car. Voucher in hand, I visited the Presbyterian Bookroom in Auckland. The old lady in charge – glittering spectacles – offered me books about heroic missionaries, but I resisted and, seduced by the knight in a mail shirt on the cover, came away with a novel about the Crusades. The cover was the best thing about it; I remember nothing of the story inside. The novels of an American called Joseph A. Altsheler satisfied me more: frontiersmen fighting Redskins in the forests of America. I borrowed them from the book cupboard at Henderson School. And somehow I got my hands on, and managed to keep, a collection of Robin Hood stories, and this displaced the *Chums Annual* as my favourite book. It met and satisfied my boyhood yearning for adventure and companionship. Robin and Little John meet on stepping-stones across a stream (I'd have called it a creek) and neither will give way. They fight with quarter staves and Little John knocks Robin into the water. The hero gets beaten, but it did not bother me because he and Little John become best friends. Who did I want to be? Robin, of course, because of his courage and his skill with a longbow, and because he was the leader; but Little John too, for his bravery and size and strength; and Will Scarlet, because he wore scarlet clothes, which really appealed to me, and was devil-may-care. But not Friar Tuck, because he was fat and greedy, and because I had taken on the Chapple anti-clerical bias. The other member of the band I liked was Mutch the Miller's Son. Robin had been uncertain about letting him join the band because he was a workman. I was enough of a Chapple/Gee to be strenuously for him because of it. My father was a workman and Mum 'believed in' the working man. Mutch the Miller's Son, although unexciting, was okay. And it pleased me immensely that Robin was robbing the rich to give to the poor.

Maid Marian was sweet and pretty and baked the venison pasties the Merry Men lived on. I liked her too.

My reading wasn't wide but was intense and, more than satisfying, involving. I travelled places by intent as well as accident, reading fast, although I wasn't in any other way advanced – was, it seems to me when I look at it, a little retarded in understanding. Now and then someone pointed me. On my tenth birthday my grandfather gave me *The Siege of Troy and the Wanderings of Ulysses*, by Charles Henry Hanson. I still have it. 'To Mossie from Grandfather', he wrote on the fly leaf. 'Learn the following verse:

> One thought I have my ample creed,
>   So deep it is and broad,
> And equal to my every need,
>   It is the thought of God.'

I took no notice of that. The book, though, with its battles and adventures, delighted me, and the Greek heroes, and Trojan Hector too, became my companions. About the gods I was ambivalent. Mars, Apollo, Venus (Hanson used the Roman names) should, I thought, keep out of things. How could the humans have a fair fight when they kept on interfering? Heroism was flawed in the battle for Troy. When Diomedes throws his spear at Pandarus, the goddess Minerva guides it so that it strikes Pandarus in the face. Not fair! And the great hero, Achilles, was never a hero for me – how could he be when his mother had dipped him in a magic stream so he could not be wounded? He must know he'd win every fight. I was pleased about his heel but puzzled that an arrow hitting it should be fatal. I wanted Hector to get away as Achilles chased him round the walls of the city. It did not bother me that he was scared. Run, Hector, run. He had a wife and baby watching from the walls. His courage revives, but again Minerva steps in, returning Achilles' spear to his hand for a second throw. Achilles thrusts it into Hector's throat. The story, as far as I was concerned, had been messed up. Then Achilles messes it up further by dragging Hector behind his chariot around the walls of Troy, while Hector's father, ancient Priam, pleads for his son's body. When Troy finally falls Achilles is dead too – from that arrow in his heel – but his son Pyrrhus butchers old Priam, along with any others of the family he can find. There's a lot of cruelty and savagery in the battle for Troy. I was surprised my pacifist grandfather had given me the book.

I enjoyed Ulysses' travels more. I liked Ulysses, although his idea of a wooden horse was sneaky. Wily Ulysses. What a good word. I started using it, not out loud, about myself. Not everything Ulysses did was all right, though. Killing the suitors was okay but I did not forgive him for hanging all Penelope's maids.

As for the names in Hanson's book, I did my best with them, rhyming Diomedes with centipedes, Penelope with antelope, for many years.

So my reading, very much boys' reading, went on, with at last some sensible interest in just and unjust behaviour and good and bad.

FIVE

If you burrowed through the macrocarpa hedge at the back of our section you came to a neglected corner of the Catholic school grounds. Wattle trees stood in a tangle, a bank of crumbling clay went down to a patch of swampy ground, with tennis courts beyond, one surfaced in gravel chips, the other in asphalt. Further off was a football field with wobbly goalposts. There were basketball courts on an upper terrace, while pine trees in a cluster grew lower down. A stream not much more than a yard wide ran round the back of the football field, through the pines and into a scrub section on Newington Road.

The school itself – Holy Cross School, a spooky name – stepped down a slope above the tennis courts. It had two classrooms, with shelter sheds underneath. Beyond, not seen from our vantage point by the macrocarpa hedge, was the convent or nunnery where the nuns who did the teaching lived. If you hid in the pines in weekends you might see them walking in pairs along the gravel path below the football field. They were on their way to and from the church – Holy Cross too – on View Road. They wore long black robes and beads and crosses round their necks, and their faces were framed in white cloth starched like collars. I was afraid of them, for their clothes, their silence, the way they seemed to flow along instead of walk, and I could not imagine being taught in school by them. They seemed more than just women. They hardly ever spoke but I heard one using strange words to the other as they went by – not English, I thought, and it made me more afraid. I suspect now that she was an Irish woman speaking with her native accent.

From strangeness came fear and hostility. Late one afternoon in school holiday time my older brother and I, aged ten and eight, stole a spade from a store shed at Holy Cross School, used it to smash a window in the lower classroom, climbed inside and broke everything breakable we could find, tore drawings and maps from the walls, tipped out inkwells, tipped out the contents of the teacher's – the nun's – drawer: Junior and Mossie at work, gleeful and afraid, while Gus, too small to climb inside, pulled out plants from the garden under the window. Why did we do it? A tribal hostility, an us-and-them response, a fear of strangeness? We were thorough, deep in enemy territory, and sanctioned, it seemed, by our mother, who had told us one day, after passing nuns from the convent in the street, that they were superstitious women with wasted lives.

Years later, supply-teaching in London, I was sent to a Catholic school down at Elephant and Castle. It was called English Martyrs, a name that brought back some of the feelings of difference and strangeness 'Holy Cross' and the passing nuns had brought on when I was a child. As a non-believer, I met hostility from one young woman teacher (not a nun, there were no nuns), but everyone else made me welcome. Teaching a class of eleven-year-olds and forgetting, then remembering, that they were Catholic, I found myself puzzling over our vandalising of Holy Cross School and, not able to find answers, became ashamed. I still feel that way – not deeply: I can find excuses; shame shades into regret and interest. I've not been able to rid myself of that melange of feelings, and find myself confused again. I don't see anything wrong with regret but would like to be rid of shame.

Junior and I were found out. Big red-faced Constable Norton came – a Catholic. 'So these are the little rascals' – which was kind of him. Dad told him he'd given us a thrashing (on the legs, with a willow stick). The incident was put away and I forgot about it for many years; but remember now the nuns going by, their robes alive, their feet invisible so that they seemed to roll along on wheels instead of walk, while I knelt behind a pine tree with my knees on slippery needles and my hands hooked in the rough bark. Some things come back with such clarity they seem to define who you were while at the same time enveloping everything in mystery.

SIX

Newington Road was grey with gravel and white with dust. In winter yellow puddles lay undisturbed. Only E. Evans Scott, the chemist, living opposite us, owned a car – a Morris Eight with red doors and a round body. We could play safely in the street if we chose, but as we grew older our territory widened: Kellys' farm behind us, with Burke's orchard down a slope beyond the paddocks, the Catholic school grounds, the derelict orchard and the willow swamp blocked off by railway houses on the north side of the street, and, through paddocks and tea-tree scrub, the creek.

Those places were forbidden in my preschool days and for several years after. The creek especially was dangerous. There were deep pools and in one or two places the water ran fast between banks of moss-covered rock. We could only go there with our parents, and even then . . . I am four years old, walking home with my mother from a visit to my grandparents in Millbrook Road. We take a little side trip down a track through gorse to a place where the creek narrows and water races between rock walls from an upper to a lower pool. I squat beside the water and watch it speeding by until, from a kind of hypnosis, I topple in. My mother said later that I floated by with my eyes wide open and my hands crossed on my chest, and having been told this I 'remember' it. I see myself clearly, eyes wide open under water, arms crossed, body rigid; and see Mum looking down at me and reaching in. She 'saved my life' – that is how it came to be expressed, and I became even more my mother's child.

People could be dangerous too. There was access to the creek by way of a tributary stream flowing through the grounds of Peacehaven. You could walk on a spongy strip between tree-ferns and water until you reached a deep pool below a timber dam built to drive a water wheel in the early days. My mother took her three sons walking there one afternoon – water running on stones, the shade deep and still, the road blocked out by ferns and scrub. No sound; cars were rare. We came around the ferns and a pool opened out, and there on the bank was a pile of clothes – trousers, belt, hat, shirt – and up to his waist in the water a man washing his chest with a piece of yellow soap. There were suds in his armpits. We knew that under the water he had nothing on. Mum stopped. Her arms came out and blocked us. The man stood frozen, one hand stuck to his chest. He had black hair plastered to his scalp and black, deep-pitted eyes that fixed on us and never moved. Absolute stillness. He did not seem to breathe but waited to see what we would do. Mum turned us round. She hurried us back down the creek and up to the road.

'Who was he, Mum?'

'A swagman,' she said; and afterwards explained what swagmen were and that they were not bad men, only poor. Then why did we run . . . ? This is not a memory squeezed and shaped by imagination or invention. The swagman stands in the pool, white upper body, dark still eyes. I put the incident in a novel many years later, dressed it up, left things out, but the fiction has never displaced the reality. The swagman lives.

SEVEN

The creek ran through my boyhood but for several years came second as a playground to Newington Road. Places and people shift aside for each other. I walk along footpaths, open gates and step on to sections and sometimes into houses, where the Lisks live, the Greenhoughs, the Kays, the Pinckneys (rarely, although only a hedge separated us), old Ben Hart and his wife, and our playmate Murray Scanlon. For a short time there were the Flynns, in the railway house next door to the Scotts' non-railway one. It was Mrs Flynn who named Gareth 'Gus'. I remember her only as a big woman with a rolling walk, wearing an apron, and remember her husband as a man in a shirt without a collar, unshaven, bellowing with anger as he chased his son along the footpath with a tomato stake. Avon wriggled into a drain pipe by Ben Hart's house and got away. The Flynn boys were wild, according to my mother, who was trying to bring her sons up to be not gentlemen but gentle men. Avon, Bill and Murray went to the Catholic school and were older than us, so we saw little of them, and they were soon gone, replaced by the Kays. We thought the Kay boy, John, a poor replacement for the Flynns. His mother believed in something called Radiant Living but was anxious and fidgety rather than radiant; and his father – we could not work it out – was always away. John did not become our playmate, although the Gees were invited to his birthday party, where they ate raisins and nuts and, hugely embarrassed, listened while Mrs Kay sang a Radiant Living song called 'Lemons in the Morning'.

The Greenhoughs lived over the road from us, and their son

Gordon, a little younger than me, was often at our house but rarely inside. It's possible his mother had told him not to go in. I was never inside his house in the thirteen years we were neighbours. Stan Greenhough, the father, was a railway signalman. He sat high in the signal box at Henderson Station and pulled the levers that shifted the points. He was a small chirpy man whose hobby was growing flowers (he had a glasshouse at the back of his house) and he was friendly enough. Mrs Greenhough was the problem. Mum said she thought she was too good for the street and definitely too good for the Gees. I can't say, but she was certainly stand-offish – a large woman (today she'd be 'obese'), with a face that closed up when she saw you. Gordon, her son, owned toys but was not allowed to bring them outside – although once he brought his Hornby train on to the front porch for us to see. He was, in spite of these restrictions, a friendly boy, eager to be part of any fun that was going, and we liked him and were happy to play with him. One day on our front lawn he gave me a friendly shove and I fell into the hedge and cut my leg to the bone (I see white bone) on a broken bottle. Mum picked me up and carried me over the road to Mr Scott the chemist, thinking he would know what to do, but unfriendly Mr Scott told her to take me home and put a bandage on the cut. It should have been stitched. The scar still shows almost eighty years later. Gordon's mother, I'm pretty sure, would have found broken bottles exactly what one would expect from the Gees. But when we finally left Newington Road in 1948 Stan bought our house and shifted his family across the street. Gordon Greenhough, unmarried, was to live there until his death more than sixty years later.

My brother Aynsley (Junior) was two years older than me and had his own friends. We shared games and adventures but he was able to roam more widely and was out of Newington Road earlier than me. Gary (Gus) and I were more together. Our best friend in

216

the street was Murray Scanlon, who lived in a non-railway house at the corner of Newington Road and View Road. Most of our after-school games included him and we were as often at his place as he was at ours. He had a cheerful grandmother, Mrs Murray, who looked after the house. She chatted with us on the back porch and gave us biscuits but did not let us inside. The kitchen was a workplace, and most women got children outside as quickly as they could. A feature of many kitchens in the housefly season was a flypaper hanging from the ceiling, with buzzing flies stuck to it. One summer day Murray, Gus and I sat on the sunny back porch and caught flies in our hands, easy when you knew the trick, but instead of taking them in to stick on the paper – our first idea – we fed them to a spider under the porch windowsill. We must have thrown twenty or thirty flies into his web and each time the large black spider rushed out of his funnel-shaped hole and, walking backwards, hauled the buzzing fly inside. Mrs Murray was amused. She gave us a biscuit.

But Mum was not amused when we told her, even though we had our own flypaper in the kitchen. She liked Murray but was never friendly with his parents or grandmother. Mum, like Mrs Greenhough, was a bit of a snob. She was polite, interested, talkative with people she liked, but passed judgement on others for reasons I did not understand. Mrs Murray was, I think, 'common', Mum's own mother's favourite condemnation. Mrs Scanlon, Murray's mother, was 'hard', a word I heard Mum use of her more than once, and perhaps she (Mum) had inside knowledge, for now and then she expressed pity for Laurie Scanlon, a thin quiet man we rarely saw (husbands were at work). Mrs Scanlon wore make-up and had permed hair. She spoke, as I remember, in flat short sentences that lifted shrilly to an edge.

When our territory widened to include the creek, Murray joined us in our games and activities. We transferred our flat-bottomed yachts and flax-stick galleons from the water tanks to a pool down from the Scanlon house. It was dark-green and still and not for swimming. You angled across an edge of a draught-horse paddock and broke through fern and scrub and picked through blackberry vines to reach it. There, from a web of pink willow roots making a peninsula in the pool, we launched our boats and fished them back with bamboo sticks. Some were lost, drifting down and speeding into rapids out of the pool, with once or twice a praying mantis or a tea-tree jack as crew. We fished from beneath the willow tree, using tiny silver hooks bought three a penny at the grocer's, and caught silver bellies and tommy cod. Worms and penny doctors were the bait. Penny doctors could be caught by poking a grass stalk into their hole in the ground and pulling it out carefully. Sometimes a grub would be clinging to the stalk. We fried the silver bellies in tin lids and picked bits of flesh from the tiny bones. Tommy cod were black and slimy; we didn't fry those.

Back from the pool was a short gully, little more than a dip in the ground, with punga ferns and thick-trunked tea-trees growing at the edges. One of the trees leaned across the gully and Junior, who could climb anything, shinnied up with a rope and tied it to a branch leaning even further out, making a swing on which we launched ourselves across the gully. He made an improvement, a longer rope for a longer ride, and started from inside the crown of a tree fern higher up the slope. We swung over the ferns and scrub on the far side, glimpsing the creek further off, and dropped from the rope to the gully floor when the swinging stopped. It was dangerous and we did not tell our parents.

Junior, inventive and practical, soon saw there was room for a second rope. He hugged his way along the branch and tied it beside the first one, and we were able to swing in pairs, starting together to avoid collisions; but a collision was inevitable, and I was the unlucky one, slamming into one of the bigger boys – a sickening jolt that threw me to the gully floor. I ran home sobbing, gasping, with my arm locked across my chest and a spreading, deep, dreadful ache in my shoulder. A broken collarbone, the doctor said, nothing to worry about. He strapped it with sticky tape and told Mum to give me Aspros to help me sleep, but I hurt and cried, then itched and complained and made the most of my injury. Meanwhile Dad and Laurie Scanlon examined our swing and Laurie took a ladder down to the gully and sawed off the tea-tree branch the ropes were tied to. We hated him for it, but perhaps he saved a life.

His own ended soon after. He locked himself in the bathroom and drank poison. Mrs Scanlon married again, after a decent while, and her new name became Murray's too.

EIGHT

There's a further boy, called Ernie. He was only a little older than my brother Junior, but they were never friends. I doubt that Ernie had friends. He lived further along the road, on the far side of half an acre of scrub, an only child whose father, a bootmaker, travelled by train each morning to his work in Mt Eden. Ernie made his way along tracks in the scrub; he seemed to be always at our house, wanting to be let into our games, but we held him off. What was it we didn't like? His almost pleading neediness? His boasting that made him better than us in every way? We were especially outraged at his claims for his father, who, he said, could run faster and lift heavier things than ours. Didn't he know our father had knocked men out? But his, Ernie claimed, was a champion sprinter and had won the hundred yards at the New Zealand championships – and it might have been true, for when we saw the father, Les, in his shorts on summer days, he certainly had muscular legs. And Ernie called us over to watch Les chop the heads off chooks in the fowl run. We might have accepted him except that he was indefinably creepy. There was something wrong in his head; his understanding of what was going on was always skewed. It might have come from an injury we witnessed one day. Ernie's mother and ours stood talking on the wooden bridge crossing the creek where Millbrook Road and View Road met. Ernie, aged about ten, was standing next to his mother while we looked through the railings at the water. An older boy, Des Hallas, came down the hill on his bike, lost control in the gravel, and came straight at us on the bridge. Ernie ducked the wrong way, into the bike, and the handlebar struck him on the forehead. I remember an egg-shaped bruise that looked more like a dent. Ernie stood unconscious on his feet, not sure who he was, or where, and I wonder about some injury to his brain. I can't remember what he was like before but there was a kind of thick aggressiveness in his behaviour, when he wasn't wheedling, after that.

Looking back, he spoiled something for us – or perhaps just for me. A shadow falls on my childhood when I remember Ernie. He found a cardboard box, too small for him to get into and close the lid, but I was small enough, he said, and wouldn't it be a great idea to put it in the middle of the road and make Mr Scott stop his car when he came home. Then I could climb out and we'd have a laugh at him. I took some persuading. What if Mr Scott drove right over the box? No, he wouldn't, Ernie said, it was too big. So, not long after, I found myself in a cardboard box in the middle of Newington Road, with Mr Scott due home and Ernie watching from behind our hedge. Did I raise the lid and stop the car, or did Mr Scott stop the way Ernie said he would? I don't remember. But the white-faced man burst out of his car, yelling with anger and fright as I scrambled out – not laughing – from the box. He gave me a good telling off, and so did Mum and Dad when they heard. But they believed me when I told them it was Ernie's idea and they watched him closely after that.

I haven't any doubt that Ernie wanted Mr Scott to run over the box.

Several years later I tried to fight him, using Dad's straight left and right cross, but he knocked me silly with half a dozen round-house punches. 'You've got to keep your guard up,' Dad said. It wasn't easy.

We made an underground hut. Junior had the idea but all three of us worked on it. We dug a hole at the top of the garden – a wider, deeper hole than any we had made for bottles and cans.

Then we dug a narrow, curving trench leading into it. We carpeted the bottom of the hole with coal sacks. Dad let us have an old sheet of corrugated iron to cover it with, and we spread a layer of soil over the iron. We roofed the trench with wood and soil, making a tunnel, and crawled and wriggled along it to our underground hut. It was dark in there. We needed a candle. Dad said no, not without an air hole, so Junior dug one in a corner and it had the advantage of letting in more light. All three of us got inside and sat cramped together. What did we do in there? Almost nothing. We took in bits of food and ate it, that was all. It was too dark for reading, and the candle smoked and wanted to go out. So we sat there enjoying the feeling of being underground, then came out and stopped using the hut after a while. Mum was happy with that. She thought it was dangerous and it made our clothes filthy. We crawled in only now and then to see how the place was getting on.

Ernie wanted to come into our hut but we said no, it was ours, and anyway he was too big, which was true. He would not have been able to wriggle along the tunnel. But the place kept drawing him back and he began to hate us. (I don't know this, I'm writing fiction now – and years later I put the incident into a novel, or was it two?) One day when Junior was alone in the hut Ernie came the back way into our section. He stuffed newspaper into the ventilation hole (in the novel or novels the Ernie character blocks the mouth of the tunnel first) and lit it with a match (wax matches) and ran away. Junior wriggled out all right and told Mum and Dad, and for a while Dad chased Ernie off our section whenever he saw him. But it's possible Junior could have died. The hut didn't last long after that. One day a bull broke away from a herd of cows being moved from the farm at the end of Newington Road. It bolted up our path and across our garden, where its front legs broke through the hut roof. No one was down there. The farmer had to dig the bull out and lead it away with a nose ring, and shortly after that Dad told us to take off the broken roof and fill in the hut. We did it without complaint. Ernie not the bull had ruined it for us.

There's more about him. By the age of nine or ten I knew nothing about sex, though I'd heard boys at school talk about it and say what happened. I thought that was just big kids' dirt, even if at the back of my disbelief a sort of knowledge moved, disguised as curiosity. But no adult had confirmed it. Nothing from Mum and Dad. Mum took us to watch a calf being born on Kellys' farm and I found it interesting but messy. When Gus asked how the calf got in there she fell back on the planting of a seed and would only say that a bull had to plant the seed in the cow's tummy. How? And what about people? She replied that it was a beautiful thing and we'd understand one day.

The kids at school knew. My brothers came to know. My younger brother told me bluntly that I was a mug. My deskmate in Standard Four was Clyde Markwick, a fierce little yellow-haired boy who grew up to be a jockey. I asked him why he bounced around in his seat like that. 'Practising,' he said. 'What for?' 'Fucking sheilas.' I drew away from him as though he were diseased. I knew but wouldn't know. What about purity? What about beauty? When a group of boys down at the swimming pool at Falls Park were talking about fucking I said flatly that I didn't believe it. My parents, I said, would never do a thing like that.

Ernie steps back into the frame. He's about thirteen and I am ten. We're at his place, up at the back of the section by the fowl run. We climb through the fence into Kellys' farm and go along past the scrub so we're hidden from the house because, he says, he wants to show me how he can make milk come out of his cock. He takes out his penis, it's big and red and looks deformed, but I watch as he rubs it and makes the 'milk' come out and squirt on a pine trunk. And then I take off, I get out of there, because I recognise it's dangerous. Ugly, shadowy, dirty, dangerous. I could write this as though it's nothing – boys learning to masturbate, it happens all the time – or as a bit of comedy. But those four adjectives are the truth of it for the ten-year-old I was.

I got over it easily enough. Just another day in the life of an ignorant, over-sensitive small boy. In the rest of my behaviour I was rough and tough, noisy and physical, and curious about all sorts of things. But about sex I remained obdurate (can't say firm). I would not admit Ernie's penis as evidence.

He comes back, bringing it with him. When I wanted to get away to read I sometimes went to the porch Dad had converted into a bedroom for Junior and lay on his bed, safe from intrusion. The room had sliding windows, and one afternoon as I was reading Ernie pushed them open and climbed in. First his head, with its red thick face and eyes seeing something that wasn't there: 'You be a girl, eh, and I'll be a man climbing in the window.' Disbelief paralysed me as he tumbled in. He took out his penis, already hard, kept me still with one arm, and rolled on top of me. He made a couple of prods, not at anything he could see because I was fully clothed; but I've never known any horror like it – horror of getting his 'milk' on me. I was a quick, agile boy and I got out from under him with a heave and slide and was at the door and into the house before he could move from the bed. I haven't any doubt that I was in danger of violence, perhaps of death. He was a big strong boy. But again I kept quiet, told no one until recently I described Ernie's attempt to my brother Gus, who said, 'Yes, he did the same with me.' Gus got away too – he was smaller than me but tougher. Like me, he didn't tell anyone. And we saw very little of Ernie after that. He kept away. I can't remember even talking with him again, although he lived in the street for the rest of our time there. He must have gone to school on the train – one of the train boys – to Mt Albert Grammar or Seddon Tech, the schools that took western suburbs boys. He simply passed out of my life, except for the memories left behind. More than sixty years later I gave him an existence after Newington Road by putting an Ernie figure into a novel and making him larger than life, a grotesque. One reviewer, with some justification, described the novel as silly.

NINE

I was safe in my family but not always safe outside, as Ernie had proved. Places too could be dangerous – the creek, the Catholic school grounds, even Henderson School where I started in 1936, even the streets of our town. I saw a man die at the creek – but that comes later. When I was a small boy I ran home from the outside world into a warm kitchen, where my mother was cooking our dinner at the stove. Dad would be coming in soon, my brothers would appear, and we would wash our hands and sit up at the table where, remembering our manners, we would eat mince stew and rice pudding and Mum and Dad would talk about their day. This was the safe place, where nothing from outside could get in, where afterwards I could read or play – after helping my brothers do the dishes, after, perhaps, in front of the living-room fire, holding a skein of wool on my parted hands while Mum rolled it into a ball. We were called on to help. That was part of family, part of being home. Later in my life, looking for symbols, I could find nothing more useful than 'creek' and 'kitchen', and they still work, although a bit of thought makes them less useful.

Why does a happy active child, in the heart of his family, sleeping in his own bed, with his brother in a bed alongside and his parents through the wall, find himself overcome with terror at something outside the window or something under his bed? I lay huddled, cramped up, listening, not breathing, and heard no sound, but something was there, I felt it as surely as the beating of my heart, and in the end, finding courage to move, I stood on the edge of the bed, not daring to put my feet on the floor, and leaped into the dark for Gus's bed, where I tumbled across him. He woke and grumbled and slept again, and I snuggled into his blankets and slept too. Some nights I could not find the courage to stir, so I lay in bed and called for my parents, Mum and Dad equally – called and called, waking Gus, who told me to shut up. Mum came and sat with me until I dropped off to sleep. I was six or seven, not a child of two or three, but they kept their patience; and in the end they put a narrow wooden bed in their own room and I slept there. It could not have been for long, perhaps just for one night. I woke and heard the sound of breathing, and, dopey with sleep, stood on the edge of the bed and jumped into the dark for my brother Gus, and crashed into the wooden end of my parents' bed. They jumped up, turned on the light, and found me stunned and bleeding on the floor. What happens next? Patched up, with a chipped tooth, I spent the rest of the night in their bed, sleeping between them. Then it fades away, I'm not certain why or how, perhaps just from being safe and warm between my parents for one night; but my terrors come to an end and I'm in my own bed again, with nothing to frighten me and keep me awake. The demons, murderers, ghosts, creatures under my bed and outside the window are gone. After that I could even, if I had to, go up to the dunny in the dark and sit there with a candle burning and the house lights hidden by the hedge, and not be afraid – more nervous of the wētās gleaming on the ceiling than of anything that might be creeping in the night.

There's another 'kitchen' in my childhood. My brothers and I were there almost daily before we started school and at least once in the weekend after that. It was always with Mum; Dad only came now and then. We walked along Newington Road and down the View Road hill, turned off before the wooden bridge and went along Millbrook Road to our grandparents' house, where the barred double gate at the bottom of the drive had the name

Peacehaven painted on a board. It could be a long walk, hot and dusty in summer (gravel roads), but the creek was down its bank on the right; a macrocarpa hedge halfway along, sheltering my uncle Holl's orchard, gave a little shade; pines above a clay bank meant we were nearly there; and then the little side-creek and the gate, the drive, the summerhouse on the lawn, the rose garden and the kitchen.

My grandmother greeted us with her exclamation, 'Ah, Lindy!', and her smile of pleasure in seeing us. There was a ritual that never failed – she reached for the cake tin or the cookie jar and our mother said, 'You'll spoil their dinner, Mum.' Grandma took no notice and we went outside with a piece of cake or a cookie in our hands. She was in her mid-sixties and she dressed in a style that looked back to the early days of the century – long skirts, long-sleeved blouses, always sober in colour, with a shawl round her shoulders and a cameo brooch at her throat. A tall woman, standing straight, she could seem stately to a child, but this was overcome by her warmth. There was never any sourness, there was always a smile and a kiss. She had rules and we knew it, but never tested them; we were automatically 'good' with her; never used 'bad' language, not even dash or darn it; always – the most natural thing in the world – said please and thank you. We got rid of our chewing gum (chuddy), not saving it behind an ear in our usual way, before going into her kitchen. Her rules for adults were harder for them to bear, even though they weren't applied directly. Certain things caused her pain and nobody was willing to cause that or see her turn away with a sad look on her face. It was a gentle sort of tyranny. Not that her dislikes were always reasonable or fair. She had no liking for easy ways of sociability, for promiscuity (I don't mean sexual), for 'common-ness'; for loose language, bad manners, too much lipstick on a woman or any nail polish at all, and, when slacks came in, 'women wearing trousers'. But this is a small part of Florence Chapple. She was loving and welcoming, and if one met the little standards she wasn't anyway aware of imposing she created warmth around her. She as much as my grandfather was creator of 'the Chapples'.

Outside, we had the freedom of the Peacehaven grounds. The house itself was a bungalow, standing above a driveway curving around to the back yard. It seemed large because there were parts closed off to us. We kept away from the back, where several pine trees overshadowed the house and where our grandfather worked in his study. We did not want him noticing us. The two side lawns were our playground, the upper one, bounded by a rose garden, several peach trees and a row of guava bushes with a vegetable garden beyond, and the lower by a loop of a side-creek that flowed into a culvert and down to Henderson Creek. A tea-tree summerhouse, built by Uncle Dick, stood in the middle, but this somehow seemed to belong to Grandpa and we rarely went in. We were drawn more to the top lawn and the path beside the rose garden leading to a brick bridge where we were able to scramble down to a pool little more than waist deep, and explore beyond it to a wider, deeper pool, home to giant eels, we believed – and, I always felt, to some other presence. A little of my fear returned in this place. We never swam there, even though we could break up through bracken and fern and reach the safety of the bottom lawn.

Sometimes we went through the culvert under the road and came to the main creek but more often chose the other way, over the brick bridge and into the cow paddock. The cow, a Jersey, took no notice of us. There were three or four acres, some flat, some climbing a steep hill to the boundary fence, the rest fenced off for an orchard, where old peach and plum trees, growing more lichen than fruit, dozed and died. The side-creek had its beginning further off, in a patch of sticky ground growing rushes. This territory stays intact, requiring different language from Newington

Road, perhaps because it has less clutter and was not filled with my daily life and the light and shade surrounding the growth of habits and behaviour. Nothing much happened at Peacehaven. We were – I was – simply at ease there. Just once or twice something upset the flow. My grandfather was likely to do that.

One day Mum and I found Grandma trying to decide what to do with a rat caught in a cage-trap Uncle Dick had set. The animal was frantic inside the wire, and threatening too, malevolent. Grandma and Mum were afraid of it. So was I. They took it down to the creek to drown but could not do it, could not drown this live thing. They dithered, they tried to nerve themselves, but in the end Grandma sent Mum for Grandpa. He would decide, it was a man's job. But he too dithered, could not bring himself to put the trap in the water, wanted to, knew – everyone knew – it was the proper thing for a rat. If Uncle Dick had been home there would have been no problem, but Grandpa, I saw, was useless. In the end he put it on me – take the trap into the cow paddock and up the back hill to the fence and let the rat go. I did that, afraid of the creature, which scrabbled in the trap and was wild with fear itself. I held it as far from me as I could, climbed the hill, put the cage down, unlatched the door with a stick and backed away fast, frightened the rat would come for me; but it was out and away in a grey flash. Instead of running into the neighbouring property, as my grandfather had insisted it would, it went back down the hill, straight and true, and vanished into the rushes by the old orchard, heading back, I saw, to where it had come from. I took the trap down to the house and told the adults. My grandfather was cross with me. I was cross with him (although I didn't show it), and, more importantly, disappointed.

I knew his story, with its three key events: his quarrel with his church and 'trial' for heresy (a word I did not understand); his shift with his family to supposedly pacifist America; and, back home again, his imprisonment for seditious utterance (although I didn't learn that name till later). This little man in the grey suit was larger than life, as long as he stayed in his study. I was nervous of him when he came out but liked him well enough, and he was interested and friendly. But I kept a sharp eye on him and inevitably a shrinkage began. His failure with the rat is an example. It seemed to me a lack of courage. Then I learned he could be mean and lacking in 'finer feelings'. Each day he fed backyard sparrows with bread, and one had gained the confidence to eat crumbs from his hand, which delighted him. Along came the Gee boys. They found an old mousetrap in the garden shed, baited it with bread and caught the tame sparrow. Grandma and Mum found us with the dead bird in the trap. Mum refused to cover up for us. She called her father, and I, knowing we'd done something terrible, expected some equally terrible punishment. He took it in his stride. He was sad and angry but not equal to the moment. He was quickly resigned and, casting about for a punishment, told us we'd each have to give him sixpence from our pocket money and save stamps for him for a month. I was outraged. Sixpence and some stamps for the bird he had trained to sit on his hand! My grandfather had disappointed me again. He went back to his study. And our worst punishment was that by killing the bird we became, for a while, small and nasty in Mum's eyes.

I'm not trying to 'get' my grandfather. I liked and admired him and still see him as brave and energetic, adventurous in his mind and full of good feeling. He might retreat to his study and his books, but he was working there, reading in his 'wider bible', writing, preparing lectures, thinking, thinking, thinking, a lot of it right and a lot of it wrong. When he came out he could be warm and funny. He could make people laugh. Mum took me along one night to hear him speak at an election meeting. There was an echoing hall, a small bald man in a grey suit standing on an empty stage. He shouted loudly – but Mum told me later that the proper term was orated. He made the crowd in the packed hall bark with laughter. I don't remember any other speakers. I don't remember the jokes. He kept notebooks full of anecdotes, quotations, funny stories, and sprinkled them through his speeches and lectures. His humour was simple, but with an edge. An example: An old Irish woman, coming back from a pilgrimage to Lourdes, is stopped by a Customs official. 'What have you got in that bottle?' 'Lourdes water.' 'It smells like gin to me.' 'Praise be! I knew a blessed miracle would happen.'

His thought was simple too, and direct, and dogmatic. I have a set of speech notes, headed: Mrs Howson candidate, Zealandia Hall, Balmoral, 6/5/35. This was probably not the speech I heard, as I would have been not quite four. The pages are largely a set of headings and reminders to himself: quotations from Browning, Bacon, Keir Hardie. Points to be made and illustrated: Illus: Mother! I die a murderer. Illus: Incinerated wreaths: Gallipoli. Illus: NZ stamp: Kiwi looking for a Worm. '1917,' my grandfather reminded himself to say, 'God laughed and emancipated Russia. 1935: God laughed and emancipated the WORLD.'

Mum and I met him outside the hall after the speech I heard. We watched people greeting him and patting him on the back. Mum was over-brimming with pride in her father. I was happy too, although I didn't know what it was all about. 'They were laughing,' Mum shouted into his ear trumpet. Almost stone deaf, he would not have heard. It was true; they had laughed and shouted applause. This little man with the big voice, grey-suited, bald-headed, blue-eyed and deaf, was powerful. It matters to me now, it confuses me about him, that while he was right about some things, he was wrong, deluded, about many more. Was he simply blind as well as deaf? Was he dishonest? A note for his 1935 speech reads: 'Russian asylums empty – ours FULL'. He must have known that Russian prisons and labour camps were full. And the thirties were the time of the purges and show trials and summary executions; the time too of Stalin's engineered famines in the Ukraine. Seven million people died while the grain they had grown was held in storage. But my grandfather ended his speech with: 'God is a Communist!' He took my mother along with him in this, and she took her sons. It was a good while before his influence died out.

But yes, I liked and admired him, and was ready to agree he was a hero. The shrinkage did not stop, though. <u>Illus</u>: playing draughts. On our visits to his study, timed by Mum so as not to take too much of his time, he began to quiz me about books. Redskins, I said, I like those. Ah, he replied, *The Last of the Mohicans*. I'd tried to read that book but stopped after three or four pages. Joseph A. Altsheler, I said. My grandfather had never heard the name and I saw I'd disappointed him. But perhaps he spotted something in me, because he invited me to play draughts. When I got the signal I'd go to his study, sit towered over by books and watched by his brass Buddha, and play a game; or, on fine days, we'd sit at a table in the garden and play there. I learned the moves and soon played well enough to give him a contest; he always won, which was okay with me, but bit by bit I was learning ways to beat him. It happened on a sunny afternoon, under the rose-garden plum tree. I worked him to the back, I jumped his king, took the double draughts off the board, rattled them in my hands, grinning at my grandfather and waiting to be praised. His face – perhaps it's time and imagination – darkened and shrank. 'I let you win that one,' he said. I felt as if he'd slapped me, stolen from me. And I knew he was lying. I was smart enough to work out that if he'd let me win it would have been to please me but telling me took my pleasure away. I liked him less from that time on; understand him better today. Beaten by a child – it was a step in aging too big for him to take.

TEN

The other person at Peacehaven was Uncle Dick. He was Mum's younger brother and the second youngest of the Chapple children. His real name, Maurice, was never used, so unlike my brother Aynsley I never had to be Junior. All the same I knew I was named after him and that we were meant to take an interest in each other. He was a quiet man, not often seen, and although usually friendly had an uncertain temper. He chased us with a leather belt for some piece of mischief and we hid behind Grandma's long skirts while she spread her arms and kept him away. During the Depression he had worked on the Chapple property – food from the garden, milk from the cow – or had laboured on relief. His younger brother Aynsley left for America and Dick was left alone with his parents. He was a balding red-haired man who smoked a pipe. He always seemed to be in the distance, up the paddock or at the bottom of the garden, turning away, or else was resting or reading in the shed where he slept.

The bond that was supposed to exist between us became real only once. I must have been seven or eight. Uncle Dick took me to a rugby match. Saturday afternoon: we walked along Millbrook Road and over the creek to Sunnyvale Station, where we caught the train to Kingsland, the station beside Eden Park. It was a big match, Auckland playing Taranaki, and I was excited. I'd only seen rugby (footy, we called it) played at school, where it was mainly the big kids barging and the little kids getting scragged. We found a seat on the terraces and watched two high school teams play a curtain-raiser. Uncle Dick was happy and easy, smoking his pipe.

'Good boy,' he said expertly when someone on the field ran with the ball. I wasn't sure what was happening, but enjoyed the sudden roaring of the crowd and the hollowing into silence as it died away.

The teams for the big match trotted out of the cave under the grandstand – it was breathtaking the way they appeared, big men in hooped jerseys, light-footed on the grass, spreading out and taking positions that must mean something. I don't know who won. I remember only one moment, in the second half, when the forwards heaved at each other in a scrum and the ball came out to the Auckland halfback, who passed, long and hard, to his first five-eighth, and suddenly, from nowhere, someone else appeared, the blond-haired Auckland winger, Jack Dunn, taking the ball before it reached his team-mate and running with no one to touch him, running into a huge space; almost, it seemed to me, running into the sky. I still find it lovely. Jack Dunn ran fifty yards before he was tackled. Then we had to leave to catch our train.

It was getting dark by the time we reached Sunnyvale Station. We walked along Millbrook Road to Peacehaven, Dick smoking another pipe. He stopped me under a row of pine trees black against the sky. 'Listen,' he said. I heard the trees breathing. 'Pine trees are never quiet,' he said.

Mum and Dad were waiting at Peacehaven. I told them about Jack Dunn, and how we'd seen a curtain-raiser between King's College and – I stopped. The name on the scoreboard had puzzled me all afternoon – 'And,' I said, 'Scared Heart.' They laughed and I didn't mind. I was filled with the excitement and pleasure of the afternoon, and Jack Dunn running into a space he had made out of nothing. Uncle Dick had given me 'footy' and I've loved the game ever since.

Dick stayed on at Peacehaven until, in 1940, he married a woman called Christine Jones. My mother tried to conceal her disappointment that a favourite brother had married a girl she found – I heard her say it – coarse. 'Common' must also have been in her mind. Christine seemed all right to me – friendly, cheerful, except when we found her and Dick, in their courting days, lying on a blanket in the orchard. They were getting ready to 'do it', my older brother said, but even this near-encounter with the physical side of love failed to persuade me that 'it' was something grown-ups really did.

Dick and Christine had a child, then Dick was conscripted and went to the war. A second child was born when he came back. Several years later the marriage broke down. Christine set up house with her newly widowed brother-in-law, Phil Reanney, and Dick, in my mother's words, 'went bush'. I met him only once again, in the early 1980s. He was living in a tiny flat in Te Kūiti, where he worked as a council handyman. I had written to him, thanking him for his kindness to me when I was a boy and reminding him of our afternoon at the rugby match. He wrote back inviting me to call. He had some books he wanted to give me. They might be valuable, he said. I did not recognise him when my bus pulled in beside the Te Kūiti railway station; then the shrunken old man with the walking stick and pipe and grey beard turned into Uncle Dick. We did not have much to say to each other as he took me to his flat just down the street. He sat me at the kitchen table and brought out the books. I'd hoped they might be rare and that I could sell them for him, but they were a two-volume Cassell's *History of English Literature* and a couple of similar things. In size and condition they reminded me of my old *Chums Annual*. I thanked Dick and said I'd be happy to take them away, and he was pleased.

'We'd better get some tea,' he said. We went along Te Kūiti's main street to a milkbar, where he bought two meat pies from the warmer. Back at the flat we drank a bottle of beer and ate the pies with tomato sauce. He had a television set and we watched for a while, then talked about Peacehaven and his brothers and sisters and my parents. He smoked his pipe and coughed a lot and spat into an old baked beans tin he kept beside him on a chair. My visit pleased him but I saw he was a loner and that he didn't want too much of it. At nine o'clock he said it was time for bed, and he dragged an old mattress from the washhouse and laid it on the floor by the table. He gave me a sheet and two blankets, and I slept there with lumps of kapok pressing in my back. In the morning a breakfast of Weetbix. We tied the books in a winebox, he came with me to the bus, we shook hands and he stood with his stick raised as I went away. Maurice Chapple, the uncle I was named after. My visit made both of us happy. I never saw him again and he died in 1989.

ELEVEN

My childhood is peopled with uncles and aunts, some in the flesh, others in story. Hollis, the third born, lived in Millbrook Road with his wife Connie and their six children. They were gone from their orchard behind the macrocarpa windbreak shortly after my memories begin. I don't know where they went, but late in his life I met Holl several times. He was living on Waiheke Island with his second wife. They had a bit of land and no pretensions. Holl, always 'artistic', painted the local scenery and enjoyed being looked after by an attentive wife. His first marriage, Mum said, had been unhappy, because Holl was – the choice is between scallywag and womaniser. A story, possibly true: Connie, upstairs at the Henderson pictures, looked over the balcony and saw Holl down in the stalls holding hands with a pretty young woman. Next day she chased him through the orchard with an axe. No, Mum said, anticipating the question, she didn't catch him.

Although taller and stouter, Holl was the Chapple son who most resembled his father in looks. In almost every other way he was different. As a boy he had begged to join the navy (perhaps the merchant navy) and his parents finally gave way. In just a few months he came to hate it and pleaded with his parents to be rescued. James Chapple had to buy him out. His life, as far as I can tell, went on in much that way; but he was a happy old man on Waiheke Island. A Chapple genealogical chart prepared in the 1990s shows that his marriage to Connie had, down the generations, produced almost one hundred descendants. He resembled his father in that way too.

They come and go, uncles and aunts. First-born Dora made

a visit from California. She was the only one of Mum's sisters called Aunt instead of Auntie, perhaps because of Mum's near-reverence for her. Dora combined friendliness with reserve. She had a quick mind and a pleasant voice but a kind of elevation and otherworldliness. One could be affectionate but not familiar. She was, we somehow picked up, rich – or, as it was more politely put, well-off. Her husband, Hurd Comstock, who came with her, was a banker (strange word), and was jolly and plump and comfortable, but the most lasting impression he gave was 'clean'. Dora's two sons, Max and David Hagemeyer, also came. Their father, Dora's first husband, had died in a car crash, a death that seemed American to me. Teenagers, dressed differently from barefoot Gees, they were the most foreign of our visitors. They took little notice of my brothers and me.

Dora was a poet (called Dora Hagemeyer). Mum made sure we knew that. She had been Mum's 'second mother' and Mum had been her favourite. Dora was encouraging her in her own poetry writing, but more important was the love the two women had for each other. You could feel it, feel Mum's happiness.

Dora was a thin woman with an ugly–beautiful face. I felt she was overrated. I felt that the Hagemeyers had dropped down from somewhere, taken a quick look at us and floated away. It was only on a later visit that I found how kind and patient Dora could be. I took her on a walk down the hill from Tirimoana Road and through Newington Road to Millbrook Road to show her the house where her parents had lived. She listened on the way to my gloomy ramblings about, as I remember it, the gap between the fulfilments we imagine for ourselves and what we're almost certainly going to get, all that I had taken from my reading of Camus. She smiled and said very little but somehow made me feel both ashamed of myself and a little better.

The two old people in Millbrook Road drew their sons and daughters like a magnet. By the end of the thirties Mum and Joyce and Geoff were in Henderson, Deorwyn was in Titirangi, Kingsley on the North Shore, and Bernice at Arkles Bay just north of Auckland. Flo and Holl and Dick were not far away. Of the others, Dora, Jean, Mercy and Aynsley were in California, and Len, the oldest boy, was teaching at Wanganui Collegiate. We did not meet Len for many years and never met Jean at all. The only thing I know about her is that she died telling a joke at a bridge party – but perhaps I don't 'know' that, perhaps it's just a story. And I don't 'know' either that she had a daughter who divorced her husband, married him again, divorced again, and married him a third time. It's better not to check, and anyway that cousin was as far away as a film star. Back in the late thirties and early forties the uncles and aunts who mattered most were Joyce and Deorwyn and Geoff. Joyce was a year younger than Mum, and Deorwyn two years older. Geoff came just before Deorwyn, so the four had a shared childhood.

Joyce married a Henderson man, Phil Reanney, in the mid-thirties. They lived by the entrance to Falls Park (to us The Falls), a popular picnic ground and swimming hole, but later shifted to a double unit state house beside Henderson School. It's there I remember them, smoking, drinking Dally plonk, playing cards, bickering good-naturedly, leading a most un-Chapple-like existence; and when Phil went to the war, remember Joyce alone there with her newborn son, Darryl. I liked Phil. Everyone liked Phil. He and Dad got on well. I think of them as a two-man mafia working to subvert the Chapple ethos. Phil was four or five years younger than Dad. He drove a delivery van and helped out in his mother's grocery store opposite the blacksmith shop on the Great North Road. His mother was German and there seemed to be no father about, but Phil was aggressively a New Zealander. He was in the Voluntary Fire Brigade. He played rugby into his thirties and had a broken nose to show for it. One day a dog was run over outside the shop. People stood around, wondering what to do as it whimpered and tried to drag itself away. Phil knew. He went into the shop and came out with a crowbar and killed the dog: 'Someone had to bloody do it.' And speaking of swearing, he was the first man I ever heard use the construction 'abso-bloody-lutely'.

Joyce and Mum bickered and disagreed and laughed a lot and, while up and down and sometimes snarly, were comfortable with each other. As girls they had shared a bed and they still fitted like that. Yet in spite of the laughter and joking that travelled with Joyce she wasn't a happy woman. She was too sharp and quick for contentment; she seemed to have nowhere to be still. When Darryl was born in 1940 she wrapped him about with anxious love. Her rushing off to check on him in his bassinet, to see that he wasn't wet, that no flies were sitting on him, that he was still breathing, became a kind of joke, but a joke that worried Mum. She thought Joyce had gone just a little bit mad.

Of all our uncles and aunts Joyce was the one we saw most frequently and, because she came down to our level, the one we liked best. She was direct and non-smarmy; I never heard 'little Mossie' from her. She seemed to go out of character when Darryl was born, but as he grew older the old Joyce reappeared. Now, though, unhappiness broke through. I was aware of something not right, of something hectic, forced, in her jokiness. My mother said much later that Joyce 'broke down at the change'. Her marriage was 'no good' anymore. All her love was for her son. But she managed to present her old self in patches. I never think of her now without Don Marquis's Mehitabel coming to mind: 'wotthehell toujours gai theres a dance in the old dame yet.'

Uncles and aunts mill around or pop in and disappear again. It becomes random when, in 1940, James and Florence Chapple sell Peacehaven and shift to a house in the suburb of Mt Albert. Peacehaven means Chapple for me and Chapple, to some extent, Peacehaven. I was nine years old when it went out of my life. It was like having a door closed. I still had Newington Road and the creek, but my territories were reduced by one and 'Chapple' as a concept taught in story and breathed in with the air began to shrink. I was getting to know a new friendly uncle, Geoff, who came to Henderson at this time, and know Auntie Deorwyn better, sweet Deorwyn (a sweetness that was natural and never cloying), but they had no connection with that haunted place. A family called Parker bought the property and Mum became friendly with the daughter, Muriel, so I still went there with her now and then – but it was gone, the Chapple Peacehaven, and quickly I grew past the loss of it and moved on. There were other things to think about.

TWELVE

One of them was school, where I was doing well. It hadn't started like that. At the little two-roomed infant school, on a plateau above the main school, I was for a while lost and unhappy. I did not want to go there, I wanted to be at home with my mother. A photo taken before I set off on my first day shows a child facing his future unwillingly. My arms are folded on my chest as though locking something in. Usually I went barefooted, but on that day I'm wearing new sandals with socks turned down at the ankles. My shirt is buttoned to the neck and my jersey looks new. Perhaps Marmee in Christchurch had knitted it for me. In spite of all this my eyes are afraid and my mouth turns down.

There's no narrative of my two years at the infant school. Instead there are vignettes and tableaux. First comes the shift between home and school, which I manage in this way: schoolbag on my back, lunch inside (marmite and lettuce sandwiches, peanut butter sandwiches, jam and honey sandwiches wrapped in greaseproof paper), I set off with Junior along Newington Road. We turn into View Road, cross the creek on the one-way bridge, climb up to Station Road and start along towards Henderson township. A hundred yards along is the jam factory, where a side street meets Station Road, and there, just before a hedge cutting off the view, I can look a quarter mile across the creek and see our house on the high side of Newington Road. My mother is standing on the front porch with a tea towel in her hand. I wave to her. She waves back. I go on and the hedge hides the house. But it's not enough. Has it all vanished, my mother, our house, everything? I run back. She's still there. We wave again, and again I go on. But . . . three times, three waves, before I can run after my brother. Mum knows if she doesn't do it I'll simply turn round and come home. It must have worried her, but for me it meant home and mother were locked in place. I don't know how long it went on – perhaps only a couple of weeks. Junior did not wait and I had to run fast to catch him up by the Methodist church. He didn't want anything to do with his dopey little brother.

My new entrants' class was called the Fairies. We were in with Primers One and Two so I stayed with the same teacher, Mrs Sutton, for more than a year. Bits and pieces: I'm sitting behind a girl with her hair in a pigtail. We're having a little exchange, some sort of game in which I tug her pigtail. I tug too hard. At once she starts to cry, and the feeling I've retained is: treachery. She doesn't want a game now, she wants the teacher. Mrs Sutton hits my hand with a ruler and I'm the one crying and the girl is looking pleased. Strange that out of more than a year there should be only this and two more things.

The Fun Doctor. He turned up once a year in a little Morris Eight, a man who juggled and did conjuring tricks. He had a long nose, blue eyes (pained eyes, I'd say now) and thinning hair, but I don't remember his conjuring tricks or his patter – there must have been patter. He played the piano with his nose. He wore a bow tie, the first I'd seen. If I were putting him in a novel I'd probably use words like seedy and brave. He's a Graham Greene Englishman. And his best trick, the only one I remember: he stacked chairs six or seven high and lifted them up and balanced them on the bridge of his nose. His arms went out to the sides, he swayed backwards and forwards and made little steps to keep the chairs balanced, before lifting them down and smiling with his exhausted face. We clapped and cheered. It was thrilling. The Fun Doctor, Norman Tate, performed at schools around Auckland until 1956. He always wore a Labour Party badge in his lapel.

I was never certain of Mrs Sutton. She was kind one minute and cruel the next. She seemed to like you, then she didn't like you. I see her frizzed-out hair, her thin face, her browny-green dress with big buttons up to the neck as she asks us to take out our handkerchiefs for inspection. Some of us bring bits of rag torn off old shirts or bedsheets. Bits of rag are acceptable in these hard times. But if you don't have a handkerchief or a rag you are dirty.

I've forgotten mine. Mrs Sutton calls me out to the front of the class. She says no one can stay in her room without a handkerchief or they'll give everyone germs. If I've forgotten mine I'll have to go home and get it. She sends me off to walk two miles through the streets of Henderson. I skulk in the school porch, knowing I can't do it. Empty streets, spooky streets – I can't. Then Roy Dally, one of my Primer One friends, comes in. He's late and he's going to get into trouble. I ask him if he's got his handkerchief and he pulls out a bit of rag. I tell him what Mrs Sutton is making me do and he agrees to tear it in half. After he has gone in, I try to work out how long to wait, and decide that counting to a hundred should be long enough. Back I go into Mrs Sutton's room, where she is waiting and the class is waiting. I show her my scrap of rag. She holds it up alongside Roy Dally's scrap. See how they fit? She tells the class I'm not only dirty but a liar, and plays with me a little more, until she has me crying, before sending me back to my seat without even my scrap of rag to wipe my nose on.

Mrs Sutton is kind to me for the rest of the day. I remember nothing else about the year I spent with her. Yet I must have been happy most of the time. There's no overall memory of unhappiness, and I can only conclude that humiliations and punishments lodge in the mind more firmly than happy events. I'll say for Mrs Sutton that she sent me through to Primer Three, Miss Wolfe's class, a good reader.

I've no fond memories of Miss Wolfe either. Our readers were the Milly-Molly-Mandy books: the adventures of a little English girl in a village of thatched cottages and bluebell lanes. The content didn't bother me: when I took any notice of it I found it rather pleasing. What I was really after was getting there first. First to finish each book, ahead of a couple of girls whose names I've forgotten. Miss Wolfe didn't like it, she didn't like me, I could tell from the sour look on her face. That was all right, I didn't like her and was confident enough to feel it evened things up. She was a woman with a twisted mouth and a heavily powdered face. She didn't praise anyone, so it wasn't only me. Yet she must have wanted to be liked, and perhaps was liked, for she stood at the classroom door at the end of the day, stooping at the waist, and pupils who felt like it kissed her cheek as they went out. I joined the kissing queue. She was surprised to see me and drew back a little. Her cheek tasted of powder, which I did not like, and I never kissed her again.

It's easy to have mean guesses about Miss Wolfe, e.g. she washed her kissed cheek in the staffroom when the last child had gone, and put her powder back on. Kind thoughts are harder. The reason is Miss Wolfe's Apple. Each day she put a Red Delicious at the front of her desk. It was meant as a lesson in healthy eating. One morning, at playtime, someone sneaked into the room and bit Miss Wolfe's Apple. In a piece about my schooldays written twenty years ago I asked, Was it me? I also suggested that I had joined the kissing queue because I loved her. That was silly. It was more likely bravado, or it might have been anxiety. But did I bite her apple? I lean towards no.

She held it up for the class to see. There were two uneven scrapes in the perfect skin. 'That,' she said, 'was made by crooked teeth.' Flexing her ruler, she walked up and down the rows: 'Open your mouth.' We obeyed. We curled our lips to show our teeth.

Mine were crooked. She found them, looked hard at my terrified grin; and although she was only halfway round the class it was enough. 'This is the boy who did it.' She held my trembling fingers and smacked my palm with her ruler, hard hits, and I sat crying in my desk. (I hadn't learned yet that boys don't cry.)

I was certain I had not bitten her apple. I remember its rich red colour but have no memory of weight or taste or of sneaking into the room. I knew the overlapping grooves in the apple's skin. I made them every time, first bite. But my strongest memory is of outrage. Mum shared it when I told her. She went along to the school and told Miss Wolfe I hadn't bitten her apple, she could tell whether her son was lying or not, and she told Miss Wolfe she should apologise to me. That didn't happen. Nothing happened. But I got on all right with Miss Wolfe after that. She taught, I listened, and finished Milly-Molly-Mandy first every time.

THIRTEEN

After two years in the primers we went down the hill to a four-roomed building at the edge of an asphalt playground. Here memories lie in a jumble; there's no end to them and no good reason for choosing one ahead of another. I'll quote from the piece about my schooldays: 'Some things were reversed. Miss Hoyle said handkerchiefs were dirty, they trapped the germs and spread them around. A much cleaner way was to use pieces of tissue paper, which could then be burned. She demonstrated, honking melodiously, and dropped her weighted tissues into the stove . . .

'In winter the stove turned red behind its safety bars. Standard Six boys brought kerosene tins of hot cocoa round the rooms and we dipped in our mugs . . .

'In summer we worked in the school gardens, growing vegetables for the War Effort. We saluted the flag, sang God Save the King, and marched into school to martial music on the gramophone. Men came and dug slit trenches in the wattle trees beside the gardens and we had air raid drill once a week. The Japanese were in the war and bombers might come over any day. Teachers left to go into the army and retired men and women took their places. In standard four we had Mr Warren, who told us we were as ignorant as Russian peasants. He strapped us with a little rubber strap that barely tickled. We tried as hard as we could to get the strap . . .'

In Mr Warren's class I sat next to the future jockey, Clyde Markwick. He didn't bounce around in his seat all the time. And I was puzzled by Mr Warren's reference to Russian peasants. Mum told me what peasants were and that Uncle Joe had made them happy and free and they certainly weren't ignorant anymore. So Mr Warren was wrong. It seemed to me too that in speaking with such contempt he was being unpatriotic. The Russians were on our side in the war.

In Standard One I was the king in a play put on at the school fancy-dress party. We stood on a real stage in the Henderson Town Hall. In pyjamas and dressing gown, wearing a cardboard crown, I spoke my one line: 'The king was in his counting house counting out his money.' I counted sixpences and shillings from one side of a desk to the other. The boy who played the blackbird pecking off the maid's nose pecked too hard and made her cry. But everyone seemed to think the play was a success.

In a photo Mum took with her Box Brownie I stand in my pyjamas, with my dressing gown tied crookedly and my cardboard crown towering over an unhappy face. I did not want to be at the fancy-dress party in pyjamas. Why pyjamas? I argued against it, but both the teacher and Mum insisted. Perhaps it's where my occasional nightmares come from, of finding myself in pyjamas or underpants or sometimes naked in public. The other boy in the photo is much happier in his pilot's helmet and flying suit. He's Peter Henderson, who lived a short way along Millbrook Road. Now and then, up a long path, we saw his father moving slowly about the yard, dressed in a homburg hat and a black overcoat. He had been in the first war and wasn't well. Years later someone told me that Peter's father was Dick Henderson, the man in the painting 'Henderson and His Donkey', bringing wounded soldiers down the hill at Gallipoli. I've no idea whether it's true. Peter remained a friend through primary school but I lost touch with him after that. I ran into him in Wellington in the nineties. He was a member of the Mormon Church and lived in Salt Lake City where, he said, he conducted a choir.

Some teachers are connected with painful events while others, often the 'good' ones, leave only a general impression. Johnny Edgar, red-faced, white-haired, bad-tempered and not much more than five feet tall, was my teacher in Standard Five. We had competed to be strapped by Mr Warren but nobody wanted to feel Johnny Edgar's strap, which didn't fold up but was rigid. It had a piece of tin held between strips of leather. He didn't use it often and he never had to strap me.

I was bold in the classroom and had become a bit of a skite. Although he never praised me – never praised anyone – he didn't seem to dislike me either. One morning it was my turn to read aloud to the class. I was going along easily, sure of myself, when I came to a word I'd never seen. I paused and tried to work it out and decided it was a spelling mistake. 'Unique,' I read, pronouncing it 'uni-cue'.

'You-neek,' Johnny Edgar growled. 'Read it again.' I peered at the word and couldn't see it – where was the 'k'? It must be a spelling mistake, so, not knowing what else to do, I read it my way again. 'Unique, boy, unique,' Johnny yelled. But I couldn't, I couldn't get the word out the way he wanted. So, again: 'Uni-cue.' Johnny exploded: 'You're stupid, boy. You're thick in the head. Sit down.' I sank into my desk in a bewildered state, with my fantasy of being best in the class broken to pieces. The next reader read 'unique' in Johnny's way. I brooded all that morning, all that day (and seem to be brooding still). Stupid! Thick in the head! He'd called me that? Whenever I see the word 'unique' I think of Johnny Edgar, and pronounce it 'unicue' in my head. I don't remember that Johnny ever told us what it means.

Our headmaster was Mr Stevenson, a tall thin stooping man with a moustache – rare then unless you were a high-up soldier. We saw very little of him and knew he wasn't well. One morning when we assembled a teacher came out and told us Mr Stevenson had died in the night. We stood in silence as a mark of respect. The unnatural hush in the yard was spooky rather than sad. The teacher told us to go home where we should try to have a quiet day. School would start again tomorrow. Most of us bigger boys didn't go home. We had our togs with us so we went to The Falls and spent the morning swimming. 'Good old Stevo,' we cried, diving off the board.

The new headmaster was Mr Moffat, a big cheerful man as healthy-looking as Mr Stevenson had looked sick. He often came into the playground and walked about talking to pupils. We liked Mr Moffat, even though he'd forbidden us to do handstands on the end of the benches where we ate our lunch. A few of the more agile boys could flip off and land on their feet. One day he came by and caught them at it and told us again how dangerous it was, and said he'd strap any boy who did it again. I was in the group and suddenly his eyes fixed on me. 'What are you grinning at, boy?' 'I wasn't grinning, sir,' I said. 'Don't lie to me, I saw you. Go into my office and wait for me.'

I stood in the little room, deeply afraid. Only a couple of boys had been strapped by Mr Moffat and they said it hurt like hell. After a few minutes he came in. He opened a drawer in his desk, took out his strap and let it roll out to its full length. He asked my name and then what I'd been grinning about. Did I think he wasn't serious? 'No, sir,' I said. 'But I wasn't grinning.' 'I saw you. Don't tell lies.' 'It probably looked like grinning, sir, but I was doing was this', and I clamped my crooked top teeth over my lower lip. Mr Moffat drew back his head. He saw my earnestness and that what I did fitted with what he'd seen. He gave a smile. 'Ah, so that's what it was.' He rolled up his strap and put it away. 'All right, sonny, off you go. Don't go doing any more flips off those seats.'

I got out of there. It was a long strap that unrolled like an anteater's tongue.

Mr Moffat gave me a grin when we passed in the playground after that.

The teacher I remember best from Henderson School is George Broomfield, who took over from Johnny Edgar. He too was a small man, but the resemblance ended there. He kept his temper, never strapped as far as I remember, and taught patiently and with good humour. It's strange that there's little more to say. There's simply a year in my life that connects with Mr Broomfield without the assistance of 'encounters'. The impression remains of a man who liked his job, which he did without showing off or performing. We obeyed him quickly while never feeling under his thumb.

It's a description without features, unenlivened by events. Yet of all my primary school teachers he's the one I liked best. If there was any excitement in his lessons I don't remember it, yet I have the impression that in 1944 my life opened out, my mind opened out, I wasn't concerned anymore just to be clever at school. It might have been that family influences, home life, street life maybe, began to run hand in hand with life at school, and my mother's influence, with my grandfather's behind it, began to fit in with the things I learned in Standard Six – language, bits of history, bits of geography, even arithmetic, all of which can be covered by the term general knowledge. My readiness on the one hand, a good teacher on the other – these produced the most satisfying school year of my life. At the end of it I took home a report with every subject marked 'Excellent'.

It's fortunate we didn't get marked for woodwork. For those lessons we travelled fortnightly from Henderson Station to Avondale, where we walked down to a workshop by the primary school. A fearsome man called Burgess kept order there with spitty-mouthed sarcasm, a bullying voice and the strap. Although I was a carpenter's son I didn't do well for Mr Burgess. I could saw and plane and hammer all right in Dad's workshop, but could get nothing to fit in Burgess's domain.

I hunt for times when I didn't please Mr Broomfield, and find only two. Both are connected with rugby, which he loved. He coached the school team for its matches against New Lynn, Glen Eden, Avondale and the Convent. We always beat the Convent, usually beat Glen Eden, but lost against the bigger schools Avondale and New Lynn. I had learned rugby by running about at lunch time on the field, kicking and catching. We punted and took shots at goal with our bare feet. By Standard Six I was good enough for the school team. I wasn't big but could run fast and duck and dodge and that was enough for Mr Broomfield to choose me as second five-eighth. Our best players were Maurice Thorne, always called Sawney, who knew how to sell a dummy (it came to him naturally), and the Ross brothers, Bill and Jack, sons of a local carrier. Jack later played rugby at top provincial level. Sawney played at first five, and Mr Broomfield decided to teach us the scissors pass. Sawney would run wide but instead of waiting for his pass I would change my angle and cut back inside him, take a flicked pass of no more than two feet, and shoot into clear space against the run of play. Mr Broomfield said I would score without a hand being laid on me. I would, I thought, be like Jack Dunn.

We tried it out against New Lynn. We saw how excited Mr Broomfield was. Late in the game we had a scrum on the New Lynn twenty-five. Mr Broomfield was taking his turn as referee. He gave me and Sawney a little nod. Henderson hooked the ball, Bill Ross sent it out, Sawney ran wide and I went on an angle behind him. The way was open; I saw lovely space in front of me, with the try-line unprotected. Sawney flicked me the ball. We'd done it in practice a dozen times. This time I was watching the line and the ball bounced forward out of my hands. Mr Broomfield, on the edge of a fulfilling moment in his teaching career, had to blow the whistle, say knock-on and give New Lynn a scrum. He frowned at me, a quick frown, full of disappointment. We never tried the scissors pass again; and as late as today I regret not giving him his moment.

In spite of my knock-on he chose me, with Maurice Thorne and the Ross brothers, to represent Western Suburbs in a primary schools competition called the Roller Mills Shield. It was to take place on a Saturday at the Auckland Domain. We usually played in bare feet but Mr Broomfield managed to borrow boots for me, the first pair I'd worn – real sprigs. On Friday afternoon I was working at my desk with my bare foot in the corridor when Lloyd Cossey walked by. Lloyd was the only boy in the class who wore shoes. (None of us wore underpants either; underpants came at secondary school.) Lloyd's heel came down on my foot and tore half my toenail off. It didn't seem a bad injury, but that night at home the toe swelled and in the morning I couldn't get my borrowed football boots on. I could barely walk. There was no chance of playing in the Roller Mills Shield. Mum wouldn't even let me hobble to school, where a bus was picking up Mr Broomfield and the Henderson boys. I should go, I said, to tell them I couldn't play. She forbade it. So I sulked about the house, thinking bad thoughts about Lloyd Cossey, with his clodhopper shoes and his shirts buttoned at the wrists and his sleeveless pullovers. He probably even wore underpants.

On Monday Mr Broomfield wouldn't listen to my excuses. His face went red like Johnny Edgar's. He shouted at me that I'd let the team down. I tried to show him my bandaged toe but he wasn't interested. A sore toe didn't stop you playing football. So my standing with Mr Broomfield dropped, and although it had recovered by the end of the year my memory of him, my liking for him, carry a stain. He should have listened.

I don't remember who won the Roller Mills Shield that year.

My toenail came off and a new hump-backed one grew in its place. It's hump-backed still. I call it Lloyd. But, a rider: at secondary school Lloyd Cossey, despised as a sissy at Henderson School, revealed himself as a friendly and likeable boy and we got on well. I never told him about the trouble with my toe.

One day I got into an argument with a boy called Harry Smith. Egged on by others, we went into a shelter shed to fight. He punched me on the forehead and grazed off some skin. In reply I hit him on the nose and blood poured out. Several bigger boys took him off to be doctored by the teachers. Going into our classroom (Standard Three) at the end of the lunch hour, I saw him lying on a bench with a wad of bloodstained cotton wool pressed to his nose. We winked at each other. He had not told the teachers how he'd got his blood nose. After that we were friends. Choosing your deskmate wasn't allowed, but outside the classroom we teamed up and spent all our time together. We even walked about arm in arm until a teacher told us only girls did that.

I infected Harry with my puritanism. When we heard kids swearing we told them they shouldn't. 'Dirty' words, like the one I was to hear Clyde Markwick use, made us especially solemn and reproachful. But our little purity squad didn't last long. Perhaps we saw it was absurd. One day I heard a boy call my brother Gus a bastard. I told him – very solemn – that it wasn't true, my parents were married, and as well as that if Gus was a bastard I was too because I was older. The boy looked at me as though I was mad – a fair judgement.

My friendship with Harry lasted through our primary school years. I went to his place after school – that little house in Henry Street, with Pat Phillips over the swing-bridge – and in the weekends he came to mine. Roy Dally, who had shared his bit of rag with me in Primer One, joined us and we became a trio. Harry and Roy were almost as close to me as my brothers, yet at secondary school we grew apart. They took technical courses and we all made new friends. Harry still came round to visit me and we played tennis together at the Holy Cross courts, but the time of linked arms was over. He left school at the end of his Fifth Form year to become apprenticed to an engraver. He grew into a big man, over six feet tall. I heard that he had become a Catholic. We exchanged letters late in his life, when he was dying of cancer. He told me he had made his peace with God. As for Roy, all I know is that his father was killed when his car was hit by a runaway horse-float. Someone told me he (Roy) played the guitar in a dance band. And his widow wrote to me after his death saying that Roy always remembered sharing his bit of rag with me.

FOURTEEN

I was driving my Dinky Toy truck on a dusty road round a hydrangea bush when Mum came out and told me a man called Hitler had sent his armies into Poland, which was a country he didn't own. Mum was upset. She said there was going to be a war. The next day there was. We heard it on the radio. But for a long while it seemed far away, even though New Zealand soldiers went overseas. Dad's younger sister, Kay, passed through Auckland on her way to England as an army nurse. Mum told us what she was doing was dangerous and brave. Kay stayed several days, looking more like a soldier than a nurse in her khaki uniform. As a goodbye present she took her three nephews to the pictures in Auckland but would not let us choose what to see. We wanted Abbott and Costello (an American comic duo, a kind of poor-man's Laurel and Hardy) but she said no, she would take us to something we would remember. So she herded us, a little sour – wasn't it supposed to be our treat? – into *Goodbye, Mr Chips*, which I enjoyed. Then Kay went off to the war.

Two of our uncles went, and we heard that a cousin, Holl's son Max, a fighter pilot, had been shot down and killed, although that was late in the war. All this was real enough, but present every day was Mum's anxiety and sadness. It increased, it overflowed and made her ill when Japanese planes bombed Pearl Harbor and the war started coming towards us down the Pacific. There were air-raid drills and filing into slit trenches at school, and blackouts and ration books. We went out with empty jam jars and collected ergot from the seedheads of roadside grass – it would be used, we were told, to make medicine for soldiers. The war had come close. We played at it, running round the playground, arms outstretched, making aeroplane noises, before changing to machine-gun fire as we strafed the girls sitting on the seats.

At about this time I persuaded my parents to let me join the Boy Scouts. Dad didn't mind but Mum saw the organisation as a training ground for the army and she tried hard to talk me out of it. But I had friends joining, it sounded like fun and I wouldn't give way. So, dressed in my hat and scarf and khaki shirt (which must have strained the family budget to buy), I went off to become a Tenderfoot. My troop was called Kotare, which I learned meant kingfisher. Very soon I found that the fun was overrated. I didn't enjoy the forming up and parading and the singing of God Save the King (felt I was betraying Mum). There was too much talking at us; it was a bit like school. The games were the best part – the Wide Game and Bullrush and British Bulldog. I lasted about a year and at the end of that time was looking for a way to get out.

One night in our meeting hall at the Methodist church when it was too wet for the Wide Game our scoutmaster told us to come out one by one and pretend to be anything we liked, a sportsman, an actor, a workman, anything, and the rest of us would try to guess. It turned out to be easy guessing. When my turn came I shadow boxed, straight left, right cross. Easy. The game ended with a troop leader, Des Hallas, who must have been about sixteen. He came out front and said, 'Now you've all got to tell what I'm doing.' He squatted in front of us, placed his hands palm up on his knees, and began to strain and groan. Plainly he was someone trying to shit. Some of us tittered, some laughed, and a boy called out, 'You're doing a poo.' 'Yeah, yeah,' came the calls, 'you're doing a poo.' Des Hallas stood up and dusted his hands. 'You've all got dirty minds,' he said. 'I was a man lifting a heavy log.' There were jeers and catcalls, but it had been a success. Even the scoutmaster laughed. But me? I was shocked. Our oath was a lie. Every meeting we said it, with right hand raised in the three-fingered salute: 'A Scout is clean in word, thought and deed.'

I didn't go back to the Scouts. I told Mum I was tired of it and she sold my hat. She did not sell my sheath knife though, I hung on to that. There must have been someone in my reading who threw a knife. I practised on the back lawn, throwing at the trunk of a pine tree in the hedge. The knife flipped over once (I couldn't make twice work) and stuck in the tree with a satisfying thud. The next step was to tack up a drawing – slit eyes, buck teeth, glasses. This was either Tojo the Japanese war leader or the Emperor Hirohito: 'Die, yellow dog.' I also shared a BB gun with my brothers. BBs were hard to get, so we didn't shoot at just anything. I drew Tojo on the side of a cardboard box and shot him there, collecting the BBs from inside the box when I ran out.

There was no stopping my belligerence and bloodthirstiness. Yet inside I remained an earnest twelve-year-old, eager to be good, eager to help, ready to believe whatever Mum told me, and confused about many things. I knew she was unhappy and I wanted to help, but the war was too strong, the war dragged me – dragged us, my brothers too – away from her lessons and her need, and turned us into wild things and made us nasty.

Junior started secondary school. He caught the train each day and travelled to Mt Albert Grammar. Someone there showed him how to make Japanese fingers and we made one at home. You got a flat tobacco tin and punched a hole in the bottom big enough to fit your finger through. You yellowed your forefinger with iodine and added streaks of red ink for blood, then poked it up into the tin and rested it on its side on a bed of rags or cotton wool. You had to hold your hand still and open the lid carefully with your free hand. 'Look, Mrs Lisk, it's a Japanese finger our cousin sent back for a souvenir from the war.' 'Look, Mrs Scott . . .' Some of them believed it. Some of them laughed. We showed it to Mum: 'Look, Mum, a boy at school's uncle sent it back from the war.' Horror, I think, and then despair. She did not know where we had gone. She made us throw the tin away and made Junior scrub his finger clean; she told us what we had done was horrible and cruel, and this lesson worked for me because I saw the pain behind it. I became ashamed of the Japanese finger, and six or seven years later, trying to write a novel, I described a group of boys showing one to people in a street like Newington Road. Along came Mr Graham, a grave young pacifist in a dark suit. The boys showed him the finger and Mr Graham repeated Mum's lesson, and the boy who was me – I forget his name – slunk away ashamed.

The novel did not get past chapter two.

FIFTEEN

When our grandmother, Marmee, died in 1939, Dad's father came up from Christchurch and lived with us for a year while he looked for a house to buy. Mum taught us to call him Pater, which he seemed to like.

I'm fonder of Pater now than I was then. He was a spirited old man, opinionated, dogmatic and impossible to hold in check. He scorned anything 'arty', and although he seemed fond of Mum thought her beliefs and behaviour were a joke. He must have scratched his head over how his son had found her. His year with us produces few memories – mainly his dog Kep, his tools in Dad's workshop, his snoring from his bed in the boxed-in front porch, and his eagerness to give us hidings which, he said, would be good for us. In that, against Mum, he never had a chance. She hid us behind her. No one was touching her boys. In all his stay with us he never managed a single hit.

Perhaps it was Boxing Day, perhaps New Year's Day when we drove to Titirangi beach for a picnic lunch. Dad parked by the stream and we crossed the bridge and laid out our food in the shade of trees. It was a simple spread – sandwiches, cold meat, tomatoes, Christmas cake. Then we saw the Greenhoughs arranging their picnic next to us. It was too late to move. Awkwardly, our two picnics joined; and Mum was mortified to see how far Mrs Greenhough's spread outshone hers. Ham and mustard sandwiches, cupcakes with hundreds and thousands, a plate of mince pies with crimped edges, jellies in little bowls, with whipped cream to go on them, a jar of preserved peaches, soft drink and a big thermos flask of tea. (Mum was going to boil a billy.) The Greenhoughs had proper plates and forks and spoons and serviettes in serviette rings. But things quickly grew easy. Stan Greenhough was talkative and Pater full of opinions which, when he was relaxed, had an edge of humour. He was at his best that day. He pushed his big-nosed face across the food, grinned with his big teeth, and jabbed his finger to make his point. I've no memory of the conversation – it might have been about building bridges, training dogs, politics, the war. Pater might have been telling Stan Greenhough, a railway signalman, how railway signals worked. Dad chipped in now and then. He had opinions too. The women kept quiet, they watched the food. So did I, fascinated by what was happening: every time Pater paused to let Stan or Dad have a say, his hand went out to Mrs Greenhough's plate of mince pies, took the nearest one and transferred it to his mouth. They were two-bite pies but he made them one – into his mouth, several chews, a swallow, and he leaned forward to butt into the talk again. He cleaned out more than half the plate, while Mum made little dabs and darts to stop him. Mrs Greenhough watched with a reddening face and tightening mouth as Pater's hand went out – he didn't even look – and another one of the pies she had crimped and baked and arranged on a flower-edged plate disappeared into his mouth.

We ran away, the three Gee boys and Gordon Greenhough, and explored the bush until our food had 'gone down properly' and it was safe to swim. I don't know who got the last mince pies.

SIXTEEN

Religious lessons played little part in my life. Jesus was the Good Man, man as he was meant to become; God was someone who watched over everything – and God, Mum felt, must be in pain at the way humans were behaving. We must try to please him and be kind to each other. The nearest we got to doctrine was: treat each other the way you'd like others to treat you. That, and once or twice: God wants you to be clean and pure, your body is a kind of temple where he lives. There was nothing heavy or insistent.

I came in contact with doctrinal teaching by accident. A local man, Cyril Griffin, started a gym class for boys in the Masonic Hall. He had tumbling mats, a springboard and a vaulting horse, and a dozen of us, mainly Standard Six boys, learned how to do forward rolls and handsprings and somersaults. Cyril was a friendly man, but no gymnast himself. He must have got his knowledge from a book. He was careful not to let us hurt ourselves, no easy job. A few of the boys were natural athletes and learned to do exaggerated dives from the springboard, and one or two could dive to the end of the horse and do a high flip on to the mat. Cyril jumped and twitched with anxiety. He was keen to get the gym part of the night over and sit us on the mats for the lessons he really wanted us for. I don't know which church he belonged to. His teaching was Bible based and fundamental: God had made us in His image, Adam and Eve had sinned and were expelled from the Garden of Eden and we were sinners ourselves, all of us. But God had sent His Only Son . . . That, as I remember, was it. Cyril kept it up for ten minutes, in the face of our fidgeting and whispering. We paid his price for the springboard and the vaulting horse and then got back to them for another session.

Cyril asked us to perform at a concert for the War Effort. We agreed to that. We thought we were pretty good. Then he told us we would start by singing God Save the King. No, no, not for anything, we said. None of us was any good at that, we couldn't sing. Cyril refused to listen, and on the night we lined up in our singlets, unrehearsed and mutinous. A lady struck up on the piano. Cyril bellowed out the words to the packed Town Hall, and one or two thin whispers, 'God save our gracious . . .' followed him and died away. Embarrassed, I moved my mouth for a little bit, then gave it up. The audience must have been embarrassed too. Cyril seemed not to notice. And we redeemed ourselves with our display. Handsprings, somersaults. The more athletic boys did flips off the horse and running dives off the springboard over a kneeling pyramid four high. We got cheers as well as clapping and Cyril went red with pleasure. Then a young tenor with a burning eye sang a bracket of songs about England and her Empire, which made Mum cross. She could not win. Even through her sons she could not win. I hoped she'd noticed that I did not sing God Save the King.

In the new year Cyril took a new class as we Standard Sixers went on to secondary school. The tumbling had done me good. I had been skinny but I put on weight and grew muscles on my bony legs. I could do handsprings and forward somersaults and kept it up on the lawn at home. Once, in my thirties, remembering that time, I tried to somersault again, on a sloping lawn for extra height, but jarred my spine so badly I had to lie down for several days.

Cyril must have jarred himself against his unwilling listeners, but he was a true evangelist and he kept on trying.

SEVENTEEN

I wanted to tell a story but fall into anecdote. I had hoped for an even flow and that finding day-to-day memories would let me present myself as a person, but happenings disturb the flow and turn the child I was into a caricature. They seem less to define than distort. Yet I can't get on without them. If I write about my older brother, will he be a caricature too?

The timeline is jagged and turns back on itself. He's my first memory, hugging his parcel from Marmee as he comes back from the letterbox. And now he's seventeen and revving up his motorbike – an Indian, I say, but he says no and at eighty-two can't remember the make. I climb on the pillion seat and we ride to Henderson Valley Road, where he tells me to hang on tight and opens up the throttle. We speed (helmetless) along the gravel road, leaning left and right, and exhilaration takes me. I trust Junior and want to go as fast as he can make the bike go. The wind whips the moisture out of my eyes and wants to rip my cheeks off and hair out. Then the bends grow sharper and he has to slow down. He makes an easy turn and we putter back. 'Now you've been a hundred miles an hour,' he says.

I don't see much of him at school, he's two years ahead and runs with the big boys, with Minnie Oldfield and Rex Banks and Joe Corban and Lew Wright. His nickname is a simple Geegee, and sometimes Horse, and for a while Creeping Jesus because of Gee, although there's nothing creepy about him. He's the most open-natured person I've known and the plainest in his feelings.

After school and in the weekends he's usually in Dad's workshop making something. In one of her pieces of writing Mum tells how he came home from school with a cinder in his eye, and when she'd got it out he fixed her squeaky wringer and spent the rest of the morning in the workshop making her a toast rack.

I'm all over the place in my memories of Junior. He worked with his tongue poking out, a sign of concentration. It poked out as he sat at the kitchen table doing his homework. It poked out as he squatted by the hind he'd shot in the Urewera bush, trying to cut out her back-steaks – but she's old and too tough. I had borrowed a rifle that wouldn't shoot straight. Dad loaned us the work truck and we drove down, slept on the tray, hunted for a day and drove back in the night. The hind wasn't our only kill. Alone in a gully I came across a fawn and shot it, and was sick with remorse, and a kind of horror, at killing the beautiful thing. I followed Junior quietly after that, and admired the way he saw the hind up a hill through trees and brought her tumbling down to his feet with a single shot.

He left Gus and me behind. His front-porch bedroom was a little home – posters on the walls: motorbikes and movie stars, actors at first and then actresses. Joan Leslie was the poster above his bed. He thought she was the prettiest girl in the world.

He knew about girls long before I did. A boy called Anderson from up View Road said his sister would take down her pants and show us her cunt for sixpence. Gus and I followed half a dozen older boys to where the girl was waiting in a shelter shed beneath the convent school. Ernie was the oldest – he was there. Junior was there. The Anderson boy is about twelve. His sister is nine or ten. She's stick-thin and bony and barefooted and I'm going to dress her in a washed-out hand-me-down dress and say Depression child, one of those half-starved children you see in Okie photographs, although the slump is over now and it's almost time for the war. She's unconcerned, patient, standing at the back of the shed. Gus and I don't have sixpence and anyway the Anderson boy says, 'You're too young.' 'Yeah,' say the big boys, 'you're too young.' They push us outside. But whatever this thing she's going to show them is, we're determined to see it. We go into the neighbouring shelter shed. The wall between the two doesn't go all the way to the ceiling and the framing is exposed on our side. We clamber up and peer through the gap and see the boys half-circled in front of the girl, looking down. She's looking down too, holding her dress up with one hand and pulling down her pants with the other, but we can't see, the boys' heads are in the way. No use stretching our necks. Whatever she's showing them and they're looking at is out of sight. She doesn't give them more than a couple of seconds anyway. With both hands up, making a single fist, she pushes through them and runs out of the shed. Her brother follows, and Gus and I, quick as cats, climb down the wall and get out of there. What did she show them? What have we missed? I can't remember that we talked about it – and Junior, moving ahead in his untroubled way, got on with his next thing . . .

Which was making rope swings and, soon after that, making bombs. He must have learned from friends at Mt Albert Grammar. He was a train boy, travelling each day from Henderson Station to Mt Albert and bringing back stories that made me envious. I couldn't wait to get to Mt Albert, where the teachers had nicknames like Itchy and Slimy and Snarler and Froggy and Butch. Junior was having fun on the train – fights up and down the carriages against Seddon Tech boys, firing acorns from forts built of squabs taken from the seats. Mum wanted him to do well at Grammar (she liked that name) and win some academic distinction, but Junior wasn't going in that direction. He made friends she didn't like. McKee and Cartwright were 'roughnecks'; they were getting him into trouble.

I don't know who he got his bomb recipe from or where he found the ingredients. As far as I remember they were potassium chlorate, sulphur and charcoal. Maybe saltpetre was in there too. I watched him mix them several times. How close did he come to blowing off his fingers? He and his mates blew up several letterboxes. And Mum records in one of her notebooks that instead of digging a root of potatoes, as she'd asked, he put explosives under it and blew it out of the ground. She heard the bang and ran into the garden, where she found him sitting by the hole with a dazed look on his face. She and Dad outlawed bombs. But Junior made one more. He packed his mixture into a length of iron pipe and puttied in his last piece of fuse. We both had bikes, mine an old balloon-tyred wreck Dad had bought second hand, and we and a couple of his friends rode along Lincoln Road to the bridge beside the radio masts. The tide was out in Don Buck's Creek. We climbed through the mangrove jungle on to the mud bank and scooped a hole in the mud two feet deep. Junior stood his bomb in the bottom and we filled the hole, leaving an inch of fuse poking out. We stood back a dozen yards while he lit it. The sound was more a whump than a bang. Mud flew everywhere and bits of iron must have gone everywhere too. The hole was deep enough to stand in up to our waists, and wide enough to hold a sack of coal. We got back to our bikes in a hurry, knowing the sound must have carried to the houses by the road and maybe to the buildings by the radio masts. Junior was satisfied. He had made a big bomb and had no need to make another.

Although he was two years ahead and at a different school and separate from me in interests and by temperament, he was Junior, my brother and, by virtue of it, in a casual, taken-for-granted way, closer to me, understood more easily, trusted more, and loved more than my friends; as Gus was too, coming behind. I spent more time with Gus, doing whatever came next, but was with Junior for 'times' that disturb the flow of childhood.

We rode off together on our bicycles (before his motorbike days), once to a farm up Sturges Road to help the farmer, Bill Cameron, a friend of Mum and Dad's, turn his hay. I was a bit young for it and found tossing swathes of heavy grass with a pitchfork almost too hard and Junior got ahead of me up the rows. We put in a dusty, sweaty afternoon, and at the end Bill Cameron, dour and Scottish, handed us a florin each. I took mine and, taught to be polite, said, 'Gosh, thanks, we didn't expect that much,' which was true. 'Didn't you?' Bill Cameron said. 'Wait on then.' He took the florins back, felt in his pocket, found some shilling coins and gave us one each. Junior waited for Sturges Road before rounding on me. 'You silly bugger, what did you say that for?' I'd been waiting for it and accepted it meekly. Silly bugger I was. But Junior was too amiable to keep on for long. He swore about Bill Cameron instead – the mean bastard. Mum and Dad agreed with him (without the bastard) when we got home, although Bill's canniness made them laugh too.

Another ride we made was to the Waikumete reserve, a pine forest on land where the cemetery would grow. We hid our bikes in the trees on the north side and headed in as though into a jungle. The silence was unbroken; it seemed part of the darkness. (So Uncle Dick was wrong when he said pines were never silent.) The needles were beautifully smooth under our bare soles. 'This is the place to come if you want to find frenchies,' Junior said. We didn't find any of those. The light increased and we found the cemetery, acres of slabs and headstones, and once a family mausoleum built like a temple. We wandered along – fresh flowers, dead flowers in vases, angels, fingers pointing skywards, broken arrows, broken columns; and names, thousands of names, thousands of dead people, and children dead, younger than us – how we enjoyed walking in the cemetery. We circled round and went back into the jungle, came across no lovers there, but rode home happy with what we'd found instead.

Junior didn't stop at toast racks and swings. From somewhere he got the idea of canoes. I decided to make one too. Dad let us have two sheets of corrugated iron, holed by nails but not yet eaten by rust. We laid them on the lawn and hammered out the corrugations, which took a long time. The noise was too much for Mum in the kitchen and she made us carry them up to the back of the garden. The flattening was imperfect but good enough. Then, another hard job, we folded the sheets lengthways and nailed in bow and stern posts. Opening the tin envelopes into canoe shapes was tricky. We managed it by using struts to keep the sides apart, nailing one in front of where the paddler would sit and one behind. Junior got pitch from somewhere – nothing could stop him – and we melted it in an old pot and stopped up the nail holes and the gaps around the bow and stern posts. A drop of pitch fell on his foot, and he shrieked and ran limping to the tap on the tank stand and doused the burn. It was, he said, the worst pain he'd ever felt. But we had two canoes. Dad looked them over and approved. We sawed paddles from match-lining, sandpapered the handles, and next Saturday, wearing our canoes like ten-foot hats, went along Newington Road, down through the draught-horse paddock, past the gully where our swings had been and launched them on our private pool. They floated, they were balanced, they worked. We paddled them round the pool for the rest of the afternoon.

Sunday, Junior said, 'Let's take them down the Falls.' He wanted to show off the canoes to the kids down there. We started after lunch and promised to be home in time for tea, but we hadn't allowed for sore behinds when we sat in our canoes or sore knees when we knelt, or the need to go slow so we wouldn't swamp (Junior's freeboard was several inches less than mine) or the flange that broke on his paddle, reducing its efficiency by half. After a while we stopped thinking about how we were going to get back;

we let time slide away and settled into the adventure and the afternoon became one of the great journeys of my life, fixing 'creek' as a place in my mind.

The half-mile below our pool took half the afternoon. The banks were overgrown with blackberry and scrub. Taller trees stood at the top. In places they leaned over and hid the sky. The water had the colour between green and black that means deep and sheer-sided in those freshwater creeks. A brownish trickle ran in from the swamp at the end of Newington Road. There were tracks along the clay banks and I recognised them as places I'd explored with Harry Smith, which meant that beyond the trees paddocks stretched away to Catherine Street. That seemed strange – a street with a town beyond it, while down here we were locked in, with the only sound the swish of our paddles and their tinny clank on the sides of our canoes.

The long stretch darkened ahead. Something white lay wedged under the bank. It took some time to recognise the body of a pig, swollen out of shape. Black eels hung like pennants from its underside. Junior poked the carcass with his paddle. The eels waved but kept their hold. We got out of there, not liking it, and soon, from the other bank, among the fresher green, an old crinkled face looked down at us. It was, we decided, one of the Dallies from the vineyard running down to the creek at the back of our school football field. We paddled on, got soaked hauling the canoes over a tree trunk rotting in the creek, and went under the swing-bridge joining the end of Henry Street to Pat Phillips' property. It was easier after that and we knew what was hidden by the banks and trees: the wattle grove with its slit trenches, the school gardens, the bottom school and the bowling club. On the other side were the yards behind the Waitemata Electric Power Board building. We went under the Great North Road bridge, which was coated underneath with moss. No cars, no faces looking down. We wanted to be seen, because of the distance we'd come and because of our daring.

The banks were lower for the last stretch. Willow trees leaned over, and back lawns and vegetable gardens ran down from lean-to washhouses and wood sheds. Round the corner, past the empty picnic ground, and into the last freshwater pool of Henderson Creek. The tide was halfway out in the pool below the rockslide that gave Falls Park its name. We wanted to float out there, waving our paddles at the kids by the diving board, but they saw us and came running, and some swimming, as we slid the canoes down the weeds coating the rocks. They were yelling for rides. We paddled out on the brown salt water, clear of the swimmers. We did not want to share our canoes and we saw that if the bigger boys grabbed them they would sink, so we paddled for the narrow mouth on the other side of the pool, into it and away, down the curving stretch to Tui Glen. The left bank was thick with trees but on the right, through skinny mānuka trunks, we saw the kiosk and the swings and the pirate ship rocking on its axle, then the diving board and the canoes for hire – real canoes – drawn up on the launching ramp.

We paddled on. We didn't know where and, as for getting back, although we didn't say it we knew there was no chance. The thing now was to get as far as we could. The tide was running out, the river, as it had become, ran fast and helped us on. Banks of mud showed between the water and the mangrove forest running to the shore. Another creek came in from the left, unknown and somehow threatening, so we made no pause. The mud banks broadened, the afternoon was running out like the tide and we weren't sure where we were. A stretch of water, shining white, lay ahead. It widened out into the upper harbour. Several launches floated there, pulling against their anchors. We ran our canoes on to the mud bank and climbed out. Our journey was over and although we tugged at the bow posts, hauling towards land, the canoes did not want to come. We sank in mud up to our knees and it was Junior who said, 'We'll have to leave them.' Both of us were willing. It was over. We left the paddles in the canoes and ploughed shin-deep in mud to the bottom of a dirt road coming down through paddocks. The canoes would float away when the tide came in. I don't recall that we looked back – none of the looking back I'm doing now. We trotted home like distance runners, up the dirt road to Lincoln Road, along past the house where our grandfather and grandmother, back from Mt Albert, now lived, down through Henderson, along to View Road and over the bridge, almost completing the circle to the pool we had started from, and along Newington Road to home, where Mum and Dad were getting ready to head out searching for us. They told us off but in a way were pleased with our adventure.

We did not talk about it again, Junior and I, we let it go and kept it, but I wondered about our two empty canoes, where they went on the tide and where they ended up.

The Falls hadn't finished with me yet. A local doctor said he would never let his children swim there, it was full of filth from drains and farms and fowl yards and dunnies. The little creek flowing in beside the boys' changing shed had a nasty smell. It came from a pig farm up there, one of our teachers said. No one took any notice. Henderson School pupils took their swimming lessons at the Falls. I swam ten times between the diving board and the rocks, dog-paddling some of the way, and was rewarded with my 220 yards certificate. Organised picnics took place on the flat land back from the changing sheds. There were running races, egg and spoon races, lolly scrambles. We felt through the green weed coating the rockslide and caught the baby eels hiding there. And at certain seasons schools of sprats swam upriver and thrashed about in the pool. We jagged them with tripartite hooks on the end of whippy bamboo poles. There was nothing we could do with them; they flapped about our feet as we sent our long lines whizzing out for more.

It was safe to use the diving board when the tide was in. At low tide we jumped off, although some of the older boys did flat belly-busters. I tried it once and came up with scratches on my stomach. We learned the dangers. None of us died.

I was at the Falls one afternoon with Junior and his friend Minnie Oldfield. We sat on the high bank above the rocks watching two men and two girls who had arrived in a car. They walked down to the grassy flat beside the board and spread out a blanket. The men changed into swimming togs in the boys' shed and the girls came past us to the girls'. They walked back in their bathing suits – pretty girls, we thought. They had permed hair. On the blanket the men opened bottles of beer and the girls drank too. Minnie and Junior reckoned they would soon start 'doing it'. We lay in the long grass and watched for a while and it didn't happen. Instead one of the men walked out on the board and started bouncing. He went higher and higher. We knew he wouldn't dive. The tide was out at the Falls. 'Skite,' Junior said.

The man dived in. It was an attempt at a jack-knife. 'Jesus,' Minnie said. We stood up from the grass. The man's back appeared, a white hump in the brown water. His head was sunk as though he was looking for something on the bottom. Junior and Minnie ran yelling down the slope, with me behind. The girls and the second man hadn't realised anything was wrong. 'No water. No water,' Junior and Minnie yelled. They plunged in up to their waists and pulled the injured diver to the steps, where his friends hauled him up the bank on to the blanket. He was worse than injured, he was dying, it was plain even to me.

The man friend and one of the girls ran to their car, with Minnie and Junior following to show them where to go. Constable

Wakelin lived nearby on the Great North Road. The injured man lay on the blanket, his eyes staring at the sky, but he saw nothing. A gash on top of his head leaked blood into his hair. I saw a lump on the back of his neck that would have filled my hand. His girl knelt beside him, making little noises more like grizzling than crying. Tears smeared her cheeks. Her hands were clasped in her lap and she rocked backwards and forwards. Falls Park was empty. Just the dying man, the girl and me. I was afraid. I wanted to get away but when I moved she turned her wet face. 'Don't go,' she whimpered. Then she resumed her rocking and crying.

Constable Wakelin's car appeared up by the swings. He came down long-striding, with the dying man's friend running in front and the girl behind. Junior and Minnie did not come back. I got out of Falls Park. I ran up the hill past the school and cut through the farm to Newington Road. Junior was home ahead of me. He had told Mum and Dad and I could only add that the police had come. Our parents must have looked for damage to Junior and me, but he felt none as far as I know, and I felt none; I had only a kind of disbelief, and a feeling close to importance, and in my mind, over the years, it became: I saw a man die.

He did not die on the blanket, as my memory insists, he died in hospital next day. He was a barman in an Auckland hotel, where the girls also worked. I found this out only recently, from a report in the *Herald* at that time. It also says police pulled the man from the water. That's not the way I remember it. When I met Minnie Oldfield again at Junior's seventieth birthday party I asked him if he remembered the man diving into shallow water at the Falls. 'You bet,' he said. 'I pulled him out.' Like me he felt no guilt at not shouting a warning. When Constable Wakelin interviewed us the day after the accident we told him that none of us had thought the man was going to dive in. Everyone knew it was low tide at the Falls.

A short while later, the Henderson Borough Council put up a post with markings showing the depth of the water by the board.

When I throw a stone into my past as often as not it splashes into Henderson Creek, which for me includes the salt pool at the Falls. So one last time. We've come out from a swim and dried ourselves and dressed in the boys' shed. Girls have been swimming too but they've gone home. Who do I mean by us? Not a single name or face comes forward out of the group – so, Henderson boys, half a dozen. I'm the only one with a name; and there's one other, hanging around. He's Fatty Walker, the butcher's son, and he hasn't been swimming. We've never seen Fatty in bathing togs. Someone says, 'Fatty was looking through a hole round the back of the girls' shed.'

We'd all thought of doing that but none of us had dared. Fatty saw us coming. He ran but we caught him by the park entrance. He started blubbing and denying but we circled him, unified in cruelty and envy and frustration. 'We saw you. You were looking. Dirty bugger.' We pushed him back and forth, he went one way and the other like a weighted doll, and we punched him between pushes, not on the face but the upper arm, where we had learned to hurt without leaving marks. (Minnie Oldfield had done it to me, all through one playtime, until my arm hung useless at my side.) Fatty cried and blundered about but found no way of escape. He was teary, snotty, abject, but we weren't going to let him go. We moved him out the gate to Edmonton Road, and might have kept going all the way to the Great North Road if a truck hadn't come round the corner and pulled up. The driver was Snow Pennell, a local carrier. He yelled out the window, 'Leave him alone.' We gaped at Snow Pennell. 'He was looking in the girls' changing shed.' 'I don't care what he was doing, leave him alone.' Fatty pushed out of our circle and ran. 'He was looking –' 'How many of you, eh? Pack of little buggers.' We were surly and disunited and directionless. Snow Pennell drove away and we went off to our homes.

When I think of that pack of boys circling the terrified fat boy I think of hyenas snapping and biting round a wounded animal. We had that nastiness. Snow Pennell had seen it. Some years later he coached a rugby team I played in. I liked Snow but was never comfortable with him, thinking he might recognise me as one of them.

EIGHTEEN

Until his mid-teens my younger brother Gus was shorter than me and looked much younger, but I could never play the big brother with him. He more than made up for his lack of size with a vigorous personality. No one was going to dominate Gus. He had hard fists and a quick temper but was also quick in his mind; he seemed to see the possibilities for fun in everything, and grabbed the opportunity quicker than I was able to. Mum tells how she found a rotten tomato in the scullery and gave it to Gus to throw in the compost bin. A moment later she heard him cry, 'Catch', then my howl of rage, and ran outside to find me with my hands smeared in 'tomato sauce' and Gus laughing from a safe distance. At times I would try to get back at him with what Mum called 'tormenting', usually about his lack of size. One day he became so enraged that he chased me with a screwdriver and threw it as I kept ahead of him. It hit me behind the knee and stuck in, and hung wobbling as I tried to keep running. We were both so appalled that we pulled it out and kept quiet, hiding the wound from Mum.

But most of the time we got on well. When we all went off, shilling in hand, to the Saturday night pictures in the Henderson Town Hall, Junior would peel off to find his mates but Gus and I stuck together, even when I teamed up with Harry Smith. We sat together downstairs through the newsreels, *The March of Time*, the shorts, usually comedies – Leon Errol, The Three Stooges, The Great Gillespie – the cartoons (*Bugs Bunny*, *Tom and Jerry*) and, after a choc-bomb at half-time, the main picture, whatever it was, a Tarzan movie, a western, a musical, a war movie or a gangster one.

Being Gees we especially liked movies with G-men in them. Then it was home to our shared bedroom, where we quickly went to sleep . . . Until, that is, a few years later. There's a line I remember from a song – it can't have been on radio. A sad/comic voice sings 'I pulla da pud, I knew I would . . .' I had arrived at that. It was a three-act drama: the battle against that could go on for what seemed hours; the inevitable surrender; and then the fall into shame and guilt, which also went on and on – not just any old shame and guilt but deep and corroding and destructive.

I would have hated Gus to find out.

When I think of Junior things like our tin canoes come to mind, but there are few big events with Gus, he's a constant presence. He was a favourite of Auntie Joyce. Their personalities seemed to chime – both outgoing, both seeing, as Joyce would have put it, the funny side of things. He also gave Mum a lot of joy as the war saddened her and seemed to destroy her faith, learned from her father, in man's, or Man's, perfectability. The anecdotes she tells about Gus mostly centre on his combination of innocence and curiosity and quickness of mind.

To me though he was tough, busy little Gus. He knew more things than me, he had more facts about how the world worked. I never had to defend him as older brother; he fought his own fights. At times he was contemptuous of me, wondering how I could be so dumb. When I remonstrated (gravely) with the boy who had called him a bastard, Gus looked at me with a kind of pity. He could not believe in me any more than the boy I lectured could. Several times in our boyhood my younger brother told me to grow up.

Mainly though he seemed pleased with me. We had, and had with Junior, a brotherly loyalty. The flip side of my silliness and puritan unreality was a physical toughness and quickness that matched, and often outdid, Gus's own. I could fight, although not as aggressively as him; I could run faster and was better at footy. As a result several of his friends became mine too. Rex Flavell, his classmate, was the school's fastest runner by a long way. He won everything. Rex had the same outgoing nature as Gus, with an anarchic streak that had him always in trouble. As the time for our end-of-year school picnic approached, my last at Henderson School, I asked him to be my partner in the three-legged race. He was reluctant, but we tried out and found that when I ran flat out and he loped along at three-quarter speed our steps matched. We practised every lunch hour and at the picnic, held on the Point Chevalier domain, we won the race by half the length of the track.

Several years later, at secondary school, Rex was winning races again. He won the school junior sprints – but could not contain his boat-rocking impulses. He romped home in the 440 yards with his school cap on backwards and a grass-stalk in his mouth, and earned himself a dressing-down from the teachers. He behaved himself later on at the inter-secondary school sports, winning the junior 220 yards easily.

An odd thing about Rex: although he was dark skinned it never once crossed our minds that he was Māori.

When Pater lived with us for a year, his Border Collie, Kep, became Gus's special friend. We all played with Kep and came to love him, but when he died suddenly – dead in his kennel one morning – Gus was the one most upset. A short while later Mum and Dad bought him a little short-legged, short-haired dog, a cross between a Corgi and a Dachshund. Gus named him Jimpy. We all grew fond of Jimpy and he became the family pet. Jimpy roamed the street. Soon, while Gus was at school, he spent most of his time with Ben Hart, a long-time resident of Newington Road and owner of the land between the north-side houses and the creek. The old man fed and cosseted the dog and Jimpy seemed almost to play the role of Ben Hart's child. He trotted happily between the two houses but more and more chose to be with Ben. Gus, with his social life widening and his interests changing in his early teens, called in one day and offered to let the old man keep the dog. Ben Hart almost wept with delight. So the little dog ate his food and had his sleeping basket in Ben's living room and trotted along Newington Road to visit us every day. After several years, when Jimpy was middle-aged, Mr Scott the chemist ran over him in his Morris Eight outside our house. It fell to Gus to tell Ben Hart and carry the body down the road to his house. They buried Jimpy in the back garden. Ben died a short while later and none of us had any doubt that it was grief that killed him.

NINETEEN

The Waitemata Rugby Football Club had a field at the Henderson Domain. Now and then we biked down to watch the seniors play, and joined in the barracking from the sidelines. 'Wot's-a-madder Wydermadder,' we yelled when the opposition scored a try. Shortly after the war ended, the club went back to fielding junior teams. Gus and I put our names down – overcoming Mum's opposition, which came from her fear that we would break our bones or, worse, injure our brains. I was the right weight for the seventh grade. Gus was too light, but the team was short of players so he got in. Our coach, Snow Pennell, tried him at hooker and he enjoyed being in the middle of the scrum. Halfway through the season Snow switched him to halfback and that turned out to be his proper place. He was nippy and aggressive, a perfect link between the forwards and the backs.

We looked forward to wearing Waitemata jerseys – black with red and green hoops – but our club could afford them only for the senior team and we turned out in pale-yellow shirts made of a tough interlocking material. We grumbled at it and felt like country hicks as we faced Suburbs in their red and blue, Ponsonby in blue and black, Grammar in pure white . . . all sixteen teams in our competition had proper jerseys. We got over it. We beat some of them in their nice colours and stopped complaining about our yellow shirts. When we played on the Henderson Domain we grinned when visiting players complained about there being nowhere to wash in our roofless and rusty tin changing shed. We told them there was a good pool in the creek down through the tea-trees. Mostly though we played on neutral grounds: Walker Park in Point Chevalier, Western Springs, the Auckland Domain. We played Eden on their home ground, Gribblehurst Park, and Eastern Suburbs at St Heliers.

In that year our team did quite well, finishing in the middle of the competition; and in the second, in brand new red, green and black jerseys, did even better. I was picked in the Auckland seventh grade representative team, for boys of sixteen years and younger and less than ten stone. We played only one match, against the Kaipara reps in Helensville. The bus picked up me and Harry Williams, the other Waitemata member of the team, in Henderson. There were spare seats, so Gus managed to get on too. The Auckland team was much too good for the country one. We had boys who played senior representative rugby later on and we won by more than forty points. Playing on the left wing, I scored two tries, one an easy run to the line but the other, from long range, needing a fend and a swerve to beat opposing players. I felt like Jack Dunn. But my day was spoiled by the team singing 'dirty' songs on the bus back home. I couldn't understand why our coach didn't stop them. The result for me, a horrifying one, was an erection. There was nothing I could do about these things; I got them at a stray word or thought, on buses, in the pictures, even in the classroom, and had become clever at holding whatever I had, schoolbag or book, firmly to my front as I exited. Several times I had to travel beyond my stop, once even to the terminus, where I got off last. The football bus drew up in Henderson and I got off with my football gear clamped to my loins, and no one, I hoped, saw my condition. What a day! Two tries for Auckland and an unwanted erection.

My rugby career didn't come to much. A couple of years after the Seventh Grade I was picked in the Auckland Fourth Grade reps but didn't get a game. I was never big enough or fast enough for senior football. I moved about the back line, playing on the wing for the school first fifteen and at second five-eighth or centre for the club. I was captain of club teams – where I did little more than call three cheers for the opposition and three cheers for the ref. It improved my confidence, which, because of my corroding inner life, needed a boost.

Mum's fear of us getting hurt came true for me. I broke two fingers and dislocated an elbow, and once, in a school match, woke up on a bench in the changing shed with a teacher leaning over me asking if I knew my name. Why did I play such a violent sport? Saying for companionship and enjoyment is too simple, and saying for the joy of it is hard for others to believe. When a player ran into space where no space had been, when he created space, like Jack Dunn, it brought me an excitement close to aesthetic. I was never in the forwards, where the rough stuff went on; I avoided most of the violence, tackled when I had to and was tackled and broke bones, but what I was looking for was space in which to run, and a way to make that space, and now and then, not in every game, it happened – a fend, a swerve, a calculated overlap, a change of pace and I was free. I invented a move, absolutely simple, running at my marker and making him cover me while the ball was still with my inside backs. I changed my line minutely as he looked away to check where the ball was, and so was a foot or two inside him when it arrived, and I ran free, untouched, as he clawed backwards, clawing at air . . . I'm exaggerating. I tried it half a dozen times and it worked only once, but in that moment, exultation, exaltation – I don't exaggerate now, and don't when I say that it was beautiful.

*

Rugby and reading kept me sane. My rugby skills and my willingness to try other sports – athletics, boxing, tennis – even when I could not do them well, made me reasonably popular in a boys' world quick to punish difference.

I tried athletics when I started secondary school but although reasonably fast on the football field wasn't fast enough for sprinting and quickly ran out of breath in longer races – where a skinny kid called Murray Halberg turned up in my second year and was soon winning everything. I did no better in tennis. There were boys who were members at big suburban clubs and played like adults, so I gave up tennis at school and went through the macrocarpa hedge at the back of our section and asked if I could join the Holy Cross Club that used the Catholic school courts on Saturdays. The vandalising of one of the classrooms must have been forgotten, or perhaps no one connected me with it, because I was welcomed as a member of the little club of a couple of dozen men and a dozen women. Harry Smith, whom I wasn't seeing much of at school, joined along with me, and our friendship revived. Nobody at Holy Cross played very well. The best was Johnny Lloyd, a middle-aged man who stayed in one place as much as he could, hitting lobs and making cunning placements, and a young Dalmatian, Nick Devcich, who slogged and bashed at every ball. Nick never had a pleasant word for me, or any sort of word – perhaps he remembered. He was the right age to have been at Holy Cross School at the time of Junior's and my attack. I played there happily in spite of him, only twenty-five yards from the scene of the crime, and tried to develop a game that mixed hard hitting with angled shots. At the end of the season we held a tournament grandly called the Club Championship. It was completed in a single afternoon, in matches of one set, first to six. I played Nick Devcich in the semi-final and let him bash his way out of the contest. He left the court without shaking hands. The final against Johnny Lloyd was harder and more enjoyable. Johnny made me run, but I was fit and made him run too, and won 6–5. So there I was, club champion at Holy Cross. There was no cup, no presentation, which was just as well. I would have been nervous of being found out.

I didn't go back to Holy Cross the following season but played now and then at a bigger club in Henderson, which I didn't enjoy as much. It was shortly after this that Harry Smith, who had left school, became a Catholic. Our friendship had faded again and this seemed a further defection to me. I judged him for choosing not the Catholic Church but any church, any religion, and judged him too, in my snobbish way, for choosing a trade for which I could not see any need. Engraving watches and cups when he might have been building houses like my father or hammering red-hot iron like his own. Harry went out of my life; but fifty years later, when he wrote to me that he had made his peace with God, it gave me the uneasy feeling that his life had opened wider than mine.

TWENTY

I had looked forward to going to Mt Albert Grammar, but at the end of 1944, as the war against Japan moved back up the Pacific, the Education Department took over an American naval hospital at Avondale and turned it into Avondale Technical High School, and I found myself going there. We were told that a full range of academic subjects would be taught as well as technical ones but it seemed a big come-down. Both Mum and I had liked the word 'grammar' – and I believed that I was good at grammar. It wasn't until 1948 that Avondale Tech's name changed to Avondale College.

There was a huge newly built assembly hall where, in the first year, we watched James Turkington, high on a scaffold, paint a series of murals of New Zealand rural, industrial and social activities. There was a gymnasium, probably the best in New Zealand at that time. The classrooms, which had been wards, were large and bright, with sliding windows that could be opened wide on fine days. We were all Third Formers, with no older pupils over us. It was a co-ed school, although girls and boys had separate playgrounds. We had good teachers (and some not so good, but I got only one of those). I enrolled at Avondale Technical High School a happy child, top of my class at Henderson School and expecting to be top at Avondale too, and ended the year nervous and bewildered and unhappy and only two or three places from the bottom of Form 3A General.

There are plenty of similes and metaphors: puberty struck me like a hammer, it sucked me down in a swamp, it split me in two, it dragged me out in an undertow. I like the last because you can fight an undertow. The earnest, eager child wasn't lost; he continued his existence alongside the troubled, furtive one. The undertow might drag him out but he struggled back and went on playing where the waves ran up the beach. That will do. There were times when I believed I was diseased and mad and dirty, and others, many more, of longer duration, for I had to live in the everyday world, when I was free and active and alive – but the sucking back could come at any time. An example: 3A General, Room 10, Froggy Martin's English class. We boys are at our desks on the window side of the room, waiting for the girls to arrive, and here they come, filing in and taking their seats, and the boy across the aisle from me (in adult life he became a radio talkback host) pats the front of his trousers: 'Down Jock, down.' And that's enough for me to go up and up. And stay up, right through the lesson, in spite of my desperate commands for the unwanted thing to lie down. I got out of the room at the end of the lesson with my school bag held tight in front of me. Priapism is a heavy word to lump on a child, but accurate enough, although with me the condition was only occasional. I let no one know, denying myself the help – just a few sensible words – that might have led to some sort of control, and control of my overheated fantasies, or might at least have made me feel better and not a freak. I struggled on alone, and it's no wonder I couldn't keep my mind on classroom work.

Bill Martin may have guessed what was happening. (I won't call him Froggy anymore.) Although he was a reserved and, it seemed, humourless man, he was a good teacher with a liking for poetry – one saw a gleam of warmth in his eyes and the beginning of a smile – and he was friendly to me, even as I slipped further behind. At the end of the year he took me aside and told me that although my results weren't good he was going to let me stay in an academic form and not go into the technical one he would normally recommend. He said he knew I would do better work if I concentrated. Although this was not the help I needed, it was a kind word, a kindly act, and possibly the saving of me.

I dropped Latin, where I had been lost in a dark wood, but kept on with French – where I couldn't see much further. The teacher, tubby and genial, was Stinger Rae. He had a store of jokes designed to help us remember. 'The French for neck is le cou,' he said, 'so if you see people necking you can say they're cou-ing.' This was innocent enough not to set me off. I climbed to the middle of the class in French, and in English and social studies too. My Fourth Form year was better than my Third, although I was no happier in my mind. I wasn't helped by the principal, L.E. Titheridge – a man I never saw smile or heard make a joke in my five years at Avondale – sending the girls out of assembly one morning and lecturing the boys for a quarter of an hour about the consequences of thinking too much about sex (although he never used that little three-letter word). 'Dirty' pictures had appeared on the lavatory walls. This was the worst sort of filth and it must stop. Did we know, he asked, that thinking about (pause) things like that could send us mad? Mental asylums were full of men who had an unhealthy interest in – Titheridge couldn't say the word.

That little narrow-faced man frightened me. I hadn't drawn – or even seen – the pictures on the walls, but I certainly had 'things' on my mind; and my head state and its penile consequences were enough to convince me at times that I was, as Titheridge said, destined for a 'mental asylum'. (There was one in Point Chevalier, just a mile up the road.) Yet my other life went on, full of long happy times – school life, home life, friendships, rugby, lots of reading. I probably seemed a normal fourteen-year-old boy.

Gus started at Avondale Tech a year behind me. Having him there helped me. But Gus had a way of finding trouble, and now and then he pulled me in with him. One morning, with teachers as outriders, we boys, two or three hundred, marched up the hill to Avondale Station and boarded a train to Auckland. We walked along to a Queen Street picture theatre where the English war movie, *The Way Ahead*, was showing. In the final scene Stanley Holloway, usually a comedian, walks his platoon, bayonets fixed, through gun smoke towards the German lines. Instead of 'The End' the words 'The Beginning' came up on the screen. Our orders were straight back to school, no loitering, but I ran into Gus and Rex Flavell on the way down Queen Street and they had worked out that they could get to the Tepid Baths, have a swim (hired togs), catch the Avondale tram and be back at school before lunch hour was over. Sneaking in would be easy. 'It'll be easy. Come on.' I took some persuading but I went, enjoyed my swim, and then, with nerves jumping and a sense of doom, went back to school – where lunch hour was over, as I had known it would be, and classes had begun.

We hid in the toilets, waiting for the period to end. Stinger Rae found us lurking in the cubicles. More sad than angry, he led us to Titheridge's office. Titheridge was outraged. That we, after that movie, could actually, actually . . . he could not believe it; and soon enough he fixed on me. I was the senior one. I should have set an example but instead I had led my young brother astray. Although I kept my mouth shut, I was open-mouthed. Me lead Gus astray? One look at us should be enough . . . He hit Rex and Gus once on the hand with his whippy cane and sent them away. Me he hit three times on each hand; and through the pain I was as outraged as he . . . What a stupid man, couldn't he see?

In the rest of my years at Titheridge's school I was in his office only once more. It was 1949, end of year. He called the prefects in one by one. 'Thank you for your service to the school, Gee.' Not a smile, not a glimmer of friendliness. He handed me a book. I said, 'Thank you, sir,' and left. It was Boswell's *Life of Samuel Johnson*, which I never got round to reading in that close-printed edition. Neither Boswell nor Dr Johnson would have liked Mr Titheridge, nor he them. To be fair, Boswell and Johnson would not have liked me either.

TWENTY-ONE

The Avondale Tech library was well stocked with adventure fiction. I plunged in. The word escapist exactly fits my reading for two years. While I was in a book – and I was in, with the covers closed around me – I had no troubles. Westerns were best, perfect for a boy who had things to get away from. Our library had Max Brand, Jackson Gregory, William MacLeod Raine and, best of all, Zane Grey. Best because his books outnumbered those of the other three writers put together. I was after quantity, full-time escape. Grey wrote more than ninety novels, and in my Third and Fourth Form years I read forty-five of them, competing with another Henderson boy, Tony Betts. I got from them the triumph of the hero, who was a tough and skilful and often lonely man. He was hunted. With the posse in a dust-cloud behind him, he rode into the badlands, rode along dry gulches, through sage brush, over mesas (I had no idea what mesas were, didn't look it up) and in the end he faced the villain and beat him to the draw. He got the girl, always, after saving her from the villain who, in some of the novels, tore her blouse from neck to waist, exposing her breasts, which blushed rosy pink. This didn't excite me because she was pure, and although brave and resourceful was just 'the girl', there for the hero to save and take in his arms. 'Oh my darling,' Buck Duane says, 'what is this madness of love?' It was silly but the book had to have a rounding off. What upset me in that novel, *The Lone Star Ranger*, was that the villain Poggin beats Buck Duane to the draw. How could Zane Grey do that? Even today I hold it against him. The hero is fastest, no one beats him. But Poggin does, by a fraction, and I can't forget his name or his 'yellow jaguar eyes and mane of tawny hair'. Poggin is Zane Grey's lesson to me.

When no westerns were available I read P.C. Wren, Jeffery Farnol, Rider Haggard, Rafael Sabatini and anyone else who looked likely – Conan Doyle (not Sherlock Holmes but the historical romances), Georgette Heyer, Baroness Orczy, who was recommended by our social studies teacher. Pirate captains, knights in armour, bowmen, foreign legionnaires, African explorers: I spent time in all their skins, although cowboys fitted me best. Any critical faculty I might have developed was impeded by my need to be away, out of my life. If I frowned now and then it was because of my – almost wrote 'political' but 'Chapple' suits it better – indoctrination. In *The White Company*, surely the subhuman creatures Sir Nigel and his French counterpart slaughtered so enthusiastically were really downtrodden peasants. (Years later I was pleased to find knights in armour categorised as 'the terrible worm in the iron cocoon'.) When Cavaliers fought Roundheads I was on the anti-royalist side and was disturbed to find the Roundheads so thick-necked and brutal and coarse. As for the Scarlet Pimpernel rescuing aristocrats, I was for chopping off their heads. But most of the stories pleased me and I might have stayed much longer if it hadn't been for Ben Hart.

There's a park in Henderson called Ben Hart Reserve. It covers part of the territory that was wasteland and swamp and lost orchard in my childhood. Ben must have owned it and perhaps had worked the orchard at one time. A few trees remained at the back of his house, a bungalow behind a high hedge on the north side of Newington Road. I didn't see Ben outside very often but he sometimes put apples in a box by his gate for neighbours to help themselves. He was short – shorter even than my grandfather – and old (ancient he seemed to me), tubby, white-haired, rheumy-eyed, and he had a small parrot's-beak nose. His wife, even tinier, dressed like my grandmother, with the addition of a white lace cap. It was hard to believe that the Harts were the parents of our heavy-limbed and disobliging neighbour, Mrs Pinckney.

I went along now and then to call Jimpy home. By the time the dog switched houses I knew Ben quite well and one day, seeing me pass, he invited me in for a game of draughts. Jimpy lay sleeping in his basket, waking only when Mrs Hart brought in tea and cake. Ben fed him pieces. I don't remember who won our game – probably not me, as my interest was more on Ben's books, in a bookcase so tall it made my head go up and down. None of them looked like my sort of thing. They had ridged binding and some of the titles were lettered in gold. Ben saw me looking and asked if I read books. I told him yes, I liked novels. 'Do you like,' he said, 'Charles Dickens?' I hadn't read Dickens and didn't want to. I was in the Fifth Form by then and Mr Martin had talked about him, but I had no time for fat old-fashioned books with small print. Ben fetched one – fat, old-fashioned – from the shelf. 'You should start with this.' It was *Oliver Twist*. I'd heard of Oliver, the boy who asked for more; how could I spend time with someone like that when I had Buck Duane and Captain Blood for company? I took the book politely and carried it home. That night, knowing I had to get it out of the way, I opened it. Double columns, tiny print swarming like black ants, and a first paragraph written like a puzzle. I was used to speeding along, easy and submerged, and here I had to turn back several times to work out what was being said. There was no chance of my seeing that the description of a newborn workhouse baby as an 'item of mortality' was perfect (perfect in information, perfect in tone) – and was, in fact, the first live thing in the paragraph. I did not know what a workhouse was; and, used to simple grammar, did not enjoy the convolutions, the deliberate slowing down, of the single sentence making up paragraph one.

Paragraph two was worse. But in paragraph three I found an old pauper woman, 'rendered rather misty by an unwonted allowance of beer', and the book, like Oliver, came to life – a hard birth, which Dickens perhaps intended.

There's a bit of invention going on here. It was probably like that. But in chapter two, after the baby farm where Oliver spends his first nine years – keeping his ninth birthday in the coal cellar after a thrashing for 'atrociously presuming to be hungry' – Mr Bumble makes his appearance, and delight overtook my humanitarian outrage as I saw how Dickens was not only getting them down, the pompous beadle and the baby farmer Mrs Mann, but 'getting' them too. I fell in love with Charles Dickens in chapter two; I grew up several years in half an hour. After that I didn't stop – the workhouse, more Bumble, the asking for more, the Artful Dodger, Fagin, Bill Sikes, Nancy, and so to the end; and I was back at Ben's in a week's time for another game of draughts and another book.

It went on like that for a year. *Nicholas Nickleby* followed *Oliver Twist*. Then came *The Old Curiosity Shop*. Ben handed the books out roughly in the order Dickens wrote them, breaking the sequence only with *The Pickwick Papers*. While I enjoyed some more than others – *David Copperfield* more than *Martin Chuzzlewit* – I was taking in a world as much as stories. The humour, the melodrama, the exaggerated behaviour delighted me, but were in a way incidental pleasures. Real human emotions lay at the back of them, connecting readily and easily with mine. Dickens made Zane Grey seem full of abstractions. Fellow feeling took the place of facile identification. Nicholas Nickleby thrashing Squeers with his own cane, and Wemmick too, a less active figure, coming home to his Aged P and changing his nature at the door, were more than adequate replacements for Buck Duane. I had lost several years of normal growth in my emotions, and in my intelligence, and might have stayed in a retarded condition, not started to grow, if it had not been for Ben Hart and Charles Dickens.

I began to cast around: Thackeray, George Eliot, the Brontës, Mrs Gaskell, back to Henry Fielding, along to Thomas Hardy. I fished for writers less well known – George Meredith, George Gissing, Anthony Trollope, Charles Reade – found forgotten novelists (Harrison Ainsworth, Theodore Watts-Dunton). I'm pretty sure I read *Lorna Doone*. It took a bit of time to like Jane Austen. With these people I did the growing up I could not manage in my everyday world.

Memory compacts this into two years but it was open-ended and I can't be sure of dates. I can be sure of Newington Road and of what I was reading there. My grandfather died in 1948. Mum brought home some of his books. One of them (fat, gold-lettered on the spine) was a selection of poems by Robert Browning. 1947 to 1949 were the years of Dickens and Browning. Grandpa had marked the poems in his usual extravagant way – underlinings, double underlings, exclamation marks, approving comments. He'd pasted a caricature of the poet opposite the half-title page, folded several newspaper articles inside the front cover and covered two blank pages at the back with references. All this intrigued me. I began to read the poems he had starred in the Contents or made notes about at the back. So I came on 'Abt Vogler', 'Andrea del Sarto', 'Fra Lippo Lippi', 'The Bishop Orders His Tomb in Saint Praxed's Church', 'The Grammarian's Funeral', the verse drama 'Paracelsus' and the enigmatic 'Childe Roland to the Dark Tower Came'. There was a great deal I didn't understand but I read over the top of difficulties. There was a fair amount of God stuff, which I ignored; ignored the argument of the poems, simply enjoyed the language and the characters and the story. Several years later I read the long – the huge – poem 'The Ring and the Book', which a contemporary review describes as 'the supremest poetical achievement of our time' and 'the most precious and profound spiritual treasure that England has produced since Shakespeare'.

Browning was thought of as a great teacher. He didn't touch me in that way. I enjoyed him for the stories he told and the people he brought to life. And sometimes there was something more . . .

'Childe Roland to the Dark Tower Came' puzzled me. The young knight rides across a 'starved, ignoble' plain. He reaches the Dark Tower and blows a challenge on his horn ('slug horn', I liked that). What comes out to fight him? Browning doesn't say. He ends the poem with the horn blast. I tried to imagine: a giant knight in black armour on a black horse; a fire-breathing dragon; a wizard throwing lightning bolts? None of these fitted, and slowly I came to understand that what must emerge was Roland's other self, the evil that lies sleeping in us all, and that was what he challenged and must fight. This bleak understanding satisfied me.

So I began to break free from the trap that held me. With the help of these writers, and others I soon found (Wordsworth in particular), I began to open out my life and confine my troubles in a smaller space. School became more enjoyable, schoolwork easier and more interesting. I gave up club rugby so I could play for the school first fifteen. I was a member of the library committee, the magazine committee, and was a prefect in my final year. I did not always manage to avoid self-importance but nor did I always conform. One afternoon a week we had military drill. In 1949 I was the only senior pupil still a private. Fourth Form sergeants were bossing me around. It was time for a stand, or at least a sit-down. I walked away from military drill to the prefects' room and sat reading a book, waiting to be fetched to Titheridge again. No one came. No one ever came. I see Bill Martin's hand in this. Early in the year I had handed in an essay arguing against militarism in an impassioned way, and although he made no comment he gave me a high mark; so he knew how I felt. I sat in the prefects' room undisturbed for the rest of the year.

It was Bill Martin again who allowed me to drop maths and

science, subjects I had fallen too far behind in to do well, and take only English, history and French. At least five subjects were needed for the scholarship exam so I didn't sit that. John Titheridge, our headmaster's son, came second in New Zealand, and Brian Craven thirteenth. I was able to behave as though I shared their cleverness. John Titheridge also scored higher than me in our school English exam, which puzzled me because I was sure he hadn't read as many Charles Dickens novels as me.

In the Sixth Form we had had a break from Bill Martin (although he took us back in 6A, thirteen survivors from the 1945 intake of foundation pupils). Maurice Hutchinson was our Lower Sixth English teacher. I got on well with him but my classroom memories are few. Dickens and Browning come into the picture. I had just finished my last Dickens novel, *Edwin Drood*, when Maurie asked us to make a list of all the books we'd read in the last year. Aha, I thought, this is going to be good; and I wrote down all seventeen, without *The Christmas Books*, which Ben hadn't given me yet. 'You haven't read all these,' Maurie said. 'Yes I have.' 'No you haven't. You can't read all Dickens' novels in a year . . .' We went on a bit and he wouldn't believe me. He was calling me a liar and all I could do in the end was shut up. I'd liked him up to that point and later on came to like him again, but he had soured my pleasure and I kept quiet in his class for a good while after that. A teenager in a reading frenzy gulps like a shark, a teacher should know.

Maurie got his comeuppance later in the year. An inspector sat at the back of the room while he took a lesson. She was a big-voiced woman with grey bobbed hair and an intrusive manner and she seemed to unsettle him. He was talking about Victorian poetry and he mentioned Browning. She butted in: 'Have you read "My Last Duchess"?' Maurie said he hadn't. 'Young man,' the inspector said, 'your education has been neglected.' Maurie went bright red, more,

I think, with anger than embarrassment. She gave us a little talk about the poem – how chilling it was as a portrait of evil. Maurie kept quiet; and went on with his lesson when she had finished. His colour remained high. I didn't quite have the nerve to put up my hand and say that I had read 'My Last Duchess' and didn't think it was Browning's best poem at all. 'Andrea del Sarto' was better, and so was 'Fra Lippo Lippi'. (They were longer too, an important point!) And 'Childe Roland to the Dark Tower Came' was best of all. If I'd spoken it would have been to show off, not stick up for Maurie. The inspector, I thought, had been showing off.

TWENTY-TWO

One effect of my reading was to start me writing. I came across a Henry Lawson poem praising Dickens. It set me off on a poem of my own, about Dick Swiveller, the good-hearted wastrel from *The Old Curiosity Shop*. I remember none of it now but have the impression it was something a precocious ten-year-old might have written. Rhyming was fun; and I had loved Dick Swiveller, I meant every sentimental word I wrote. Other poems followed, sub-Wordsworthian excursions. I felt, probably because of the creek, that I had a bond with hills and trees and dark still pools, allowing me to call them Nature with a capital N. I was reading *The Prelude* and the poems I wrote in imitation made me feel wise. I showed them to Mum, and she, understanding her role, said she thought they were very good. I don't see any need to shoot myself down, so I'll simply say that they were no improvement on my Dick Swiveller poem. I began to see it: a slow understanding there was no appeal against. But it turned out I had one more poem left in me.

Maurie Hutchinson and another teacher, Des Mann, wanted to start a school tramping club. It was to begin with a weekend at Tongariro National Park – just the two of them, with one pupil, to see if a trip like that would work. Maurie invited me to go along. We travelled down by train, got off at National Park Station in the small hours and hitched a ride in a baker's van to the start of the track, where we slept for a few hours in a shelter before starting out for the Maungatepopo hut. We soon hit snow, and I found the going hard after my lay-off from rugby with a dislocated elbow.

We reached the hut by early afternoon and had it to ourselves. There was enough time left to climb Pukekaikiore, the hill that stands as a footstool to Mt Ngāuruhoe. The teachers were not teachers for this trip. We were friendly and relaxed. A week or two short of eighteen, I was not much younger than Des Mann. The next morning, with snow on the ground, we set off to climb Ngāuruhoe. It's not a hard climb – no obstacles or difficulties – but it's steep. We simply trudged, one foot after the other, and every time we looked back the land had opened wider – low hills, snowfields turning to tussock, silver creeks, lakes Rotoaira and Taupō gleaming, and round the other way, higher and more jagged, Mt Ruapehu. Wordsworth would have liked all this, I thought. We reached the top; stood on the crater edge, where steam with a sulphurous smell swirled round us. We sat and ate our lunches, pleased with ourselves, then glissaded down and tramped back to the hut. I stored it all, still thinking I might be a poet. The next day, in a snow storm, and in some danger it seemed to me, we slogged our way to the Chateau, slept for several hours, then caught the night train at National Park Station.

With all that scenery in me, and memories of being awed and moved and taken out of myself and stretched into the distance, I wrote a poem. Maurie and Des wanted me to write the story of our trip, preferably in a humorous way, and put it in the school magazine. They were disappointed when I said no, and I couldn't understand why they didn't see my poem was better. In fact it was no improvement on my earlier ones – although for a while I thought it was. I put it in the magazine – and I look at it now and see, what? A lump of verse. I should have written the funny story Maurie and Des had asked for.

I imagine most story-writers start with verse. It's quicker, for one thing. It brings you close up against language and you find out if you like it and can use it. I liked it all right, but couldn't use it in that way – and other things were missing as well. I took a looping track into poetry and was relieved when I came out. I had found Dostoevsky to go with Dickens and I wanted to be like them.

TWENTY-THREE

I've told my parents' story in 'Double Unit': Mum's breakdown, Dad's immersion in his work and his near-affair with the wife of a Henderson businessman. Junior and Gus and I saw what was going on but could do nothing. Dad seemed to have gone away from us. Mum, although she struggled out – and struggled on for the rest of her life – was lost for several years in the illness that had begun during the war. There were good times still to be had, but for our last two or three years in Newington Road uncertainty, fragility, underlay them.

I was more affected by Mum's unhappiness than Dad's 'absence'. Social life, sport, school, reading, my troubles (not an adequate word), home life, my companionship with my brothers, my love for my parents, these are the parts I find when I break myself down. Mum's sadness was always there. I belonged to her and she to me – so it was, or seemed to be, for the duration of my childhood and youth. I don't know whether I was a naturally sensitive child or whether she created 'sensitivity' in me. I kept away from it, stayed out as often as I went in, but once in I was helpless and had to stay. Sentimentality was a component, but so was good feeling. It's hard now to separate one from the other. Which was it – or was it something else – that made me, twelve years old and pre-pubertal, mope and droop about the house for most of a week after seeing a film about Edith Cavell, the British nurse mistaken for a spy and shot by a German firing squad in the First World War? Mum finally asked me what was wrong and I found myself sobbing: 'I didn't want Nurse Edith Cavell to die.' I was a noisy, football-playing boy, but my grief was real. Perhaps there was some morbidity in it and Mum should have resorted to the most common of her cures: 'Get out in the garden and do some digging.' (Sometimes she called it 'straight digging'.) This time she comforted me, pleased, I think, as much as troubled, by such a degree of 'sensitivity'. For me there was something else. As well as being brave, Edith Cavell, as played by Anna Neagle, was beautiful and soulful and pure. I looked for those things in women's faces – not in their behaviour; behaviour was across the divide. I entered, for that week, a state of pre-erotic love for the brave, pure nurse. Straight digging might have sweated it out. Instead, Mum's sympathy fixed it in – helped fix unreality in, my certainty that women were brave and good and pure. A conflation of the pure and the romantic took place. Then hormones kicked in, colouring and darkening my life.

The influence on my fiction is not hard to see.

My mother had a nature both earthy and transcendent. I responded to both parts, enjoyed the former but became, as time went on, more alive to the latter. There was a quieter, stiller child living inside the rowdy active one. My mother had access. When she struck a note it echoed there. The whole of good and right and loving behaviour was encompassed, and it's no wonder that with my dependence on her I began to participate and invent. I heard what she said and took it into myself. I might fail, I might relapse, as I did with the squashed soldiers and Private Schmidt's head, but I heard at once that what I said was wrong. 'Wrong' stayed with me, became part of me.

Evil? She didn't call it that, but used words like cruel and bad instead. The cruellest, 'baddest' man was Gaston Means. He was an American extortionist and friend of gangsters. Among other schemes he conned a rich socialite out of $100,000, supposedly to pay off the kidnappers of the Lindbergh baby. Gaston Means grew up in 'a loving family'. For Mum his worst crime was that he 'broke his mother's heart'. His name sounded nasty. Mum had only to say it to make me determined to be good.

I was eager and adventurous but grew up hedged about with moral choices. I don't blame my mother. She was filled with love, she overflowed with concern. I was the one who constructed places that must and must not be gone into. I found things to believe in and things I must not think. There was no strict teaching, no heavy emphasis. I made restrictions and imperatives for myself, using her feelings and beliefs as material. If she'd seen my unhappiness she would have been filled with grief, while my twisted view of right behaviour would have appalled her.

TWENTY-FOUR

I began with gravel roads but in the postwar years the roads around Henderson were being sealed. Newington Road had proper footpaths. No longer blind, it cut through the farm beyond the turning bay and met the Great North Road not far from Henderson School. State houses went up and our street became suburban.

Our house was too small for two adults and three adolescent boys. And Mum's father had died. Her world had shifted on its base – the war had shifted it too – and she had lost her sure grasp on family and home and her place in things. When Dad suggested we move to a bigger house, she was happy to agree.

Tirimoana Road runs off Te Atatu Road not far from Te Atatu Corner. In 1948 it was semi-rural – a paddock on the corner, another halfway down behind a row of pine trees, the asphalt seal giving way to gravel where the road turned sharply left and dropped into a gully filled with scrub. There was only one family down there, the Loncars. The house Dad bought, a bungalow in more or less Spanish style, fitted our family well. It was built on a section sloping down from the place where the seal ended and the gravel began. Dad bought the paddocks alongside and behind the house. At last he could run the horses he had always wanted to own. Mum had a view over a wide mangrove creek, with Rangitoto Island rising beyond the distant city. I had my own bedroom, with shelves for my growing collection of books and a desk for my homework. No longer a train boy, I caught the bus to Avondale each morning. My last lazy year at Avondale College moved to its end. In his final report Bill Martin said that I had 'a sensitive quality', which pleased Mum. For my part, I wondered what he had seen.

Dad was willing to support me at university. I started a BA course in 1950, before I was fit for it. I was seriously under-educated and entirely without ideas. The criticism I was capable of came largely from feeling, not from thinking. I had, of course, prejudices and obsessions but they made me assertive and silly. Quick responses were perhaps the most valuable thing I had. So I went off to university with insufficient equipment, and with no coherent self.

My reading included few living authors and no New Zealanders. All the same I thought myself clever. And I was determined to work hard so Mum and Dad would not be disappointed in me, and Dad wouldn't feel he had wasted his money. I had no idea what I would do after I had got my degree.

The asphalt seal ended outside our house with a clean cut; the gravel road ran down the hill to its blind ending. But 'blind' and 'gravel' attach themselves to Newington Road, and Tirimoana is a different place. Our shift there brings the story of my childhood and youth to its unsatisfactory end.

RUNNING ON THE STAIRS

ONE

It began with the clatter of footsteps on stairs. The door thumped open and a bright-faced young woman burst into the room.

His life changed direction in that moment, although it took him more than a year to find out.

That's how a novelist might have written it – feet on wooden stairs, a young woman bursting into a room where a not-so-young man sits reading at a desk. That's me, aged thirty-four. She was eight years younger – but I'm going to leave her to get on with her life for another year while I say how I came to be in that room high up under the roof in a Wellington house.

I had travelled down from Rotorua, leaving behind my partner of seven years and our six-year-old son. Our life as a family was over. Now I expected to start a new life as a librarian, with a new partner, a young schoolteacher I had met in my last few months in Rotorua. She had agreed to break off her engagement (to a doctor about my age) and come to Wellington to live with me. I rented a small flat and waited happily. My writing ambitions were on hold. I did some study in preparation for my year in the diploma course at the New Zealand Library School.

The room at the top of the stairs was in the Alexander Turnbull Library. The deputy librarian, Ray Grover, had decided that I would make a good research librarian. He had taken me to the room high up in the house in Bowen Street, Alexander Turnbull's old house, to show me collections of letters written by New Zealand politicians. I found them uninteresting, drab, except for one in which a Minister of Works confessed to building an unnecessary road along a lake front where an opponent had his house, because he 'wanted to spoil the bastard's view'. Yes, good stuff, I told Ray, but felt it would fit better in a novel than a research paper. At this point we heard footsteps running on the stairs.

She had come to find a file for a reader. For a moment she was confused, finding Ray and me in the room, then grinned and apologised for bursting in. Ray introduced her: Margaretha Hickman, who worked in the reference room. We said hello and I saw she recognised my name from the two novels I had published. Ray explained that I was starting the Library School course. 'Ah,' said Margaretha, 'I hope you like it.' She found the file she wanted and went away, as fast on the stairs going down as coming up.

I saw her several times in that year, behind the reference desk or coming and going in the streets. Once, standing with Ray at the top of steps leading down to Bowen Street from the grounds of Parliament, we saw her hurrying into the library. It was mid-winter. She was wearing a fur hat that might have done for a Siberian winter. 'She seems a nice person,' I said.

'You can forget about her, mate,' Ray said. 'She's married to a mad anarchist.'

By that time I was in an unhappy state. Early in the year the red-headed teacher from Rotorua, Leigh Barron, wrote to say that she had changed her mind and was marrying her fiancé, David Minnitt, after all. It must have seemed a sensible decision: the penniless writer and half-hearted librarian, or the doctor? No contest. I could not see it that way. The bottom fell out of my life for a second time, and to stop looking into the hole I wrote Leigh an angry letter I came to regret. She never replied. Fourteen years later David Minnitt shot and killed her after an argument.

I ate alone in my scungy flat. (How could I have believed that Leigh would live with me there?) I ate alone in restaurants and came to think I would spend the rest of my life alone. I had been in this state before, in and out of it, and seven years earlier, in my first stay in Wellington, had written a story about a young man (me in unconvincing disguise) who loses a girl he had in fact never had to a charming and experienced older man. He falls into a deep loneliness from which he believes there is no way out – until one night, walking up Willis Street behind two young lovers, seeing them hug each other, hearing them laugh, he comes to believe that he holds them in the palms of his hands, that his way is not to participate but to watch and understand. (I had just read Thomas Mann's *Tonio Kröger*). I wrote the story in an attempt to struggle out of self-pity and find a way to be alone. It was never published, and is lost, which is a good thing.

I did not give up hope the way the character in my story did, or believe for more than the time it took to write that my role was to watch and understand; and a short while later found a partner in Hera Smith. Our son Nigel was born. Rachel Barrowman has told the story of the sad and bitter, and sometimes ugly, years that followed in the biography *Maurice Gee*. There's no need for me to tell it again. Hera had other men, I 'found' Leigh Barron, and it ended.

So here I was in Wellington alone again, working at a course of study less interesting than the jobs as hospital porter and postman I had held in that city in 1957 and '58. At the end of the year, with a diploma in my hand, I had to decide what sort of librarian I wanted to be, while knowing that the answer was no sort at all. I would be standing off to one side of any job I took, because the only work that satisfied me was writing stories. I had written nothing in the Library School year but told myself it was because I had too many other things on my mind.

Several vacancies came up in the Turnbull Library. Margaret Scott, the one lasting friend I had made at the school, was appointed as a manuscripts librarian, beginning a career as successful and distinguished as mine was to be inconsequential. I applied for a cataloguing job, a good fit for me in my state of mind. It called for close attention, while each book or item that came under my hand was different from the one before. Under chief librarian Graham Bagnall and head cataloguer Nancy Irvine I prepared the Monthly List for the *New Zealand National Bibliography*, and helped with the Annual Cumulation. It wasn't hard, it wasn't easy. The cataloguing room, with a staff of six, was a friendly place. Nancy Irvine had an unobtrusive style of command. She suffered from arthritis and must have been in severe pain at times but kept her cheerful manner by a strength of will that seemed almost magical to me. Everyone in the room was half in love with Nancy.

Graham Bagnall was genial and well liked. He had come as chief librarian when the National Library swallowed the Turnbull in 1965. Most of the existing staff had hated the idea. They enjoyed the Turnbull's independent status and feared the 'heavy hand'; feared sackings, changes, bureaucratic meddling, the knock on the door at 2 a.m., as Ray Grover put it. That none of this happened was probably due to Bagnall and Ray, whom he quickly won round. The library ran on in its even way. As editor of the *National Bibliography*, Bagnall kept a close eye on my work. He seemed easy-going but wanted perfection in a publication carrying his name. I liked him and we got on well, in spite of his opinion that reading novels was a waste of time. He was easy to grin at and he usually grinned back. My work satisfied him most of the time. My one serious mistake went right through to publication – I don't remember exactly what it was, some misattribution involving the national librarian Geoff Alley and his connection with the Somerset family. Bagnall brought the Monthly List into the cataloguing room and slapped it on my desk. His grin had the appearance of a snarl. 'When you make a mistake you make a real beaut.' He handled the correction for the Cumulation himself. 'Don't worry,' Nancy Irvine said. 'Every cataloguer makes at least one bad mistake.'

I got to know Margaretha Hickman as I got to know everyone else on the staff. She spent a lot of time at the reference desk and finding material for users. She seemed to be scooting across to the General Assembly Library or the National Library almost daily, and to spend days at a time at the Ford Building in Courtenay Place, where parts of the Turnbull collections were housed. Tony Murray-Oliver, the art librarian, a cheerful eccentric middle-aged man, seemed especially fond of her. She helped him feed the tribe of feral cats that gathered each morning outside the library back door. Her husband, Stuart Hickman, never appeared. He drove a book van for the Country Library Service. It began to be rumoured that the marriage was not working well.

Several months into the year I brought my son Nigel down to Wellington to live with me. The bed-sit wasn't suitable, even though I had made it less scungy, so I rented a house in Wadestown, where he had already started school, and where he was looked after by Margaret Scott's child-minder until I picked him up after work. We went on in that way for the rest of the year.

In 1968 I began to look at Margaretha Hickman differently. There was a change in perception – I began to 'see' her, perhaps a little sooner than she began to 'see' me. The absence of Stuart Hickman removed a kind of invisibility. And getting to know her easily, as a workmate, over more than a year, gave me a place to stand in relation to her.

In May that year I went to several sessions of the Peace, Power and Politics conference held in the Wellington Town Hall.

Margaretha was also there. In one of the lunch breaks she invited three or four people to her house for a cup of tea. She lived in one of four old cottages in Footscray Avenue, a blind street off Abel Smith Street close to Cuba Street. I watched Dick Scott, a well-known Auckland historian, try to work his charms on her. Skinny, grinny, bespectacled Dick seemed an unlikely womaniser but rumour had it that he was one of the best. I saw that the main components were confidence and a quick tongue, and watched with interest as Margaretha responded with an easy impersonal friendliness. Dick made no ground, and Margaretha and I found ourselves more in step after that. Perhaps she had seen me watching Dick and a message had crossed and an answer come back. An attraction dormant until now began to work on both sides. Both of us were aware of it but did nothing to bring it into the open.

For several months we circled round each other, coming close, moving away, in friendly conversations that failed to become intimate. I had never met Stuart Hickman and had no idea whether he came home to Footscray Avenue from time to time, and Margaretha did not say. He blocked the way, while she continued to be friendly, vivacious, quick to laugh or become serious, and indefinably inviting. I stopped being lonely as we circled round but did not become unreasonably excited. We went on in ever-decreasing circles for a while, both of us waiting for the right time and place – which came at a staff party in Hataitai. There, down wooden steps at the back of the house, on a deck overlooking Evans Bay, the circling stopped and we were able to stand still, talk sensibly, and meet each other properly. We walked from Hataitai through the tunnel to the Basin Reserve and along to her cottage in Footscray Avenue, where I stayed the night.

For both of us a new life had begun.

TWO

Margaretha was born in Sweden in 1940, in the town of Uppsala north of Stockholm. Her mother, Greta Norlen, came from Orbyhus further north. While working as a hotel receptionist in Stockholm, Greta met Oscar Garden, a Scot, whose job as a mail pilot for British Airways brought him to Stockholm regularly. Flying made Oscar a romantic figure. He had a cheerful, outgoing manner and was good-looking, and Greta was an attractive young woman. There's a rumour, no more than a whisper, of an illegitimate child. No evidence has ever been found.

Oscar grew up in Tongue on the north coast of Scotland, one of four children: Oscar, May, Violet and Rose – the girls obviously Gardens. When his mother left a stormy marriage to her merchant husband, Oscar was sent to board at Dollar Academy, near Stirling, but later joined her and one of his sisters on the Isle of Man, where Mrs Garden had grown up. He had some schooling there, then moved to Manchester with her, and at the age of twelve left school to help support the family. When he was seventeen he joined his father, who now lived in New Zealand with two of his daughters. He worked for four years in his father's cordial and bottling business in Timaru, then went rabbiting. Soon he was in business for himself – a cycle shop in Spreydon, then a garage in Southbridge. None of this led him anywhere he wanted to go. In 1930 he returned to Britain. A chance remark from a fellow passenger on the boat going back led him to take up flying. He quickly gained a licence, and just as quickly bought his own plane, a second-hand De Havilland Gypsy Moth. Then, with only thirty-two hours' flying experience, he set off one morning from Croydon Airport, heading for Australia. He had a spare propeller strapped to the side of the plane (named 'Kia Ora'), and carried a bundle of clothes in the cockpit, and a packet of sandwiches in a brown paper bag. He 'was not even wearing a hat', his mother complained later. His aim was to accumulate enough flying hours for a commercial pilot's licence.

A report from a British newspaper reads:

Mystery Airman. A light aeroplane landed at Croydon yesterday and from it stepped a young man who announced his intention of starting at 4 a.m. today on a flight to Australia.

This morning he reappeared and after stating that his name was Oscar Garden and his home was in New Zealand, he climbed into his machine and flew away.

Aerodrome officials have no idea where he came from.

Oscar made several forced landings on his trip. One flipped the plane over in an Indian paddy field. Villagers righted it and pulled it to dry ground. He fitted his spare propeller and flew on; and eighteen days after leaving Croydon was spotted by a passing motorist servicing his aircraft at the isolated Wyndham airstrip in Western Australia. His unannounced arrival earned him the sobriquet, The Sundowner of the Skies. He was the fourth and youngest flyer to make a solo England–Australia flight.

Oscar shipped the plane, no longer named 'Kia Ora' but 'Miss Mobil', to New Zealand and made a sponsored tour of the country, taking passengers on two-shilling flights, then called joyrides. Once he was arrested for making paid flights on a Sunday. He landed on Tahunanui beach in Nelson, a town where his daughter Margaretha was to spend part of her childhood, and made the first landing on Stewart Island. Then, with 'Miss Mobil' sold, he headed back to Europe, where he worked for John Tranum's Flying Circus, doing aerobatics, joyriding and wing-walking, before settling down to serious flying, first on mail runs in Africa, then with British Airways, making several inaugural night-mail flights throughout Europe and Scandinavia. He was on the London–Stockholm route when he met Greta Norlen.

Greta too came from a broken family. Her father, a pastor in the Lutheran Church, left for America one day and never came back. No one in the family ever heard from him again and Greta's mother brought up her children alone. As pastor's children, in a country with strict class divisions, they were entitled to a good education. Greta grew up well spoken, well read, but carried an air of melancholy throughout her life.

She and Oscar married at Epsom in Surrey in December 1937 and settled in England because of Oscar's work – and ever afterwards England was for Greta 'that awful country'. She claimed that the only meat one could get was tripe. She pictured 'aristocrats' (it's unlikely she ever met one) living in stately homes heated by one-bar heaters or by fireplaces breathing coal smoke into the surrounding estates. Tall skinny lords and ladies, she said, with long thin noses always dripping because of the cold – an image Margaretha was to carry throughout her childhood: thin stooping women with 'long reddened noses and a drip poised at the end'.

Although a British subject by marriage, Greta remained a foreigner in habits, appearance and in her accented English. As well as this, Sweden had strong pro-German sympathies. As war began to look likely, then was declared, neighbours started treating her with suspicion and dislike. Oscar was now with Imperial Airways and flying seaplanes to South Africa and Asia. When Tasman Empire Airways chose him to deliver its second Short S-30 flying boat to New Zealand in March 1940, she became even more isolated. And she was pregnant. Three weeks before the baby was due, she fled back to Sweden.

Margaretha was born in her mother's country 'by the skin of my teeth'. Her birthplace, Uppsala was 'Sweden's answer to Oxford', a university town. 'It was spring. I was born in a hospital. I have the Dagantecknigar, 4 de May 1940 at 5.51 formidd. That's a nice early arrival.'

There's also a telegram from Oscar, in New Zealand: 'Call the baby Margaretha.' So Lillemor was crossed out on the certificate and replaced by Margaretha. 'What did he think he was doing, importing that "h" into New Zealand.' He condemned his daughter to a lifetime of correcting the soft 'th' of English speakers to the Swedish hard 't'. Years later Margaretha was to give up the fight and drop the 'h' except in official documents. I'll leave it out from now on.

The stay in Uppsala was short. Greta shifted north to join her mother in Orbyhus. Here the persecution began again. Greta might be Swedish, and speak Swedish, but she was, by marriage, a British subject and in Orbyhus pro-German sympathies were as strong as elsewhere in Sweden, even though Denmark and Norway had by now been overrun by the Nazis. People threw stones against the window of the room where Greta slept. She took this as a sign that she must leave Sweden to safeguard her mother and her two brothers who also lived in the house. Margareta believes that her mother's experiences in England, 'that awful country', and being driven out of her own country, Sweden, began the paranoia that afflicted her bit by bit later in her life.

But, Margareta writes, in that bitter year, 1940, her mother's life 'still had one glow of promise'. She would go to her husband in New Zealand.

'It is hard to picture this woman, poised for her huge adventure, as any other than vibrant, attractive, daring . . . Greta Garbo, people called her, even in Sweden.' She had already made sure that her daughter was christened. 'I'm in a long christening gown. My mother is holding me. She looks proud and cheeky. She is wearing a pill-box hat and a dark fashionable padded-shoulder dress, with sleeves not quite to the elbow. The minister, Mormor and my Moster Gun are there too . . . I have an angel certificate: En litet minnesblad fran Margaretha Garden, dopden 23/6 1940 i Tegelsmora forsamlings kyrka. I still have engraved silver spoons, a christening mug. This sort of thing was taken seriously in Sweden, land of the state church until 1961. The Lutheran Church is still the registrar of births, marriages and deaths in Sweden.'

Greta planned her trip with great care. It would, she thought, take about two weeks. She and Margareta set out from the Stockholm airport at Bromma on 29 December 1940, on a flight sometimes known as 'the last plane out of Sweden'. It was mid-winter when they left Greta's cold homeland 'for the even colder, darker land of Russia'. Greta's planned two weeks quickly began to stretch out. The journey would not have been possible at all if she had not been breastfeeding Margareta. On the first leg of the 'slow chundering flight to Riga, the capital of Latvia', Margareta writes, 'she breastfed Averil Harriman's daughter as well as her own. Mr Harriman had been appointed American ambassador in Moscow and Mrs Harriman was going to join him. Following American custom, she did not breastfeed her baby and she also did not have enough baby-food supplies for the trip . . . Can you imagine – Northern Europe, the end of 1940, food shortages, blackouts, Germans crossing which-way, Finland dithering, Russia not sure whose side she was on? And here was one woman quietly breastfeeding the child of another.

'From Riga the group went to Moscow by train. It was New Year. The Russians on the train were "very friendly men", who carried me in my cane basket, like those baskets now used for laundry. Years later, in Nelson, New Zealand, my mother lent it

to a Norwegian woman for her first baby, and never got it back: a
sore point.'

From Moscow Greta made the long journey by train to Baku
on the Caspian Sea, which she crossed by steamer to the Persian
coast. Then came a thirteen-hour car journey to Tehran, mostly by
night, over rough roads, through desolate country, where, the New
Zealand *Weekly News* was to report, 'the fierce demeanor of the
natives terrified her'.

More travel, to the Persian Gulf, then to Basra (in present-day
Iraq) where, at last, on 16 January, she joined the Empire air route.

'I wish I could say that from Basra all went well,' Margareta
writes. 'But it got not just worse but really worse.' They flew to
Karachi, then in India, and on to Bally Reach Airport in Calcutta.
'I was a good baby. I didn't cry much. I didn't want more food than
she had, and I didn't need water. I didn't try too hard to crawl. "I
had to stop you crawling," she told me later. But I did need milk.
And in Calcutta, in the five star Great Eastern Hotel, Mamma got
a breast abcess – not a minor eruption but the real thing. There was
no leaving on the 18th January for Singapore (dinner en route at
Bangkok). Tossing, turning, in the fan-swirled heat. Oh yes, it was
a good hotel, but it was wartime, it was India, and what was worse,
it was Calcutta.'

Many years later, when Margareta told her mother that she was
going on a guided trip to the Himalayas, Greta's face crumpled with
grief, tears poured down her face, 'they just tipped over'. No words.
She was not frightened by the Himalayas. She was remembering
Calcutta, which had come to symbolise 'everything that was awful
in her life from the time she married Oscar'.

No doctors were available. Her fever was as high as it could go.
But somehow the abscess was lanced and cleaned, and the fever
reduced. '"And all we had Mar-garee-tha, was aspirin. Aspirin!
Can you believe it? Oh, I cried and cried. And they told me I

couldn't feed you. But I did.'" And at last they could leave, and on 23 January flew, with dinner in-flight over Bangkok, to Singapore; and then to Surabaya, Darwin and Sydney. There, as one newspaper report put it, 'she was reunited with her husband'.

'What did Mamma and Oscar do in the week they had in Sydney? I hope they liked each other . . .' It was ten months since they had met. 'It hadn't been smooth in England. Would it be better now?'

Margareta has a certificate saying she had flown over the equator (in a plane called 'Circe'). 'The next certificate is signed by my father, the great Oscar Garden. He wasn't just The Sundowner of the Skies. He'd flown Miss Mobil the length and breadth of New Zealand in 1930. He had brought the second TEAL flying boat out from England in 1940. And now he flew his wife and daughter to New Zealand in the flying boat RMA Awarua, probably against company rules.'

The *New Zealand Free Lance*, the *Weekly News* and other papers ran stories about Greta's and Margareta's journey. '15,000 Mile Zig Zag, Mrs Garden's Odyssey', said the *Free Lance*. '"The Russian people are depressing,"' Greta said of her stay in Moscow.

There are also newspaper photos of the family landing in Auckland. Oscar, immaculate in his uniform, holds the baby awkwardly. He had met her for the first time only a few days earlier. Greta looks relaxed and happy, and Margareta fat and happy – complacent if a baby can be that. She's wearing 'an exquisite Alice blue crepe de chine frock and a matching sun-bonnet'.

The *Free Lance* added that 'like so many of her compatriots, Mrs Garden is very adept on skis and a bobsleigh'.

'Captain Garden and Mrs Garden will make their home at Rata Street, Parnell . . . Everything in the Garden is lovely,' said the *Auckland Star*.

It was the first of many childhood homes for Margareta. Oscar could not settle. Seemingly cheerful, he was inward-looking and self-centred – well suited to long-distance solo flying. Greta was strong, determined, resourceful, as her 'Odyssey' demonstrates. She enjoyed company and conversation and made friends easily, some of the new ones Swedes who had settled in Auckland. Oscar did not have much in common with these people. His work took him away from home; he was not there more than he was there. The couple quarrelled. It was a marriage destined to fall apart. There were no more children.

Margareta doesn't remember her childhood as unhappy. 'There should be memories of a breaking marriage,' she writes, 'but the photographs show sun, and picnics, and me with a small wheelbarrow, and happy, smiling people. There are even some of me being washed outside with no clothes on. Later, my mother was told coldly that "in New Zealand we do not go naked".' This, Margareta remarks, to a woman from a country where Anders Zorn painted natural round-bellied women pouring water on each other in saunas, and Carl Larsson showed children playing naked by lakes and rivers in the Swedish summers.

'No photos of my father,' she writes, 'though his life was public. He flew backwards and forwards across the Tasman, he went to parties, the races. He drank a lot, he bet at the totalisator and goodness knows where else . . . I think he also liked women.'

He also changed houses obsessively. From Parnell the family moved to Mission Bay, then to Green Bay where, on a two-acre section, Oscar tried his hand at growing a commercial crop of tulips, hiring a gardener to look after them. The house itself stood at the top of cliffs; and here, Margareta says, 'my mother loved and hated her way through the rest of her marriage'. She had a good singing voice and sang snatches of opera and Swedish folk songs. Oscar hated it and told her to stop. One of Margareta's memories is of her mother 'playing the piano and singing behind a locked door, while screaming and crying at the same time'.

The Swedish language also went the way of singing. Between two and three years old, Margareta chattered to her mother in Swedish. Then Oscar decided it would be sensible to stop it, and Greta agreed or seemed to agree. For a while Margareta spoke a mixture of English and Swedish until Swedish faded away, leaving only phrases and exclamations her mother still used.

Yet Green Bay remains a happy place in her memories. Three years old, she woke one morning while her parents were still sleeping, and made her way down flights of steps, carrying her doll, and was found wandering on the beach several hours later. Less happy was her attempt to help her father. With a friend, Maria, she decided to harvest the tulips, and 'cut every flower with a two inch stem and brought them into the kitchen'. Greta 'sat down and wept and wept . . . No doubt my father used this in various ways to undermine my mother, who was without family or support.'

Somehow Greta cut herself free. 'One day the car was packed, the dog and cat left behind, all my things were in a suitcase. My rocking horse had been given to the war orphans. I cried about that, loudly and passionately, although I'd never enjoyed playing on it. All my mother's things were in the car too. The drive was tense and polite. We arrived in the city at an old house that had stairs up the back and Mother and I were in our new home. We had left my father. The flat was in Parnell and we lived there for a few weeks until we moved to Campbells Bay, right by the sea. There the flat was one of three. The dunnies were out the back and across a yard. In front was a covered porch where I slept, a small bedroom at the back for my mother, a bathroom, and a dark living room right in the middle . . . But it was always summer . . . the beach was sandy, there were rocks at the south end towards Milford and a shelf of rocks to the north. There were lupins, a small general store, it was country. Getting to Auckland was a bus ride and a trip on the ferry.

'After the isolation of Green Bay this place teemed with children. We were all different ages but we all played together.' There were lots of cats and dogs. There was even a Norwegian family. And games of all sorts. She remembers the terror of being 'he' in Hide and Seek. She remembers Doctors and Nurses, where 'I seemed to be the main improviser. It was all based on enemas', which she knew something about. Trying to find a solution to 'their crumbling marriage', her parents had sent her off to the Sunshine Home for a weekend – 'it seemed to be much longer'. The rules were to move the bowels before breakfast. 'Those who didn't were placed on their backs under an enema device – four or five children could be done at once. Did I imagine this?' The experience made her in demand for Doctors and Nurses, 'but I don't think we got very far in any form of experimentation. It was a secret game as opposed to the noisy hide and seek.'

Oscar sometimes arrived on Sundays or off-work days to take them driving. 'This didn't work for me. They bickered. And bickered. The best bickering day Dad had driven us up country and the car got stuck. There we were stuffing tea tree and broom under the wheels and they were bicker, bicker, bicker. I don't think this happened always, but they both swore they never bickered. Years later I found a book called *Snip, Snap, Snorum* which seemed to sound the way they were. I was definitely a child who preferred my parents apart!

'I also spent weekends with Daddy when he wasn't flying. He lived in a flat in Mt Eden and he had a woman friend called Helen, who was a nurse. She didn't live with him. What do I remember about these days? There was a large koala bear – Daddy had brought him back from Australia. I loved him (the koala bear). My grandmother Rebecca was often there too. Daddy had to have a woman when I came because he couldn't do any housekeeping things. He couldn't make a bed. I don't think he could even make a cup of tea or a sandwich.

'I do remember once finding a sack full of chits. Tickets, cards, bits of printed stuff. I took some back to Mum – she told me it showed Daddy was gambling. I didn't know what gambling was, but I found out later. Any spare cash he had he spent betting on horses. He was always broke.

'Years later Dad said, "Your mother was mad, of course, quite mad. I don't know if she ever got better." And my mother: "Your father was quite mad of course. I don't suppose he'll ever be quite right in the head."'

'Mother wouldn't let me go to school because she thought five was too young. In Sweden they don't start till seven. But when I was three months over five she allowed me to go, and what a dreadful experience it was. I went by bus. All my Campbells Bay friends were in other classes. The infant class was peopled by children I'd never seen before. There was strapping, telling off, howling in front of the class, standing in the corner, wetting of pants. We had sleeps in the afternoon and in winter the whole school got together for cocoa.'

Her memories of this school are jumbled, not surprisingly. The next phase of her life was to go on for years.

'I got sick. It was measles. Mother got quinsy. The doctor came and he wouldn't lance her boil. My measles hurt inside and out and I refused to go to the toilet. I wasn't allowed to read because you could end up blind with measles. I got better and went back to the dreaded school and was put in the next class. I still didn't know anyone. Then I got sick again. This time it was flu . . . Back to school. Another class. Somewhere in there I had a birthday. It might have been between two bouts of flu and two bouts of pneumonia. There's a photo of me looking wan and sickly. By now

I was eating halibut liver capsules as though my life depended on them. It probably did. One day, back at school, one of my capsules broke and the smell went into my woollen gloves and everywhere through the classroom. I can't remember if I confessed.'

When summer came Oscar took her to Rotorua to recuperate. It was one thousand feet above sea level and good for 'chests'. At Whakarewarewa she met Guide Rangi. Oscar had known her since he flew in air shows around the country. Then back she went to Campbells Bay School, where she got pneumonia again. This time it was Greta who took her to Rotorua, where they stayed at Brents Hotel. Swimming was prescribed, which she did at the Blue Baths – and one day, walking back to the hotel, she collapsed and, lying on a trolley in the hotel kitchen, had an out-of-body experience where she watched from the ceiling as people rushed around looking after her.

'And then nothing for days, until I lay listening to voices whispering in the dark, hands smoothing me, it was eerie. I'd been transferred to Rotorua Hospital, to the critical section – we didn't all make it out of that room.' Then she was in a room of her own, overlooking the back yard. 'The verdict was empyema . . . Staphylococci in the lungs producing pus. "It will dry up in time," said Dr Bridgeman.'

A new drug, penicillin, was tried on her. 'For the first injection everyone came, Mummy, the doctors, two nurses. They apologised for it being painful.' She remembers a huge metal machine but has no idea what it was for. The second and third injections saw fewer people, and after that it was left to two nurses every three hours, night and day. In desperation she learned to sleep through it. 'But,' she says, 'the staff were wonderful. One special Maori porter brought me orange fizzy drinks, which helped my convalescence no end.

'Soon I graduated to the women's ward, everyone in together, except the really disturbed females. It was tougher. I managed to eat my Macleans toothpaste, get skin rashes from Lux toilet soap and collapse the first time I got out of bed' – not surprising after two months on her back. There was postural drainage too, where she lay helpless with the bed tipped up.

There were x-rays, lots of them. The hospital was supposed to ask permission but Greta never found out about it till years later. Margareta remembers 'a great metal chunk' being lowered on her. 'And I was bombarded with rays I presume.'

And cured, presumably. She left Rotorua Hospital at the end of 1946 and joined Greta in a house she had rented nearby. 'Poor Mum,' she writes, 'up there on the plateau for a holiday and trapped for three months. No friends, no support, just watching and waiting, and visiting when it was allowed.'

Yet Greta decided to stay in Rotorua, where the air was better for Margareta's health. So no more Campbells Bay, no more time at the beach 'with the endless summer'. But Margareta was never to forget the sand and the sun and the wild tribe of children she had run with.

They holidayed in Auckland, in 'a splendid mansion in St Martin's Lane just below Grafton Bridge', owned by friends of Greta's, the Gregorys. Esther Gregory was a Swede, who ran a massage business. 'I remember one night being in bed while a group of Swedish women were playing bridge and I was able to understand quite a bit of what they were saying.'

But in Auckland 'the worst happened'. Margareta fell sick again and went for a hospital check-up with a surgeon, Douglas Robb. 'And Dr Robb said I had to go to hospital for a lung operation because I had hydatids. Hydatids? "Well," he said, "you get hydatids from dogs and sheep. Your x-rays show you've got it. A large shady area in your right lung." So it was into Green Lane hospital, loads of penicillin jabs; a large ward of children; a tube in my back, taking out pus' – even though Dr Robb's diagnosis had been wrong. It was empyema again. 'After about ten weeks I was up and I walked around, peering into the TB room – kids dancing about, one doing somersaults up to the ceiling. And then down to the tonsils ward – loads of kids lying in bed with blood draining out of their mouths . . .'

After those ten weeks it was back to Rotorua, with a long jagged scar on her back. Greta rented 'a wonderful old villa with a large garden with apple and plum trees'. She started a job in the office at Horrocks's Fine Fashions and took in boarders, one of them a Caltex tanker driver, who took the convalescing child on a long drive (against company rules) to Taupō and back. It was a mixed neighbourhood of Pākehā and Māori. Margareta played happily with children from both groups, although was puzzled by one Māori family who made it plain that they were superior to the rest. It seemed like Pākehā behaviour.

Her bad luck in schooling went on. Just as she was making good progress in Primer Four at Rotorua Primary, a polio epidemic closed all schools. Lessons came from the Correspondence School. 'It was rather like being sick – no school.' But a neighbour who had disowned her daughter for getting pregnant gave Margareta the errant teenager's 'wonderful collection of L.M. Montgomery and Enid Blyton novels', so her reading went on apace.

When the schools reopened she went back to Primer Four at Rotorua Primary, but found it hard integrating into a class of children who had been together since Primer One. Promotion to a huge Standard One class was even harder. 'I couldn't quite grab what it was all about. Strapping of course, no talking, no giggling.' Although she made one good friend, Rhonda Pearce, 'who later became Air New Zealand's "hostess of the year"', she was happy to transfer to the newly built Glenholme School, closer to home. It could be reached by walking with her neighbourhood friends.

Glenholme School provides few memories. There was Mr Hahn, who 'must have been good because he left none'. And the inaptly named Mr Civil, who 'had a fixation on discipline and focused on particular boys. It was horrid. There was a really nice kid, Terence, who lived not far from me, who was picked on nearly every day and taken out the back for his six-of-the-best. I never noticed Terence did anything wrong. I only got strapped once – a group of us girls were eating Throaties, a forbidden thing in class . . . Each of us got strapped once on the hand.'

The happy street life went on: winters with iced-over puddles and summers as hot as Auckland's had been. But one Pākehā woman refused to let her children play with Margareta because in warm weather Greta let her wear shorts and no top. A child from that family gave a second reason: Greta was divorced.

She wasn't yet. There was no formal custody arrangement. In the school holidays Margareta went to Oscar, who called in his mother or sisters to look after her when he was away on flights. He was now chief pilot at TEAL. The minding arrangements did not always suit the sisters. Violet, a spiteful and unstable woman, wanted Oscar to claim custody. Greta should be sent back to Sweden, she said, and she herself would take care of the child. Oscar was too canny for that. He seemed satisfied to share his daughter and call in one of his band of helpers when she came to stay. He was fond of Margareta; fond enough, or perhaps possessive, perhaps revengeful enough, to say no, with full sisterly support, when Greta made an effort to shift back to Sweden. She was pining for her own country but she remained trapped in New Zealand until Margareta grew up.

They moved to Picton. Greta was following a man but it came to nothing. Where to next? Nelson was close. They went there and Greta took a housekeeping job in Brightwater for several months, while Margareta went to Brightwater School. They shifted to a rental house on the Rocks Road hillside above Tahunanui beach outside Nelson city. Here Margareta, now nine years old, began the longest settled spell of her childhood. She was on the Rocks Road hillside, in two different houses, for five years.

Oscar's life had changed by now, more dramatically. He was promoted to head of operations at TEAL and was soon in a bitter dispute with the company's managers. They wanted to buy more flying boats. Oscar saw that the future was in land not seaplanes, and he argued stubbornly for the new four-engined Douglas DC-4s. When the TEAL management went against his opinion and bought more flying boats Oscar resigned. At almost the same time his and Greta's divorce came through, and he quickly married Helen Lovell, the Westport nurse who had helped him when Margareta stayed. He went north to Kerikeri and began a new life as a citrus grower and never flew an aeroplane again. At various times he grew oranges in the north, owned a milkbar in Paeroa and grew tomatoes in Tauranga. It was a curiously earthbound existence for a man who had been The Sundowner of the Skies. He and Helen had two daughters and a son, and Margareta spent most of her school holidays with the family. She remembers these as working times. She picked tomatoes and helped look after the babies. She and Helen got on well. Oscar too remained fond of her, although he never seemed to know quite what to do with children. One of Margareta's half-sisters believes that he married Helen only to secure a minder for Margareta and that he liked his first daughter more than his second and third.

In Nelson Greta rode her bicycle along Rocks Road each morning to Griffin's biscuit factory near the centre of town, where she worked in the office. Margareta went to Tahunanui Primary School, the fourth of her nine schools. She was happy and adventurous and made friends easily; and learned easily too. At Nelson Intermediate School she spent two years in a class for quick learners, taught by a woman called Alexandra Gordon Kane, who is remembered to this day by elderly men and women around Nelson. 'Ah,' they say, 'Miss Kane.' They talk of her quick sympathies, the interest she put into her lessons, and her demand for hard work. Margareta thrived. The territory, Rocks Road, the beach, that school and that teacher take a central place in her memories. She roamed the hillside, often followed by her white cat, Sessan – short for the Swedish Princessan. Sessan went with her to the beach, tagging along, and waited while she paddled or swam in the shallows where the stream draining the hillside flowed out. It did not follow as far as the back beach, a tidal flat behind Tahunanui spit, a favourite playground as she grew older. The back beach was a meeting place for local children and here she had her first encounters with boys, running madly from a pursuer who was allowed to kiss her if he caught her. She ran fast.

Her mother was the most important person in her life, her father and his family an interesting diversion. She might be called away every holiday but coming home to her mother gave her the security she needed. There was never any question in her mind about who she belonged with. In her infant days she had written notes and birthday cards to 'my darling mummy' and 'the best mummy in the world', and these were more than exercises in sentimentality. The closeness continued into her early teens. Greta's fractured life found its steady centre in Margareta. The loss of her country and the failure of her marriage produced an even deeper melancholy in her, but her determination to give her daughter a happy childhood never wavered. Greta became a formidable person. But she was always under the strains of insecurity and shortage of money, and so she kept on changing jobs.

During Margareta's Third Form year at Nelson College for

Girls, Greta shifted to what must have seemed more settled work in Wellington, leaving Margareta boarding with a family called Grossmith, who lived higher up the hillside overlooking the beach. This arrangement was to last for almost a year. The loss of her mother did not cause Margareta pain or grief. She had not lost her neighbourhood or school or friends, and her equable nature seemed in any case suited to change. She liked the Grossmiths, found them different, stimulating, interesting, and their daughter Lucilla was her own age.

Different the Grossmiths certainly were – in habits, outlook, background, social standing – but they were also warm-hearted and welcoming and were pleased to have a companion for Lucilla, an only child. They were English, very English. The term that comes to mind for imposing and opinionated Mrs Grossmith is 'County', although she was without snobbishness. George had taught at Eton and now taught at Nelson College. He had a family connection with the Grossmith brothers, George and Weedon, who wrote the comic novel *Diary of a Nobody* that had been popular in late-Victorian England and is still read.

Margareta stepped into this family without strain. She enjoyed their difference, coped well with their rules and formality, and got on with Lucilla easily enough. She enjoyed George's practice of testing the girls in world and current affairs at the dinner table. It suited her quickness of mind. He read *The Times*, which came by sea, and many of his questions were about England – so the girls read *The Times* too. He dropped them off at Nelson College for Girls as he drove to his job at Nelson College. (One had to be careful to get those names right.) Margareta did the Professional course while many of her intermediate school friends were in General. Some of the friendships fell away; others persisted and went on for years. The lessons caused her no trouble. She was liked by both teachers and fellow pupils. Everything ran smoothly. She and her mother wrote back and forth, and although Margareta still spent school holidays with her father and his family her connection to Greta stayed close.

They were able to see each other during the Royal Tour in 1953, when Margareta was included in a group of Girl Guides chosen to represent the Nelson district in the presentation of a giant jigsaw puzzle to the Queen. Margareta fitted in the Nelson piece of the puzzle. A newspaper photograph shows her as a neatly uniformed, blond-haired thirteen-year-old pointing out Nelson in the completed puzzle to a group of dignitaries and parliamentarians, with Keith Holyoake prominent among them. She looks confident and in full control.

Religion was the only thing causing trouble. The Grossmiths were Catholic while Greta, although a Lutheran, had sent Margareta to a Church of England Sunday school and then to an Anglican church, where she was confirmed before Greta left. There were things she enjoyed about the services but religious belief never took a strong hold on her. When the Grossmiths went to Sunday service they saw to it that Margareta went off to the Anglican church, as they had agreed with Greta. But Margareta circled back and spent her Sunday mornings with a friend, Caroline Brett, who had been a year behind her at intermediate school and who lived on Rocks Road almost next door to the house Margareta had been in. The Bretts were anything but religious – they were atheists and left-wingers and provided a healthy antidote to the Grossmiths.

Mrs Grossmiths found out and reported her to Greta, who asked that they take Margareta to Catholic services with them. She went only once. The incense made her feel sick, or so she claimed, and the Grossmiths, who had not wanted to convert her anyway, let her run free on Sundays after that. She spent her time happily with the irreligious Bretts.

At the end of 1954 Greta took a job as matron of House 4 in the dental nurses' hostel in Woburn, Lower Hutt. She also kept her daytime work in the office at Griffin's biscuit factory in Petone. One of her conditions when taking the hostel job was that she could have her daughter living with her. So Margareta joined her mother again. She had liked the Grossmiths and enjoyed her time with them, and had been happy at Nelson College for Girls, but she made the change without distress or even regret, pleased to be back with her mother.

The new environment was exciting too. The hostel was a busy, noisy place, with dozens of student nurses, most of them in their late teens, setting off in pairs and groups over the nearby footbridge to Woburn Station in the morning, heading for the Dental College in Wellington, and returning late in the afternoon, flooding into the hostel and transforming it into a hive of active, lively young women. Margareta loved it. At first she shared her mother's room but this didn't work out, so she went in with one of the nurses, changing room-mates as the intakes came and went, learning each new partner quickly and (mostly) enjoying them. She ate breakfast and dinner in the dining hall with the nurses, and learned to fill in on the telephone switchboard for her mother. She was at the hostel for three years.

Greta had no worries about Margareta mixing with older girls. She could keep an eye on her and see that she did not become precocious or get 'led astray'. School, however, was a different matter. The Hutt Valley scandal had filled the papers the year before: teenagers meeting in milkbars and running wild at night, sex in parks and cemeteries, Teddy boys, bodgies and widgies, a generation out of control. *Truth* in particular (an uncle of Margareta's on her father's side was managing director) let itself go. Soon the government set up a committee and the Mazengarb Report, named after its chairman, was published and a copy sent to every household in New Zealand. The report came down heavily on the need for the teaching of morals, for a strict home life and more religious teaching, and suggested that co-ed schools were to blame for much of the delinquency. Hutt Valley High School, co-educational, was where Margareta would normally have gone. Instead Greta, stretching her finances, enrolled her at Chilton Saint James, an all-girls private school run by the Anglican Church.

Margareta was an accepting fourteen-year-old with a happy nature, so she did not mind. For her school was school and she did not see why she should not make friends at this one. She had come from single-sex Nelson College for Girls and was used to not having boys around.

She got on well at Chilton Saint James, socially and scholastically. The girls, she found, were no different from the ones at Nelson, although speaking and behaving properly was very much a requirement. Margareta spoke 'properly' after her year with the Grossmiths. Her mother's Swedish vowels had rubbed off on her too. There were no problems there. The fact that she had a divorced foreign mother and lived in a hostel with dental nurses across on the 'wrong side' of the railway tracks did not seem to worry the other girls; they were interested, some of them envious perhaps. Margareta's diary for this year describes friendships, which began and lasted or changed; lessons – French, geography, English, science – which she seemed to have enjoyed one day and hated the next; examinations that she was always nervous about but did well in and was sometimes 'top'. There were some failures. In the 1955 mid-year examination she was third in arithmetic but with only 49 per cent. 'Ginny got 89% and came 1st. The next was 59% and I think it is disgusting! However apart from Divinity it will be the only subject I fail in which is lucky.'

It's an entertaining diary. At the hostel the intakes come and go, the room-mates change. 'I do not like these girls but the next draft should be better.' Her closeness to her mother continues. She had a 'horrid gym practice' for the exam but 'didn't feel scared' because 'Mummy said I should do my best. She's an awfully good adviser'. Several times she decides that she'd like to be a writer. 'The trouble with me is that I can't start off a book properly and I think it's the first few words that count. I don't want to be like George Joseph's character who bought all his own books because no one else would.' There's a picture theatre in the street next to the hostel and she goes there often with school friends or trainee nurses, always naming the picture and passing judgement. She worked at friendships, seeming to change frequently. In the school play 'I am Cassius in Julius Caesar . . . "the one who says little but thinks much" and who is jealous. I play opposite Madeleine. She is a likely friend and I'm going to cultivate Patricia Muston and Diana Halstead.'

Greta continued to hold down two jobs but somehow made time for friends, some of them Swedish. Margareta often went visiting with her, and on shopping expeditions to Wellington – but 1956, her School Certificate year, was the year she began to take notice of boys. A boy called Merv has a large place in her thoughts. 'I still would like to see Merv. Haven't seen him for two months but it sure gets stronger.' Later she declares that she loves him. Then there's a boy who drives her home from a dance and kisses her but stops because he wants to be 'honourable'. She doesn't say whether she's relieved or disappointed. There's a Peter too, who realises 'that I only want to see him platonically'.

In this year she found her vocation. In Nelson she had been a student helper in the public library and enjoyed it. In Wellington she volunteered for after-school work in the Lower Hutt Library and enjoyed it even more. 'I always feel really good after it. I don't know why.' She decides in this year that she will be a librarian when she leaves school. There's no more mention of writing books.

Merv is out of the picture and there's Brian now. 'Brian rang!! I am going out with him on Saturday. – I don't want to be in a dance hall all the time either. Hope he doesn't!' The day before, 'Judy and I were in the stackroom and discovered "The Physiology of Sex". Most interesting. Gee, when I think of Brian . . .'

The diary is reticent, but whatever happened was well short of Mazengarbarous (Allen Curnow's word).

She passed her School Certificate exam and changed from Chilton Saint James to Hutt Valley High School for her Sixth Form year, a decision made jointly with her mother. She soon decided that 'Hutt was seventy times better than Chilton St. James.' It's a co-ed school to begin with, and this year, 1957, is definitely the year for boys. She's clear-eyed about them, lists the ones in her class and gives them names: Long-nose, Sailor Boy, Blob. Others are 'Quiet, short, nondescript. Useful.' 'Too young. Not poetic.' 'Shorty, crewcut. Stares at me.' One 'just gets me here'. She had 'a real dinkum attraction for him'. But she's always clear-headed as well as clear-eyed, and school work and after-school work in the library took up most of her time.

It's a busy year, with University Entrance accrediting looming, weekend visiting with her mother, holidays with her father (picking tomatoes), tennis, basketball (as netball was then called), and a new activity, tramping, which she really loved. Her social activity kept up its hectic pace: dances, parties and the activity known as necking, or petting, which she sometimes enjoyed and sometimes didn't.

Towards the end of the year Greta started looking for a house to buy. Living in a hostel and having two jobs was wearing her out. Somehow she had put money by. A friend helped with a loan. She and Margareta went house-hunting in weekends, in Wellington mostly but also in the Hutt. They rejected houses – too small, too big, too far out of town – but at year's end Greta bought a small colonial cottage in Ascot Terrace in Thorndon, an inner Wellington suburb. Before they shifted, though, trouble erupted between mother and daughter. Greta must have been worried that Margareta was going to so many dances and seeing so many boys, and perhaps neglecting her school work. Just what was her seventeen-year-old daughter getting up to? She went to the diaries to find out. They didn't give much away, just 'necking' outside dance halls and in cars, but she must have been alarmed by Margareta being so excited by a certain Paul: if he wanted to she would too, she wrote. Greta confronted her daughter, who was horrified, then furious, that her mother had read her diaries. There was a lot of anger on both sides, of arguing and denying, followed by tears. Yet mother and daughter were close enough to ride the crisis out. The 1957 diary becomes skimpy after that. There's no new one for 1958.

Margareta had her UE accredited. She and her mother shifted to the house in Ascot Terrace, and her hostel and school days came to an end.

THREE

Greta's time of authority was over. They were now two women sharing a house, cemented together by affection and care, although Greta continued to worry about where her daughter's life was going. Margareta had no worries of that sort. She knew what she wanted to be. She got on easily with people and they with her. She was strong-minded, able to work hard and with purpose. Her life had been one of almost constant change but she had come through it – through living, in a way, on the edges – without emotional damage and with an outlook almost entirely cheerful. At seventeen she was an attractive young woman with a healthy and vigorous appetite for life. The way ahead seemed straight to her.

She enrolled in the New Zealand Library School certificate course – three years of study done largely by correspondence. She enrolled for Stage One English at Victoria University. And using her Hutt Library experience and her University Entrance as qualifications, she applied for and got a job as junior assistant at the Army Headquarters Library in Aitken Street. She either walked down from Ascot Terrace or, after an 8 a.m. English lecture, down The Terrace to Bowen Street, both ways taking her past the Alexander Turnbull Library where she was to spend many years of her working life.

The Army Headquarters Library turned out to be a good choice. It was staffed by a librarian, an assistant librarian and a junior assistant. She learned to handle a wide range of material, for the headquarters staff and for sending to the various military camps – non-fiction and fiction, professional and recreational reading. It was a relaxed institution, busy always but without strains or pressures, and the military staff using it proved to be friendly and were no doubt pleased that the new junior assistant was competent and lively. She was called on to help at staff social functions. At one of them she filled several glasses of beer with froth and a patient officer took her aside and taught her how to pour properly – a useful lesson.

There were also other ranks, equally friendly. One who came in often to see his librarian wife was part-time soldier, part-time law student Michael Bungay. He was, Margareta says, 'a hilarious fellow', who now and then presented himself as an ex-London barrow boy. Michael Bungay was soon to become New Zealand's best-known criminal lawyer, defending many high-profile cases.

She tried to learn the guitar and became a good strummer but never went further than that. On a flight to Wellington from Westport, where she had travelled for a weekend to help Helen Garden with her children (Margareta's half-siblings), the plane was caught in bad weather and circled Wellington Airport for half an hour waiting for a chance to land. Margareta played her guitar to help calm nervous passengers.

There were, of course, parties and dances, and a serious though not long-lasting boyfriend, but she spent most of her free time in these two years on weekend trips with the Hutt Valley Tramping Club. There are many tramping photographs in her 1958–59 albums – taken in the Orongorongos and the Tararuas, and on longer trips to Tongariro National Park. With three male friends – not HVTC members – she made the difficult and sometimes dangerous four-day traverse from the Lewis Pass road to Rotoiti in the Nelson Lakes. In these tramping years she made a close long-standing friend, Malcolm Ford, who went on to a career in Antarctic research and whose early death in 1996 caused Margareta great sadness. Malcolm, open-natured, a large and friendly bear, was the nicest man she had ever met, although she made it clear to him that their friendship was 'platonic'. This was because, at nineteen, she had met the first man she felt might become a serious partner – a life partner perhaps. He was Syd Jackson, later a well-known Māori land rights activist and trade unionist, but at this point in his career a personable young university student. The affair lasted some months but Syd failed to reach Margareta's level of commitment, and to her sorrow he ended it. She felt ever afterwards that he wanted, perhaps needed, a Māori wife.

By the end of 1959 she was ready to move on from the Army Headquarters Library and to shift out of Wellington. Greta still lived in the Ascot Terrace house, but she too was restless and in the years that followed would move from job to job and change houses several times. With Margareta no longer dependent she was free to go back to Sweden, but she chose to stay in New Zealand a few more years. She was reliable in the jobs she took and close to her few friends, but not a neighbourly woman and not easy to get to know. The neighbour over her side fence, on Newman Terrace below Ascot Terrace, was the artist Rita Angus, but it seems the only contact between the two women was a heated argument when Greta cut branches growing across the boundary fence from Rita Angus's side.

It was time for Margareta to leave home. She applied for a job in the Ardmore Teachers' College library just south of Auckland and shifted there early in 1960. Once again she was the youngest on the staff. The librarian, Christina Troup, found her able and intelligent. Christina was a boss who kept strict control, but Margareta got on well with her. Just as importantly, she enjoyed her contact with the students. Many were trainee teachers from Samoa, Tonga, Fiji and other islands. She formed close friendships with several and they became part of her social life. Living in the campus hostel – her second hostel – she fitted in easily and went out with groups to parties and dances. So, with work and friendships and study for her certificate, it was a full life. Weekend hitch-hiking trips to Wellington became part of it, and these were mostly made without incident. She had several frights though. With another young woman from the library she was picked up by a middle-aged man who stopped the car on a lonely part of the road and said, 'Which one of you is going to be first?' Margareta was by the door. She flung it open and ran back up the road, hoping that with one victim free the driver would have to let the other go. He saw it that way too – pushed out Margareta's friend and drove off, stopping several hundred yards up the road to throw out their packs. On a later trip, alone this time, she was picked up on the Desert Road by a trustee prisoner from Rangipō prison farm, driving a van. They talked in a friendly way and then politely he asked for sex. Margareta said no, to which he replied 'Okay', and they drove on. She remembers other scares, in one of which she grabbed the car steering wheel and forced the vehicle into the gutter. Yet she persisted. Hitch-hiking remained her chief method of long-distance travel in her Ardmore years.

At the end of 1961, her certificate course completed, she began looking around for a job with more responsibility. Sole charge was what she wanted, hands-on experience, and she was likelier to find that in the country. The opportunity came through an older woman, Dorothy Grover, who had befriended Margareta at weekend Library School courses. Dorothy had to give up her job to nurse a sick daughter and recommended Margareta to take it over. So, at twenty, Miss Garden became librarian in charge of the Taumarunui Public Library.

She could not have found a place further from the city: 'Taumarunui on the main trunk line', as Peter Cape's song describes it, lies almost in the centre of the North Island, equidistant from Wellington and

Auckland and with no other town of any size close. Freight trains ran through. The Express and the Limited made after-midnight stops so passengers could buy a pie and a cup of tea at the station tearooms. The main north–south highway, only two lanes wide, became the town's main street for half a mile. The population at that time was not much more than a thousand.

Margareta found board with an old woman in the railway settlement across the river from the town. At work she had two part-time helpers but all essential library functions – book selection and buying, cataloguing, library policy – were hers to control. Council soon saw that it had a competent librarian, and an agreeable person too. She reported to the Library Committee chairman, who was happy to let her get on with the job. The local bookseller and sole supplier of books to the library became a good friend. The borrowers and browsers seemed satisfied. Enrolments increased. But Margareta had one disappointment. At Ardmore she had enjoyed getting to know the Pacific Island students, had made friends among them, lived in the hostel with them and had had a Samoan boyfriend, and had felt that shifting to Taumarunui would give her the chance to get to know Māori too. There were many living in the town, which sat in the middle of a wide Māori hinterland. Almost none were enrolled at the library. She was eager to get more. It did not happen. Perhaps they saw it as a Pākehā institution. And in those days, and in that town, there was division and discrimination: pubs and clubs where Māori were not welcome. The sign 'No Maoris' still appeared in boarding-house windows. In her two years in Taumarunui Margareta never managed to attract more than a handful of Māori to the library and did not get to know any socially.

She kept up her visits to her mother, hitch-hiking still; and, less frequently, to her father, who was now growing tomatoes on a property near Tauranga. She made friends in the town. One,

Michael Mattar, was a dress designer and was openly gay (a word not in use in the early sixties). He lived with his partner but suffered no discrimination either for his sexuality or his profession in a town – and at a time – where one would have expected ridicule, bigotry, or worse. Michael made a ball dress for Margareta. She kept it for many years before donating it to Te Papa, where it is, presumably, still held. Through Michael she met another Lebanese man, not gay, and went with him to parties and dances. By this time she had shifted from the railway settlement to board with a couple closer to work. They, Mae and Tom Morrison, were deeply religious and can hardly have approved of her free behaviour. They remained, however, friends for many years, appointing themselves almost substitute parents.

But Taumarunui, for all its work experience and social pleasures, was no more than a stopping-off place. After two years Margareta wanted a spell away from libraries. Others her age were setting off on that rite of passage, the great OE. But 'Overseas' never attracted her. Why go there when New Zealand was waiting to be explored? Living in a country town and working in a profession had made her aware that there were places to see and different jobs to do here at home.

She gave up librarianship and joined a shearing gang. It was run by a Taumarunui couple, Doug and Therese Morris, and was only five strong. Doug and a man remembered only as Alkie were the shearers; Therese, who had to mind two young children who travelled along, was cook; and Margareta and another young woman, Anne, were fleecoes, or rousies as they were sometimes called in this gang. It was hard work, dawn to dusk, but she was strong and fit and quick to learn, and she enjoyed her fellow workers and stayed for the whole season.

The contracts were sometimes on small runs along the upper reaches of the Whanganui River but the gang often joined with others on larger blocks and once worked in the huge sheds on the government block in the Tongariro National Park. Writing to her mother, Margareta describes the life: 'Our day starts with a loud yell from one of the boys. If we are at Therese's it is usually Doug but at other sheds one of the others has a go. At first we used to spring up without a second thought but now we stay in the sack until the last possible moment. Then we swill down a cup o' char and several slices of bread, as many as we can get through, and make our way to the shed. At first I tried not to eat before breakfast but I got so hungry by 6 that I just had to start . . . Shearing is a fascinating business. Every chap shears differently and at totally different speeds and styles. Anne and I have fleecoed for 11 different shearers and we like comparing them all. Doug is lovely to watch, he is the fastest, his highest tally is 365 a day. Most shearers in a gang do a steady 200 . . . Some gangs with some real "gun" shearers may have a couple doing 300 a day but they are hard to come by. Doug's style is very neat and strong. The prettiest line in shearing is coming from the tail to the neck in a long back stroke and he is lovely to watch on that . . . At Moerangi we were fleecoes for two shearers, at Hura's for three, and were sorters as well . . . In the last shed I was at, I had to keep the board clear with only six inches or so to walk along and in certain shearing positions I couldn't get through at all. There was hardly room to pick up the fleeces and on the table they couldn't be thrown properly because it was too small . . .'

Hard work, the non-stop rhythm of it, short breaks, joking, camaraderie, a cold beer when the day was done and a meal of mutton from a freshly-killed sheep – she loved it all and remembers it as one of the great times of her life.

The season ended. It was either back to libraries or another country job. In Nelson it was apple-picking time. She went there. Eastons Orchard on the coast road between Māpua and Motueka was one of the larger ones, and she worked the whole season there, enjoying the physical work, the ten-hour days, the companionship at night in the pickers' huts, and trips to Motueka to dances and, on Sunday, over the hill to Golden Bay. Ivy Brett, at whose Tahunanui house she had found refuge from church-going as a schoolgirl, now lived alone on a small farm above Ruby Bay, and Margareta sometimes went there, renewing a friendship that lasted until Ivy's death in the 1980s.

Other jobs followed, the most memorable being a stint as housemaid at the hotel on Kawau Island, north of Auckland. Somewhere along the way she worked with a Latvian woman called Aino Krumins, a connection that was to prove important. But the time was coming when she had to think of a permanent working future. Short-term, physical country jobs were exploratory expeditions outside librarianship, where her real interest lay. She was never to forget her year of shearing work, apple-picking and the rest, and always held that it gave her more interesting travel than the year in London with side-trips to the continent that so many of her contemporaries had chosen.

The Army Headquarters Library; a small-town public library – she decided to try for a different sort, and in Wellington where her mother still lived. A vacancy for a cataloguer came up in the Alexander Turnbull Library, and although her experience did not exactly fit she applied for it. Perhaps it was her broader work history together with her rural working adventure that appealed to chief librarian John Reece Cole, perhaps her confidence and cheerful personality. Whatever it was, he decided to appoint her. Yet there was a small hiccup. For some reason she changed her mind and joined an advertising agency instead. It was a crazy decision, as she realised almost straight away. Everything about the agency and the work she was given to do bored her. So she quit and headed back to the Turnbull – where she found the cataloguing job still unfilled and John Cole ready to overlook her scattiness and take her on.

So, in June 1963, she began the first of her three periods of work at New Zealand's leading research library.

Everyone who worked in the old Turnbull House at the foot of Bowen Street grew fond of the building, even though it tested them. There were three floors linked by stairs, with workrooms, stack rooms, a reading room, offices and a staff room taking up large and small spaces that had been Alexander Turnbull's living areas, bedrooms, bathroom and library. It wasn't ideal for a research library but the makeover was carefully thought out and, with efficient and interested staff, it worked. (For an account of the library, its beginnings and history, see Rachel Barrowman's *The Turnbull: A Library and Its World*.)

Margareta fitted in and was soon at home. At first she lived at Ascot Terrace with her mother, but then rented a cottage, one in a row of four early working-men's houses, in Footscray Avenue, a blind alley off Abel Smith Street, close to its meeting with upper Cuba Street. From here she could walk to work in half an hour, or take a tram if she was late.

Cataloguing needs close attention and concentration. The publications Margareta handled were not the more demanding ones, which went to senior staff or were done by head cataloguer Nancy Irvine, but the material that came to her was usually interesting and the procedures for getting it catalogued and described were ones that appealed to her orderly mind. She became an efficient and well-accepted member of the half-dozen cataloguing staff, even though her interest began to veer towards other areas of the Turnbull's work.

Among those who became friends in her five years at the library her favourite was Tony Murray-Oliver, in charge of pictures. He was middle-aged when Margareta came, was artistic and had wide interests, and was thoroughly on top of his job. Largely self-named (Tony Oliver somehow became Anthony Audrey St Clair Murray Murray-Oliver), self-created it almost seemed, he inhabited the building like an overgrown sprite. Margareta always thought he rather fancied her, but then he rather fancied young men too. Tony was the only member of the Turnbull staff she invited to her wedding.

Before long she shifted from cataloguing to the reference department. She had enjoyed cataloguing, closed off from the public though it was, but enjoyed reference, learning the collections, making them available to researchers – people like J.C. Beaglehole and Ormond Wilson – even more. One afternoon, well-known Wellington provocateur, raconteur and literary fringe-dweller Brian Bell rushed into the reference room asking for a place to hide because, he said, the police were chasing him. Tony Murray-Oliver showed him the back way out of the library and how to get down to Lambton Quay without being caught. No chasing policemen ever turned up. (I should add that Brian Bell was a talented and busy photographer. His images are being used more and more.) Margareta's employment remained in the reference department, or Archives and Manuscripts as it came to be called, in all three of her times at the library.

Work, mother, father, parties, dances: her life was full. It was her love of the outdoors that led to the first big change. Her Latvian friend Aino Krumins and her husband Gundars, an Estonian, ran canoe camping trips down the Whanganui River. Margareta knew the Whanganui in its upper reaches. It flowed past Taumarunui, at the back of town, and she had worked as a fleeco on farms along its banks. The chance to follow it on its 180-mile journey through wild bush and twisting gorges, past tiny settlements and down to the sea appealed to her sense of adventure. She booked in for a trip early in 1964.

Paddling along was a young man called Stuart Hickman, who also worked in a library. He was a year younger than her but they got on well, sharing a canoe. Stuart was bright, intelligent, funny, and had a mind that went off in unusual directions. He claimed to be an anarchist, which intrigued Margareta. By the time the canoes reached Whanganui they were also sharing a tent.

It turned out to be more than a holiday affair. The relationship developed; they lived together in the Footscray Avenue cottage; Margareta met Stuart's friends, some of them also claiming to be anarchists (and indulging in mild acts of lawlessness). She found them childish but entertaining. It was, on the whole, a happy time. As for Greta, she had accepted by now that Margareta would go her own way. It was at this time that she (Greta) made an attempt to shift back to Sweden, but she found the country so changed that she could not settle down, could scarcely recognise it; so back she came to New Zealand, where she did not want to be, and resumed her lonely and embittered life.

Margareta and Stuart married in November at the Wellington Registry Office, Margareta dressing for the ceremony in a new dress and hat (and seeming out of character). Stuart wore a full beard and a suit. Tony Murray-Oliver, smiling his cat-like smile, acted as witness.

For a while they got on well with each other. There were areas of compatibility. It's hard to say why they drifted apart. Margareta seems unsure – perhaps not enough shared intellectual and emotional territory. She sometimes found the antics and opinions of his friends a strain, while continuing to respond to his sometimes wild humour, to his kindness and his charm. She was, possibly, older in the head than him, even though his range of knowledge and opinion was in many areas wider. A need for independence began to show itself in both of them.

In 1966 Stuart took up work with the Country Library Service, driving a book van to outlying settlements. Margareta went along with him on one trip and saw how the work suited him. They kept their off-and-on marriage alive, neither seeming anxious about it or more ambitious for it. It was early in this year that she came bounding up the stairs in the Turnbull Library and found me half-heartedly reading politicians' letters in the little room at the top of the house. We liked the look of each other but then forgot. Our paths crossed once or twice. She was busy with her failing marriage, while I was busy with my library course, and trying and failing to write.

It changed in the following year when I took a cataloguing job at the Turnbull. We gradually, then with increasing momentum, became visible to one another – and over that year she and I became Margareta and Maurice.

FOUR

I never met Stuart. He had no ghostly presence. Margareta and I did not talk about him, or why their marriage had failed, or when it might, officially, end. She kept up her rental of the Footscray Avenue cottage. It was never a case of lover sneaking in the back door when husband went out the front. I had no sense of Stuart at all.

My nine-year-old son Nigel was living with me in the Weld Street house, high on Tinakori Hill. Our life together was always under threat, which made the ground shaky for Margareta and me. Hera, not Stuart Hickman, was a presence.

Yet we became a unit. Oddly enough our happiest times were at work, where some of the excitement of 'affair' kept on. We were, it seems, not quite grown-up there. We kept up the pretence that nobody knew, a game that lasted several months. We took the same lunch hour, left the library separately and met in the Bowen Street cemetery, where we talked and ate sitting on the grass among the gravestones. Our friends at work were not deceived; they watched with amusement.

I met Margareta's mother. She was no more than polite to me, and I saw that I did not measure up. If her daughter's marriage was ending – she did not mind that – then she wanted a partner for her who had a 'proper' career, providing security and a comfortable life: a man in business perhaps, or mounting the ladder in a profession, not a penniless librarian with a child in tow. I was always a disappointment to Greta. She tried to talk Margareta out of me and accused her of 'making a religion of

353

this man'. This was so absurd that Margareta only laughed. We continued on our way.

I soon learned, though, that I could not take Margareta for granted. I learned what I came to call her 'suddenness'. She arrived at Weld Street to spend the weekend. On Saturday we decided to walk in the Wilton Bush and up into the hills. But before we could start Ray Grover arrived and we sat down to watch a Bogart/Chandler film on TV. Margareta left the room and did not come back. I supposed she was busy in the kitchen. When the movie ended I went looking for her. She was gone – no word, no note. When I phoned her at Footscray Avenue she said, 'If that's what you're going to do we're finished,' and put down the phone, and did not come back that weekend. We repaired the breach. But I had learned that she was not a busy-in-the-kitchen sort of woman.

Hera arrived to claim Nigel back. He was happy with me and did not want to go. I began custody proceedings and Nigel became a ward of court, in my care, with Hera allowed access for holidays. She came at Christmas and took him for a two-week 'holiday up north'. Hera was a pragmatist and just as 'sudden' as Margareta. To her a court order was scratches on paper. From up north at her sister's place she and Nigel vanished – to Australia, I thought, or somewhere even further away?

It led to an even shakier time for Margareta and me. I resigned from my job at the library and went hunting for Nigel – 'up north', in Rotorua, around the Bay of Plenty, where Hera also had family, and in Sydney. It took me three months to admit defeat. Margareta had already begun divorce proceedings and was in a kind of limbo. She left the Footscray cottage and rented a flat in Wadestown, halfway down Oban Street towards the Ngauranga Gorge. She waited there while I kept up my hunting – but would not wait forever. For a while it seemed our time together would come to a stuttering end. I chased several more false leads, and then – there was nothing else to do – gave it up and went to the place where, it seemed, I belonged. I joined Margareta in Oban Street and our lives as a couple, married in a way, at last began.

We needed to plan for the future, and in the meantime meant to save money if we could. Margareta kept on at the library, while I worked at two part-time jobs, the first in the mail room at the Manners Street Post Office, heaving mail bags around, and the other at the Broadcasting Library as a reference librarian, which meant, largely, finding material for programmers. I enjoyed both jobs in their different ways and still managed to meet Margareta for lunch. Broadcasting left my mornings free for what I looked on as my real work: writing a novel.

This was to be *In My Father's Den*, a title that came to me halfway through. In the beginning were two things with a third lying behind them. I had read a newspaper account of the murder of a young woman by a boy, a late teenager, who was 'sexually disturbed'. That was the first thing – a common enough story but always horrifying. The second: his appalled community, perhaps in a kind of denial, perhaps in an attempt to cleanse itself, banded its men together, some women too, and burned, in an almost ritual burning, the macrocarpa hedge where the murderer had tried to hide the body. The place looming at the back of this tragedy was, for me, the small 1930s town of Henderson, where I grew up – its slow, green creek sliding by, its row of shops across the road from the railway station, its vineyards and orchards spreading outwards to the ranges which stood blue and easy against the western sky, and a concrete road leading to Auckland city on the eastern horizon: Henderson, tamely called Wadesville here and not the Loomis it became in later novels.

I stepped into the story with confidence, aware that I was no longer an apprentice; and it came easy and hard, tangled and free.

I wrote fast and had very few second thoughts (not until later). It was a satisfying and sometimes sweaty job. An added excitement was that each night as we lay in bed I read Margareta what I had written that day. Just now and then she said, 'I don't think you can do that,' and I agreed or disagreed. She did not like my protagonist/narrator, Paul Prior, and nor did I, although I developed a storyteller's fondness for him. I recognised the good sense she was bringing into play, and welcomed its modifying pressure, and I made adjustments. I saw how she struggled against the story while it forced her to accept; I saw how it wrapped itself around her. Reading *In My Father's Den* to Margareta underlined for me what I already knew: that writing was my job. And it helped tie us together. We were going to need that bond.

I could not make a living from writing novels. I was determined that one day I should, but more important now was the life together Margareta and I had found. When her divorce came through we would marry. And, before or after, it did not matter, start a family. I had to have a job that would support us. We talked it over. She would work too, as long as she could, both for pleasure and the money, while I would take a full-time job until our children reached school age. Then, perhaps, she could go back to work and I could go back to writing. It sounded all right. It even sounded easy. And I was confident that even with babies in the house I would find bits of time to get away somewhere with my biro and notebook and find stories to write.

The question was, what sort of job should I look for? I did not want to be a cataloguer in a specialist library, or in any sort of library; I wanted a wide range of books and activities and some sort of daily give and take with users. I was also hankering to be boss. It narrowed the field to public libraries in small or, we hoped, middle-sized towns. We watched the advertisements and soon a vacancy of the right sort came up in a town that called itself a city: Napier, in the Hawke's Bay, thriving again after the earthquake that had destroyed much of it in 1931. It seemed ideal: a library with a staff of ten, running smoothly (we supposed) under a boss moving on to a bigger job; a city of twenty thousand people, on the coast, surrounded by orchards and vineyards. I had never been much aware of Napier. It had seemed lost out there, midway between Auckland and Wellington, and well away from the main road and rail route between them. I had passed through it once on a road trip with my brother. It left no impression. Margareta had never been there. None of this counted. We were making a new start. Why not a new place? I applied.

Perhaps no one else did. I never heard that there had been a shortlist. The town clerk, Pat Ryan, and the Library Committee chairman, Lloyd Duckworth, drove down to Wellington, looked me over, listened to me, and were satisfied with what they saw and heard – although I detected a hint of uncertainty in Pat Ryan's eyes. My lack of experience probably worried him. I liked them both – practical and straight-speaking men, it seemed to me. I had said in my application that I was married, which I felt was only half a lie. I told them now that I had published two novels. It made Pat Ryan blink. Lloyd Duckworth did not seem to know what I was talking about.

Several weeks later I flew up to Napier and faced the full council, who, after asking me for my account of myself, which I gave as honestly as I could, quizzed me half-heartedly for twenty minutes – questions easy to answer. Then I sat on a chair outside the council chamber while they talked me over – half an hour. Pat Ryan called me back and the mayor told me I had the job and took me to his office for a chat – and maybe a drink, I hoped, but no. All I remember of it is his remark that in his experience male librarians tended to be effeminate. If I had been quicker-witted I would have replied that the present National Librarian was an ex-All Black, and one of the hard men, a forward not a back. The mayor's name was Peter Tate. I came to think of him as Potato Pete.

We bought a little bungalow on Bluff Hill, overlooking the town and the bay and taking in Cape Kidnappers in the distance. I made the pleasant walk down to the library each morning. Margareta found a part-time job in the library at Napier Boys' High School, and for our first few months was almost Napier's closet city librarian as she advised me and tutored me in the not-so-easy task of running a public library. With her behind the scenes, with a bit of bluff and cunning, I got through and soon was doing the job confidently.

The editor of the Napier *Daily Telegraph* dropped in to tell me that it was an accepted part of the city librarian's job to write a weekly book review for the paper, and half a dozen short ones as well. No pay, of course, and as the review copies came from the library's new acquisitions no free books either. I saw that my standard response, 'I'm not clever enough to write reviews', would do me no good in the town or in my job. When I told Margareta that night she said at once, 'I'll do them.' She would love to do them. And she did, with the editor's cautious but soon happy agreement; wrote the main review each week while I did the 'Quick Flips', which lived up to their name.

Our problem of concealment was solved when her divorce came through in June. Early in July we slipped away to Hastings, half an hour round the bay, and were married in the registry office. It made little difference to us, we felt we had been married for six months already, but the ceremony was exciting in its clandestine way and in its difference from the usual white and frilly, over-bonhomous, teary affair. Just the two of us and the registrar, the simplest vows, and a clerk called in as witness at the end. It made us laugh, still makes us laugh. The registrar's office, with pipes crawling down one wall and a dusty photo of a horse-drawn coach with Edwardian-hatted ladies sitting by the coachman, was a bonus.

Afterwards we went to a Hastings hotel for a buffet lunch, our wedding lunch, incognito. Margareta was five months pregnant. Emily was at our wedding too.

Margareta experienced the satisfactions and difficulties of pregnancy, while keeping on with her part-time work and later, at home, writing her weekly book review. Back in my Wellington days, a friend who was often busy with cooking and housework when I called, while his wife loafed and yawned, had said to me, 'I never wanted a hausfrau anyway.' (I think he wanted her for sex and her good looks.) I did not want a hausfrau either, but Margareta was never that as she cooked and tidied. We shared what needed to be done. But she loved getting out of the house – and loves it still. I've just looked up from my desk, forty-five years on from the time I've been writing about, and seen her coming in the gate after the second of her four daily walks. She chats with people she meets. She starts conversations with strangers. I go with her on three of them. I'm not such a ready talker though.

In Napier we walked on Bluff Hill, and round the town, and along Marine Parade. She had 'taught' me to walk in Wellington, on the hills between Johnsonville and Karori. There, on my first long walk, I turned up wearing jandals, a stupidity she could hardly believe. Deservedly I got a beesting between my toes. In Napier we had less time and were more restricted, and we needed to work on our section as well, but we managed a long or longish daily walk, even as Margareta's pregnancy advanced. We fitted a table-tennis table in our narrow sunroom and played in the weekends and after dinner each night. She had a quick eye and quick hands and usually beat me, even in the last days of her pregnancy.

Emily was born on 7 November 1970, at the Salvation Army's

Bethany Hospital. Napier holds its place in our memories mainly because our daughters were born there. (Abigail, who does not belong in parentheses, followed on 15 August 1972, at the same hospital and two weeks after I had been fired from my job – another story.) Emily's birth was the harder, although the Major, as the head nurse was called, described it as quick and easy. 'Red hair,' she said. 'A girl.' In a letter to her mother Margareta says, 'Maurice . . . became quite authoritarian which is the opposite of what I expected. And of course he saw her first. The doctor arrived when it was all over and stitched me up. And as there was a nurse short Maurice came in handy with instructions on breathing, using the mask, and even supporting my leg! I couldn't have done it without him.' That's generous, but the hard work (it didn't look 'quick and easy' to me) was hers. Her own view of it: 'Well, it's all over, and so quickly. We found I wasn't a textbook case so the day-long leisurely preparations – a last meal, a hot bath, etc. didn't come off. We were all a bit surprised at the speed . . . one nurse was chastised for not realising I was "there".'

Even in that first letter, written on the day of her birth, our daughter was Emily. The other possibility, Ingrid, was quickly put aside. It did not fit with the awkward little name Gee.

Margareta's Napier letters to her mother are largely about Emily: 'She had three extra feeds during the last 24 hours plus some very odd desserts. I'd feed her, get her all dopey and changed, put her down – half an hour later she was wanting more. I've given in to all her demands and expect her to decide on something more co-operative next week! . . . I washed nappies out this morning and then had a long lie-down. It's so marvellously peaceful here and the view and weather make life very relaxed.' So it goes on – Emily's alertness, her 'milestones', her waking hours, which were all over the clock, and feeding habits; the way she refused to crawl but went along by hitching at an alarming speed, which worried us because hitching, we read, can affect left–right coordination – and so on until walking. She tired us out and made us happy.

Our plan was for two babies. Abigail was born, a second red-haired girl, although her red was lighter. Neither parent had red hair but recessive genes were at work. She too arrived before the doctor, and came at such speed that the Major just managed to grab her leg before she shot off the side of the table. Abi was in character right from the start.

Emily was nearly two years old and Abigail only a month when we left Napier to settle in Auckland, where our life as a family of four began.

Perhaps I'll write about that another time, but I'll finish now with some comments culled from letters, and adapted slightly, that give some idea of how we got on:

'I sometimes say, over-dramatically, that Margareta saved my life. I was sliding when I met her and I don't think I would have survived as a functioning person, or as a writer, without her. Nine tenths of my writing has been done since we began living together in 1968, when I was thirty-seven. Up until then I'd written two apprentice novels and a handful of stories. All the rest, more than thirty novels, have been done since that time . . . I found emotional stability with her (at last) and settled into adulthood at that late age. With her support I was able to put all my energies into family life and writing. It's gone on from there to this day . . .

'She kept our heads above water financially, from the time we shifted from Auckland to Nelson in 1975 and I settled down to write, not quite full-time. We both took casual part-time jobs, in bookshops, delivering a community newspaper round town, and so on, but it was the jobs she took when Abi started school that kept us afloat. For several years she was librarian at the Nelson

Provincial Museum at Stoke, then worked as a technical secretary at the Cawthron Institute. Later she compiled an oral history of the Cawthron. Her longest period of employment was at the *Nelson Evening Mail* as a proof reader – 1983 to 1989. Her wages from these jobs, along with my earnings from writing, not only novels but TV scripts, allowed us to live and raise our daughters comfortably.

'When we shifted to Wellington she worked for a while at the Dictionary of New Zealand Biography, then was at the Turnbull Library from 1989 to 1991 . . . Her third and longest stint at the Turnbull, again in Manuscripts and Archives, was from 1995 to 2005.

'These Nelson and Wellington years were good ones. I can't remember happier days – in Nelson seeing the girls off to school and Margareta to work, writing all morning, walking down town and eating lunch with her on the banks of the Maitai, then back to my little room under the house for more work, and welcoming Emily and Abigail home from school, in summer sliding down the steep paddock below our house for a swim in the river (in a hole aptly named Girlies Hole), and so on – happy days, all made possible by the way Margareta and I worked together.

'We settled into a good routine in Wellington too, through the nineties and up until 2005, when she retired from the Turnbull. Each morning she'd drive to the top of the Ngaio Gorge, park the car and walk on the bush path down through the gully and up to Wadestown, then down Wadestown Road and Molesworth Street to work. Later in the day I'd have my walk to pick up the car. I collected her after work, drove home, and one of us would cook. Later we changed the walk: I'd drive her to the top of Wadestown Road at 7.30, walk down with her to the bottom, come back, drive home to a morning's writing; then go down again for lunch, which we often ate on the wharf. I'd pick her up by car after work. As I said, good days, and hugely productive for my writing.

'The so-called marriage sabbaticals. They were not a response to a marriage under strain . . . Margareta had been getting very tired, almost to the state of collapse, on our longer walks – most noticeably when all four of us walked the Routeburn Track in the company of a friend who was a guide there. Margareta was not able to keep up or do some of the climbing side-trips. Her doctor diagnosed severe anaemia. The cause was found to be a large fibroid in her uterus. She had to have a hysterectomy, at the end of which a junior doctor entrusted with the sewing up botched it. This meant more surgery. Back home in Nelson she was run down and tired, and we decided time away from house and family might give her the rest she needed. She applied for and got a job at the General Assembly Library in Wellington; went across, found a flat in Upland Road, then shifted to Bill Manhire's mother's place in Karori. (Mrs Manhire was away.) The six-month break did her good and she came back in good health.

'Two other "sabbaticals" followed: a month-long Himalayan trek in 1987, which she loved, and in 1991 a visit to Sweden to see relatives, do a Swedish language course in Uppsala, her birth town, and a trek in Lapland. They were good breaks for her and good for me, working at home with Emily and Abigail for company . . . I don't say our marriage was perfect; we had arguments, periods of stress, disagreements, got on each other's nerves at times, as in almost all marriages. But the "sabbaticals" were not caused by that. Quite soon after the Lapland trek we were off to Menton together.

'Margareta had introduced me to long walks – hill walking we called it – along the ridge from Mt Kaukau to Karori. Up to that time I'd only walked when I had to . . . In Nelson we walked on the Nelson hills and in the Arthur Range, while in Menton we went out almost every weekend high into the hills and along their tops, from Mont Agel above Monaco to Grammondo over the Italian border, and came down to the villages that dot the area. Back in New Zealand we walked the Milford Track.

'Equally important, she filled a huge gap in my life by taking me to concerts, both classical and jazz, in our Wellington years. We went as often as we could to orchestral concerts at the Town Hall and especially to chamber music concerts in the Ilott Concert Chamber. For the first time in my life I began to get real pleasure from music. We also went to lunch-time concerts (her "wonderful boss" at the Turnbull, David Colquhoun, let her take long lunch hours) at St Andrew's on The Terrace, Old St Paul's, the music department at Victoria University, and especially the lunch-time jazz concerts put on by staff and students at the Massey campus. Over the years we went to dozens of those – they had some great musicians on the staff. We also went to plays at Downstage (Margareta had been a waitress there when it started), Circa and BATS. We visited Wellington's dealer galleries regularly and bought paintings when we could afford them. We made a number of road trips, the most memorable being to Auckland for my agent Ray Richards' eightieth birthday in 2001 – up the coast in our reliable little Toyota, through Whanganui and New Plymouth and along gravel roads to Kāwhia and Raglan. In Auckland we saw the Cirque du Soleil (enjoyable), and on the drive back stopped to visit Maurice Shadbolt, in an advanced stage of dementia, in his Taumurunui rest home (not so enjoyable).

'On Margareta's initiative we joined a hosting organisation called Servas, and were active in this during our time in Nelson. Over the years we had dozens of people stay – Americans, Germans, Scandinavians mostly, but also French, Israeli, Canadian. We met some interesting people. A large Dane calling himself The Hiking Viking was an out-of-control diabetic, always on the search for something sweet in our kitchen. Two young Swedes who wanted no more than to put up their tent on our lawn became good friends. In 1982 when we took the girls out of school and went on a six-month tour of Europe, using Eurail passes, Youth Hostels, B&Bs, kind friends, cheap hotels, starting in Greece, getting as far north as Narvik in Norway, and finishing in England and Scotland; they, Inger and Broren, vacated their Stockholm flat and gave it to us for two weeks. On that trip we spent ten days on a tiny rock island in the Stockholm archipelago owned by Margareta's cousin. Its highest point was not much more than ten feet above sea level. Silver birch trees and berry bushes grew in the thin covering of soil. We swam, sailed, fished for our food and had (our daughters agree) the most enjoyable holiday of our lives.

'Margareta sponsored three Kenyan children, a girl and two boys. She paid for their schooling for many years. One boy, Patrick, became an engineer and the other, Ayub, a doctor. Ayub keeps in touch. Margareta never discovered what happened to the girl.

'Margareta and I have sometimes been accused of being anti-social. The word isn't right but I don't know what the right one is. We don't usually enjoy formal social occasions – don't enjoy dinner parties, and gave up trying to give them ourselves. Neither of us is a good "conversationalist". But there are exceptions. At dinner in a restaurant during the Sydney Writers' Festival, with half a dozen other writers and two publishers, the English writer, Margaret Drabble, asked me, unexpectedly, what the racial situation was like in New Zealand now (she had been to the Wellington festival several years earlier). Caught off guard, I began a stumbling response when Margareta, seeing my difficulty, jumped in with a succinct, informative, and I thought brilliant two-minute description of how things were that satisfied everyone, and the dinner rolled on. As for casual conversations, she's great at those. We go for several long walks a day, into town and by the river (where she feeds the ducks while I feed the sparrows). A walk seldom ends without her having stopped for a chat with someone, now and then strangers she has approached with a friendly remark.

'She laughs a lot. The comment I hear most from her is "How funny". Her sense of humour is situational, visual sometimes, rather than verbal. She's puzzled by irony and sometimes doesn't get jokes that depend on word play. I wonder if this is the result of her having to change languages at the age of three. But she sees the humour in situations quicker than I do and is able to laugh away catastrophes. When she finally left the Turnbull Library one of her work mates remarked, "What we're going to miss most is Margareta's laughter."'

She still laughs, and still gives me lessons. Yesterday she came in from one of her walks and showed me a dead thrush she had picked up outside a house. It was a young bird, still warm, and must have broken its neck by flying into a window. We stroked its wings and admired its spotted breast. Then she took her garden trowel and buried it under the lemon tree.

'I couldn't leave it lying on the pavement,' she said.